THE STUDY OF RELIGION

Morris Jastrow, Jr.

CLASSICS IN RELIGIOUS STUDIES SERIES OF
SCHOLARS PRESS
and
THE AMERICAN ACADEMY OF RELIGION

Number One

Introduced by
William A. Clebsch and Charles H. Long

Scholars Press
The American Academy of Religion

Distributed by
Scholars Press
PO Box 2268
Chico, CA 95927

THE STUDY OF RELIGION

by

Morris Jastrow, Jr.

Introduction Copyright 1981
Scholars Press

Jastrow, Morris, 1861–1921.
    The study of religion.

    (Classics in religious studies [S.P./AAR]; no. 1)
    Reprint. Originally published: London: W. Scott,
1901. (The Contemporary science series) With new
introd.
    Bibliography: p.
    Includes index.
    1. Religion–Study and teaching. I. Title. II. Series. III.
Series: Contemporary science series.
BL41.J3 1981   291   81-9184
ISBN 0-89130-519-X   AACR2

Printed in the United States of America
1   2   3   4   5
Edwards Brothers, Inc.
Ann Arbor, Michigan 48106

INTRODUCTION

At the dawn of the century this little book analyzed, described, and did much to refashion the scholarly discipline concerned with the general or comparative history of religions. Eight decades later, at least in North America, the liveliest and most provocative debates about that discipline still turned on the very points and issues that the book advanced, but by then both the book and its author had been virtually forgotten. Thus, this reprinting of *The Study of Religion* by Morris Jastrow, Jr. (1861–1921), appropriately inaugurates this "Classics in Religious Studies" series under the sponsorship of Scholars Press and the American Academy of Religion.

There are two reasons why the choice is appropriate. First, the book cannot help but enliven discussion of the discipline's nature and destiny, and it is a cardinal feature of any classic to have power to stir discussion down the generations. Indeed, this particular classic may be serviceable today in introducing the student to this discipline. (Of course, the bibliography is dated.) Second, the republication and this introduction may serve to restore to the discipline's memory the author, who was America's most prolific historian of religion down to, and of, his own time—and who since then has outdone him?

It is a book that speaks for itself. Therefore, an introduction highlighting the two or three themes of greatest interest to the introducers would tend to thwart the discovery of the many themes that will be of great interest to each reader. Therefore this introduction will sketch a profile of the author as a major contributor to the discipline and ponder, briefly at the end, why the book literally and the author figuratively went out of print.

The author's father was a scholar and a rabbi, Marcus (later Morris, Sr.) Jastrow (1829–1903); his mother, Bertha Wolfsohn Jastrow. The author would grow up to be a more famous scholar than his father, but would not last as a rabbi. A brother (there were seven children) would become a scholar and a popularizer but would leave the Jewish religion. Joseph Jastrow (1863–1944), who earned at the Johns Hopkins University what was probably the first doctoral degree in psychology conferred in the United States, became professor of experimental and comparative psychology at the University of Wisconsin, established the nation's third laboratory for psychological experimentation, and became famous as a popularizer of self-help psychology through books, articles, and radio talks.[1]

Storms began breaking over the father's career even before Morris, Jr., was born. A native of Rogasen in what was then Polish Prussia, he earned his Ph.D. through studies at Berlin and Halle. Soon after marrying in 1856, he became rabbi of the German synagogue in Warsaw. Early in 1861 Russian troops, deployed to repress home-rule movements, killed five citizens. At their memorial service Rabbi Jastrow preached a fervently patriotic sermon, of which 10,000 copies were surreptitiously

---

[1] Morris Jastrow, both senior and junior, were written up in the the prestigious *Dictionary of National Biography*; Joseph Jastrow, in *DAB Supplement III*.

printed and distributed. After three months in prison, Jastrow was deported, then recalled and readmitted, then again banished to Germany. The family moved from Worms to America in 1866, where Marcus served the conservative Synagogue Rodeph Shalom in Philadelphia. There he promoted the controversial movement, Zionism, opposed Reform Judaism, and labored over his extensive *Dictionary of the Targumim, the Talmud Babli and Yerushalmi and the Midrashic Literature* (1886-1903; 1926).

In Philadelphia Morris, Jr., received his education, winning the A.B. at the University of Pennsylvania in 1881. Three years of study followed in Breslau, Paris, Strassburg, and Leipzig—perhaps also Leiden. He returned as a Ph.D. of the University of Leipzig, to serve for a year as lecturer to his father's congregation. The next year (1885) he resigned, withdrew from the ministry, and joined his alma mater's faculty. The University appointed Jastrow professor of Semitic languages in 1892 and, as an additional appointment, University librarian in 1898. He held both positions until his death.

Perhaps stability of place throughout a long academic career had something to do with Jastrow's flexibility and vitality as to scholarly topics and academic interests. Arabic grammar was his first love, but he turned to the new and far more volatile study of ancient Babylonian and Assyrian life, especially religion. Although the bibliographies do not identify which work was his doctoral dissertation, the maiden publication was a long article in German on the works of a tenth-century Arabic grammarian.[2] After 1889 he published

---

[2] See Albert Tobias Clay and James Alan Montgomery, comps., *Bibliography of Morris Jastrow, Jr., Ph.D., Professor of Semitic Languages in the University of Pennsylvania, 1885-1910* (Philadelphia: privately printed, 1910) p. 5, and *idem,* "Bibliography of Morris Jastrow, Jr.," *Journal of the American Oriental Society, 41*

no more in this field, although his verve for comparing religions led to later lectures and essays on Muhammad and Islam. Also an accomplished Hebraist, he worked extensively on the Hebrew Bible and on Judaica. From the beginning of his academic career, and with increasing intensity, his lifelong loves were two: technical scholarship in Babylono-Assyrian religion and culture, and, more generally, the scope and method of the history of religions.

Leading scholars in both areas were among the lecturers he heard abroad, both in France and Germany, perhaps also in Holland. Mesopotamian studies were then novel and exciting. Excavations as recent as those led by Austen Henry Layard (1817–1894) in mid-century allowed scholars to decipher cuneiform and learn the literature and life of a very ancient, very high civilization. In France Jastrow heard Jules Oppert (1825–1905), an authority on the Assyrians, Babylonians, and Sumerians. There also was Joseph Halévy (1827–1917), who advanced the theory that the Sumerian people had never existed, that the writings attributed to them had in fact been in a secret code invented by Babylonian priests. At Leipzig he heard the young Friedrich Delitzsch (1850–1922), who during his career taught most of the leading Assyriologists of his time; his theory of almost total dependence of the Old Testament upon Babylonian prototypes is one that Jastrow countered in his mature works.

(1921) 337. This number of *JAOS* contained a section entitled, "In Memoriam Morris Jastrow, Jr.," that included the later Clay-Montgomery bibliography plus Julian Morgenstern, "Morris Jastrow Jr. as a Biblical Critic," pp. 322–27; George Aaron Barton, "The Contributions of Morris Jastrow Jr. to the History of Religion," pp. 327–33; Albert Tobias Clay, "Professor Jastrow as an Assyriologist," pp. 333–36; and the "Bibliography, " pp. 337–44. Jastrow had been president of the American Oriental Society (1915) and of the Society of Biblical Literature (1916).

That studies and travels in Europe brought him in touch with scholars who would pique the more general interest in the history of religions may fairly be surmised. During Jastrow's sojourn, Joseph Ernest Renan (1823–1890), if not a grandfather then surely a godfather of the history of religions, became director of the Collège de France. "I recall a remark that Renan was in the habit of making in his lectures" there, Jastrow said in his presidential address to the Semitic Religions Section of the Third International Congress for the History of Religions (Oxford, 1908).[3] The remark itself is beside the point; namely that Jastrow remembered Renan's lectures. He had just noted that since the second Congress (Basel, 1904) the field had lost the two men who inaugurated these meetings. They were Jean Réville (1854–1908) and his father Albert Réville (1826–1906). The latter was lecturing on the history of religions at both the *Collège* and *l'École des Hautes Études* in Paris during Jastrow's studies. He did not say outright that he studied with these men, but the inference that he did seems persuasive.

At the latter institution, noted for its special attention to *sciences religieuses*, Jastrow may have studied with James Darmesteter (1849–1894), a Jew, an authority on Zoroastrianism, and a promotor of comparative religion, who translated the *Zend-Avesta* and edited it for *Sacred Books of the East*; he translated into French the *Lectures on the Origin and Growth of Religion* (1878) by Friedrich Max Müller (1823–1900). In the year after Darmesteter died, Jastrow and his wife—she as translator, he as editor—

---

[3] Morris Jastrow, "President's Address," in *Transactions of the Third International Congress for the History of Religions*, ed. P. S. Allen *et al.* (2 vols., Oxford: Clarendon, 1908) *1*, 240.

published the *Selected Essays of James Darmesteter.* What could be more typical of academic-filial piety?

The typical respect of student for professor also suffuses the dedication of *The Study of Religion* to Cornelis Petrus Tiele (1830–1902). This Dutch Egyptologist and theologian was from 1877 professor of the history of religions and of the philosophy of religion at the University of Leiden.

Tiele's schemes for classifying religions, set forth first in the influential article, "Religions," occupying twenty-eight columns in the ninth edition of *Encyclopædia Britannica* and revised in his Gifford Lectures (*Elements of the Science of Religion*, 1897, 1899), received extensive treatment as well as intensive criticism in Jastrow's book. Already in 1900 Jastrow commemorated Tiele's seventieth birthday in a brief article for *Open Court*; its author was personally acquainted with its subject. Two years later he wrote an obituary of Tiele for the *Independent.*

The point of reporting what is certain and surmising what is plausible about Jastrow's early associations with great scholars is not to reflect their glory upon him. It is to note that by age 40, when he published *The Study of Religion*, he was an internationally acquainted scholar, both in his special field and in the general science of religion. His lifelong bibliography lists more than two hundred publications, not to speak of literally hundreds of entries in dictionaries and encyclopedias. By 1900, fifteen years into the profession, Jastrow had published three books, two monographs, one edited book, nearly fifty articles, and nearly fifty more scholarly notes, ranging over Arabic, Hebrew-Old Testament, Judaica, and other Orientalia, as well as in the central scholarly and academic fields. In addition, he

wrote on current political topics, including Zionism, on
academic affairs at the University of Pennsylvania, particularly its libraries, and on American Jewry. He lectured across the United States and in Europe.

To the early phase of his career, through the initial
publication of *The Study of Religion*, belongs the English
version of his magnum opus on Babylonian and Assyrian religion. Through the Ginn Publishing Company in
Boston he was editing a series called "Handbooks on the
History of Religions." The first, by Edward Washburn
Hopkins (1857–1932) of Yale on the religions of India
(1895), was followed by Jastrow's book, then by Pierre
Daniel Chantepie de la Saussaye (1848–1920) of Amsterdam and then Leiden on the religion of the Teutons
(1902), then Crawford Howell Toy (1836–1919) of Harvard on the general history of religions (1913), and finally John Punnett Peters (1852–1921), a scholarly
clergyman of New York City, on Hebraic religion
(1914). Also planned and announced, but apparently de-
railed by World War I, were Abraham Valentine
Williams Jackson (1862–1937) of Columbia on the Zo-
roastrians and Jastrow himself on Islam.

His two-volume handbook on *The Religion of Babylonia and Assyria* (1898) provided "the first scientific and
adequate account of this religion," according to George
Aaron Barton (1859–1942) of Bryn Mawr College, who
in 1922 succeeded Jastrow at Pennsylvania. Further,
"The book placed Professor Jastrow at once in the front
line of the world's Assyriologists."[4] The book grew into
a tome of nearly 1800 pages and included an album of
plates in its German version, *Die Religion Babyloniens und
Assyriens* (3 vols., 1905–1912), and that tome in turn was

---

[4] Barton, p. 329.

recast as Jastrow's American Lectures on the History of
Religions. Each version or edition pondered the latest
scholarship in a fast-moving specialty.

Jastrow founded the American Lectures in 1892 and
managed them until his death. Late in 1891 he convened
a meeting of scholars in Philadelphia to explore
establishing a course of lectures on each of the major religions. Each course was to consist of at least six lectures, to
be available for presentation in each sponsoring university and in various cities, and to eventuate in a book. The
preparatory committee reported at Union Theological
Seminary in New York early in 1892 to a meeting com-
posed of persons representing major universities in the
United States. Columbia, Cornell, Harvard, Johns
Hopkins, Pennsylvania, and Yale were among the in-
augural sponsors. Toy of Harvard was the president. The
secretary and moving spirit was Jastrow, who used the
series to present lectures by renowned experts from any-
where in the world dealing with the history of religions.

Buddhism was the topic for 1895, and the lecturer
Jastrow invited was the world's authority, Thomas
William Rhys Davids (1843-1922) of University College, London. The religions of primitive peoples followed, by Daniel Garrison Brinton (1837-1899), a pioneer
anthropologist at Jastrow's own University. The German-
trained biblical scholar who held the Oriel Professorship
of Scripture at Oxford, Thomas Kelly Cheyne (1841-
1915), lectured in 1898 on Jewish religion after the exile.
Next came lectures on the pre-exilic religion of Israel,
which issued in the widely influential book, in English
and German, by Karl Ferdinand Reinhard Budde (1850-
1935) of Strassburg, later Marburg. In 1903 Georg
Steindorff (1861-1951) of Leipzig lectured on early
Egyptian religion.

Jastrow's own lectures, delivered in 1910, were published as *Aspects of Religious Belief and Practice in Babylonia and Assyria* (1911). The famous Berlin Sinologist, Jan Jacob Marie de Groot (1854–1921) lectured during the academic year 1910–1911, followed by Franz Valéry Marie Cumont (1868–1947), curator of the Brussels Royal Museum, on Greek and Roman astrology and religion. High standards prevailed throughout Jastrow's management of the series—and have continued down to our own time under the American Council of Learned Societies.

The management of the lectures, the editing of the handbooks, and the encouragement that Jastrow gave to younger scholars combined to represent one of his three major contributions to scholarship in comparative religion. His own scientific writings stand first, and the development and teaching of scholarly methods for the study of religions rank next. But they do not dim the importance of his "organizing enterprises which called forth the contributions of others," wrote a colleague soon after Jastrow died. Moreover, "America has had but one other scholar (the late Professor C. H. Toy of Harvard), whose stimulating influence called forth from others a degree of labor at all approaching that which Professor Jastrow elicited. Such men stand far above their contemporaries in the scholarly influence which they wield. They evoke in others a devotion to the search for truth which multiplies many fold the mere labor of their own hands."[5]

That judgment rests squarely on the assumption that effectiveness in the scholar's own specialty is a necessary condition for the wider influence. Jastrow amply met

[5] *Ibid.*, pp. 332, 333.

that condition. One example of his scrutiny of details must suffice. To the commemorative volume presented to Toy on his seventy-fifth birthday Jastrow contributed an essay on "The Liver as the Seat of the Soul."[6] Astrology and divination in Babylonia and Assyria fascinated him. Among one of his more noteworthy scholarly attainments stands his discovery of the importance of hepatoscopy, or divination of future events by examining the livers of sacrificed sheep, in Babylonian life. Jastrow always studied original sources, in this case not only the divination texts in cuneiform but also the livers of sheep. It was said that he wrote on this topic with a sheep's liver on his desk.

Writings in his major field are crammed with studies of omens and signs as well as with philological investigations and commentaries on the great texts (especially Gilgamesh, but also Job and Ecclesiastes and Song of Songs. The liver commanded a large place in the German magnum opus and in the volume publishing his American Lectures. There were articles on liver-divination in scientific medical periodicals, in *Proceedings of the American Philosophical Society*, in *Proceedings of the Numismatic and Antiquarian Society of Philadelphia*. He compared Babylonian, Etruscan, and Chinese divination in a lecture at the fourth ICHR at Leiden in 1912. Jastrow knew his subject matter inside-out—including the livers.

But such trees of scholarly specialization never hid from Jastrow's sight his field's forest. On the religion of Babylonians and Assyrians he wrote the basic handbook in English, at a time when the field was undergoing sharp reinterpretation, to which he contributed. He

---

[6] In *Studies in the History of Religions*, ed. David Gordon Lyon and George Foot Moore (New York: Macmillan, 1912).

embodied others' new findings and announced his own in the German tome that was received as definitive. In the American Lectures he drew widespread attention to the latest findings in the field. In the Haskell Lectures at Oberlin College (1913) he compared the Babylonian with the Hebrew traditions, giving each its due and showing, against the currents of leading German scholarship, that the Hebrews were not wholly dependent upon Babylonian prototypes. Yet he never forgot that the scholarly forest consisted of individual trees demanding meticulous study. Albert Tobias Clay (1866–1925), professor of Assyriology at Yale, wrote in eulogy, "Especially in the subject of the religion of the Babylonians and Assyrians, Jastrow made himself without doubt the leading authority in the world."[7]

The second claim to fame came from his devotion to clarifying the scope and method of the general discipline, and now *The Study of Religion* may again speak for itself. On that theme he addressed academics of several disciplines and the wider public in many diverse articles, but none rivals in importance this quite successful book. Its early printings carried the publisher's partial catalogue at the end, a common usage of the time. "This work presents a careful survey of the subject, and forms an admirable introduction to any particular branch of it," ran the succinct—and accurate—blurb.[8]

The Study of Religion was originally published in 1901 as number 41 in The Contemporary Science Series, edited by the English psychologist-sexologist Havelock Ellis, in London by Walter Scott and in New York by Scribner's. Reprintings in 1902, 1909, 1911, and 1914

---

[7] Clay, p. 336.

[8] Morris Jastrow, Jr., *The Study of Religion*, The Contemporary Science Series, ed. Havelock Ellis, no. 41 (London: Walter Scott, and New York: Scribner's, 1902) p. 463. This reprint copies the pages of this second printing.

bore the double colophon. "The book," wrote Barton in 1921, "fulfilled a two-fold purpose: It was designed to serve as an introduction to the study of religion—an introduction in which a student could learn the limits and aims of the study—as well as to teach a scientific method of pursuing it. In accomplishing this aim Jastrow made an advance at many points over his predecessors and so contributed materially to the development of the science to which he aimed to introduce the student." Further, "Now, after the lapse of twenty years, the book is without peer in its special sphere."[9]

Given such praise and the lively success of no fewer than five printings over thirteen years, what could account for the book's later near-oblivion? Certainly its conception of the scope and method of the study of religion had value and relevance after it went out of print. After World War II, for example, one of the most active world centers for graduate training in the history of religions was the University of Chicago, under the regime of Joachim Wach (1898–1955). That training followed almost to the letter the structure of Jastrow's text, as we have it from one of his students, yet Wach, himself a walking bibliography, never referred to this book. In fact, only by happenstance did each of the authors of this introduction "rediscover" Jastrow in the early 1980s and realize that the work can still be commended as a guide to the field so long after it was written. Why the lacuna of interest and currency?

Despite the fact that desuetudes are the despair of historians, we can suggest three answers. They are by no means mutually exclusive.

First, the world changed, beginning with the latter half of the year in which the book was last reprinted

---

[9] Barton, p. 328.

(1914). Many who lived after World War I tried to forget or repudiate what was accepted before it. In one such change of mind, the Christian exclusivism and the negativism toward all religion that had forestalled until the nineteenth century the comparative study of religions once again took hold, the former fostered by Karl Barth (1886-1968) and his disciples, the latter by Sigmund Freud (1856-1939) and his. On Barth's reading all religions but Christianity, and on Freud's all religions without exception, were a snare and a delusion. Why study them at all?

Second, the book developed, as Barton noted, a scientific or academic-scholarly method for studying religions. After World War I, a self-conscious and largely successful effort was made to bend efforts on behalf of religion in American academia toward providing a theological ideology of higher education. Graduate training in religion largely passed from the departments (like Jastrow's), teaching the philologies and histories of the several religions impartially, to the theological seminaries, both Christian and Jewish, where existential and neo-orthodox theology dominated the scene. Since World War II, the scientific-scholarly approach has staged a gradual, by no means yet universal, comeback. On this reading, the principles of Jastrow's book themselves, and thus the book also, went into eclipse. The desuetude was natural. Now that the eclipse is waning, the renewal that this reprinting proposes is also natural.

The third suggestion has to do with the spirit of the times, both Jastrow's and ours. While his book contains all the intellectual ingredients to speak to the cultural situation after World War I, it did not exhibit a fitness for the new intellectual and ideological ferment. In a word, the eclipse was hermeneutical. Surely, Jastrow was aware of methodological issues, as the book makes clear from page one on. He relied on the methods of history and philology, but the philosophies of which he was aware were those of Hegel, Kant, and Hartmann rather than those of Husserl, Sartre, or James. The book is not hermeneutically oriented to the modern sense of intellectual crises, of cultural discontinuities, of personal ambiguities. On the other hand, the book breaks with the nineteenth-century hermeneutical orientation toward evolutionary optimism. It explicitly points away from the spirit of the times preceding it, but it points only implicitly toward the spirit of the times succeeding it. With that point in mind, the book's lessons can be absorbed into the spirit of our times—unknown to and therefore unaddressed by Morris Jastrow, Jr.

WILLIAM A. CLEBSCH,*
George Edwin Burnell Professor of Religious Studies
and Professor of Humanities,
Stanford University

CHARLES H. LONG,
William Rand Kenan, Jr., Professor of Religion
University of North Carolina at Chapel Hill,
and Professor of Religion,
Duke University.

*The introduction was prepared while this author was a Fellow at the Center for Advanced Study in the Behavioral Sciences and of the National Endowment for the Humanities (#FC-0006-79-1229); both sponsors are gratefully acknowledged.

THE CONTEMPORARY SCIENCE SERIES.

Edited by HAVELOCK ELLIS.

THE STUDY OF RELIGION.

THE
STUDY OF RELIGION.

BY

MORRIS JASTROW, Jun., Ph.D.,

PROFESSOR IN THE UNIVERSITY OF PENNSYLVANIA.

THE WALTER SCOTT PUBLISHING CO., LTD.,
PATERNOSTER SQUARE, LONDON, E.C.
CHARLES SCRIBNER'S SONS,
153-157 FIFTH AVENUE, NEW YORK.
1902.

TO

C. P. TIELE,

PROFESSOR OF THE HISTORY AND PHILOSOPHY OF
RELIGION AT THE UNIVERSITY OF LEIDEN.

———

In asking you, my dear Professor Tiele, to accept this dedication as an offering on the completion of your seventieth year, I feel that I am repaying in poor coin a heavy debt that I owe to you. Your works have guided me in my studies, your friendship has encouraged me, and I shall feel satisfied if you find the result not altogether unworthy to be associated with your honoured name.

PREFACE.

THE study of religion has taken its place among contemporary sciences, and the importance of the study can be denied by no one who appreciates the part that religion has played in the history of mankind, and still plays at the present time. It is, however, a subject beset with singular difficulties—difficulties due in part to the wide scope of the theme, in part to the intricacy of the problems involved, and in part also to the close relations existing between the study and the actual concerns of life. The existence of these difficulties makes it all the more important to develop a proper method in the study; and it is the main purpose of this work to unfold such a method.

To accomplish this end, it seemed desirable to set forth in the first place the history of the study itself, as the best means of emphasising the significance of the historical method at present adopted by scholars in the investigation of religious phenomena. In further illustration of this method, such fundamental questions as the classification of religions, the definition, and the difficult problem as to the origin of religion are next taken up, and by a criticism of the leading systems of classification, of the more important definitions, and of the most significant solutions proposed for the problem as to the origin of religion, the reader will be prepared to estimate at their value not only the result of the studies undertaken by the author himself, as set forth at the end of each chapter, but also further researches that may be carried on by others within this field.

A second and distinct part of the work is formed by a consideration of the several factors involved in the study of religion itself. These factors are in the main—Ethics, Philosophy, Mythology, Psychology, History, and Culture in general. A chapter is devoted to each, with a view of determining the part proper to each in a sound application of the historical method. The desire not to extend the work beyond undue proportions has prevented as full a treatment of some of these factors as they deserved. More particularly, the relationship of Religion and Psychology merited fuller treatment in view of the interest aroused in this aspect of the subject by the "New Psychology." Although one may feel strongly that the hopes of those who look forward to psychological researches for a final explanation of the causes of religious phenomena are destined to disappointment, yet the great importance of such investigations as those undertaken by Dr. Starbuck,[1] and embodied in his volume prepared for this series, must be admitted, and it is a safe prediction that the "Psychology of Religion" will absorb even more attention during the next decade than in the one just past. Neverthe-

[1] *The Psychology of Religion: a Study of Conversion*, London, 1899.

less, it is the investigation of the course actually
taken by religion that must remain the chief goal
of the student. The proper study of religious history
is not only the sound basis upon which all speculation, whether of a philosophical or a psychological
nature, must rest, but it must form the starting-point
even when we enter upon a study of the emotions
involved in religious acts and experiences.

I take my stand therefore as an advocate of the
historical method in the study of religion as the
conditio sine quâ non for any results of enduring
character, no matter what the particular aspect of
religion it be that engages our attention. Whatever
the defects of the exposition may be, it will, I trust,
at least justify the correctness of the general position
here taken. It is my earnest hope also, in some
measure to contribute through this book to the more
general interest in the historical study of religions,
and with this in view I have embodied in the third
part of the work a consideration of the practical
aspects of the subject. In this division chief stress
has purposely been laid upon the historical study of
religions, and only incidental reference made to the
philosophy and psychology of religions which, as
aspects to be taken up by mature minds, not only
lie beyond the province of popular study, but also
beyond that of collegiate and university work. Courses
of a general character in these aspects of the subject
fall within the range of a university curriculum, but the
real study of them must be postponed until one has

secured a safe historical basis. The university and seminary will fulfil their function if they succeed in training students in a historical method. The Philosophy and Psychology will then take care of themselves.

Needless to add that in so large and inexhaustible a field a bibliography will only have practical value for the readers for whom this series is intended if it represents a selection out of the great mass. With few exceptions I have read and consulted the works, monographs, and articles enumerated, and recommend them therefore from personal knowledge of their contents. With a view of presenting the Bibliography in a more systematic fashion, it has been divided up into sections corresponding so far as possible to the main divisions of the book itself. The preference has been given to publications in English, though of course German, French, and Dutch works come in for a large share.

My very dear and esteemed friend, Mrs. Caspar Wister, has placed me under lasting obligations by kindly undertaking to read one proof of the entire work; and as I go over the pages for the last time, I find everywhere traces of her most skilful revision. The index has been prepared by Miss Katherine S. Leiper, and I wish to take this opportunity of thanking her for the intelligent care and painstaking accuracy with which she has carried out what was necessarily an arduous task.

My last word is to express a deep sense of obligation to my wife, who has, as on former occasions, copied most of the manuscript, and by her suggestions and in various other ways helped to make the work much less imperfect than it would otherwise have been. If the preparation of the work, involving prolonged study and reading, and extending over many years, has been a labour of love, it is largely due to the encouragement I have received from her.

MORRIS JASTROW, Jun.

University of Pennsylvania,
June 1901.

CONTENTS.

————•◦•————

PART I.—GENERAL ASPECTS.

PART II.—SPECIAL ASPECTS.

PART III.—PRACTICAL ASPECTS

I.

GENERAL ASPECTS.

THE STUDY OF RELIGION.

CHAPTER I.

THE STUDY OF RELIGION—ITS HISTORY AND CHARACTER.

I.

METHOD may be said to constitute three-fourths of any science. Discoveries may occasionally be due to accident, or to what appears to be such, but a genuine advance in any science is always accompanied by a change in method, and new results are but the application of improved methods of investigation.

There is a special reason for emphasising the importance of method in the study of the various religious systems of the past and present, and of religious phenomena in general. In the study of religion, a factor that may be designated as the personal equation enters into play. So strong is this factor that it is perhaps impossible to eliminate it altogether, but it is possible, and indeed essential, to keep it in check and under safe control; and this can be done only by the determination of a proper method and by a close adherence to such a method.

In one sense the study of religion is as old as human thought, but in another and more pertinent sense, it is the youngest of the sciences. The moment

I

that man in a self-conscious spirit ponders over the
religious beliefs which he holds, or which have been
handed down to him as a legacy, he is engaged in the
study of religion ; and we know that such a moment
comes at an early stage in the development of human
culture, if not to the masses, at all events to certain
individuals.

Corresponding to the religious strain present in the
earliest literary productions of a people, its earliest
thought is either directly religious or has a strong
religious tinge. A crude theology follows close in
the wake of a priesthood in process of organisation.
The study of religion in this form, while it must not
be confounded with the mere attachment to a certain
form of faith, yet springs from this attachment, and
as a direct consequence the limitations of the study
are soon reached. Egypt, Babylonia, Judæa, India,
are notable examples of the fertility of religious
thought in antiquity, but the theoretical phases of
this thought are overshadowed by the purely practical
purposes which it served. The study of religion in
close affiliation with a special form of religious faith
may lead to far-reaching results in practical theology,
may result in the formulation of a religious system,
and in the adjustment of the cult to an expression of
certain religious ideas and aspirations, but religion as
a historical phenomenon in the life of man will have
had a very insignificant part in these results. The
personal equation being entirely unchecked, and constituting, in fact, the source of the strength displayed
by man's activity in the early civilisations within the
domain of religious study, formed an insurmountable
barrier to the progress of the study beyond certain
narrow and sharply defined limits.

The general attitude of ancient thinkers—whether priests or philosophers—towards other religions than the one of their environment was that of pure indifference. Only rarely, as in the case of Herodotus or Plutarch, is their curiosity aroused to find out what others believe. If the question were put to a Greek, or an Egyptian, or a Babylonian, as to the reason for the existence of various religions in the world, he would have failed to understand what the question meant. It was perfectly natural to a Greek that the religion in Egypt should be different from the one prevailing in Hellas. How could it be otherwise? The countries were different, and therefore the gods were different. A difference in religion was accordingly accepted with the same complacency as was a difference in dress or in language. The Hebrew prophets, in their denunciation of other cults than that of Jahweh, appear to form an exception to this general attitude of indifference, but it must be borne in mind that the prophets were primarily concerned with the people of Jahweh, who should have been faithful to Jahweh, and whose disloyalty to their god excited the prophets' anger. It is true these prophets go to the length of virtually denying the existence of other gods besides Jahweh, but they content themselves with merely brushing these gods aside, whereas the problem involved in the *belief* in so many gods, and in the existence of such various religions, enters their minds as little as it does the minds of Babylonian theologians or of Egyptian priests, or, for that matter, of Greek philosophers. Before its rough contact with the Eastern world, through the prolonged conflict with the Persian power, Greek philosophy pursues the even tenor of its way, undisturbed by the reflection that beliefs and practices current outside of Greek limits must be taken into account in formulating a system of theology and ethics. There follow some feeble attempts at identifying certain gods of eastern nations, and more particularly, of Egypt, with Greek deities, or a sceptical attitude is assumed towards the existence of gods in general—whether in Greece or elsewhere; but even Plato and Aristotle, though evidently acquainted with other religious systems than the one prevailing among the Greeks, and in a measure influenced by foreign ideas, share the general indifference as to the manifold manifestations of religion. Their theory of the gods, though susceptible of general application, is intended to explain Greek religion only. We must descend to the period of the decline of the Greek religion, to the time when Greece herself had no further message to give to the world, before we encounter in Plutarch one who makes a serious effort to study the religion of Egypt,[1] and who, as a result of his comparative studies in religion, works out a theory foreshadowed by Plato,[2] of a distinction between gods and demons, which is noteworthy as having been evidently suggested by the endless number of "higher beings" to whom mankind pinned their faith. This essay is significant in several respects. It reveals an extensive knowledge of ancient religions. Not only is Plutarch well versed in Egyptian mythology, but he knows the leading principles of Zoroastrianism, and discusses them with admirable thoroughness; and other ancient cults are frequently referred to. His theory, too, of the manner in which symbols came to

---

[1] In his discourse on "Isis and Osiris."
[2] See Campbell, *Greek Religion in Greek Literature*, p. 372.

be mistaken for realities is interesting, and illustrates not only the acuteness of his mind, but the serious manner in which he carried out the task he had set himself, which was to account in a rational manner for the curious and complicated phases of the myth of Isis and Osiris. Still the limitations of Plutarch's studies are no less noticeable. He contents himself with superficial resemblances as a basis for constant comparison between Greek and Egyptian mythology, and his etymologies, upon which great stress is laid, are puerile and fanciful. To this same period belongs Lucian, who, if he is really the author of the essay on the Syrian goddess,[1] merits to be classed with Plutarch as among the earliest students of the history of religion who approached their task with at least a fair conception of the significance of the problems involved. It might have been supposed that the union of Hellenic and Hebraic thought in the schools of Alexandria, during the second and first centuries before our era, would have stimulated the comparative study of religions, but important as this period is for the development of religious thought in the ancient world, even in the writings of Philo Judæus, who is the best representative of the result brought about by the combination of two essentially different forms of culture, there are but few indications of a real interest in the study of religious phenomena as such, apart from their practical bearings; and there are surprisingly few references to such phenomena.

To this indifferent attitude there was added, in the case of the Romans, a pride and feeling of superiority which precluded them from approaching religions other than their own in that sympathetic spirit with-

[1] "De Dea Syria."

out which an understanding of religious phenomena is impossible. Tacitus, in his *Germania,* well represents this feeling. There was nothing which the polished Roman could learn from those whom he despised as "barbarians"; for him, as for Lucretius, the sublime monotheism of the Jews appeared merely in the light of a superstition. Indeed, the utterances of later Greek and Roman writers about the Jews and Judaism[1] furnish the best illustration of the utter incapacity of the best minds of the time to penetrate to the core of a religion like Judaism or early Christianity.

II.

We are approaching the terrible era of religious conflict. During the century before the advent of Jesus, a proselytising spirit had seized hold of certain groups of the Jews. The decay of heathenism seemed to furnish a favourable opportunity for making Jehovah, in practice as well as in theory, the god of the world, so that the apostles and early Christian missionaries found the way well prepared for them, when they passed beyond the confines of Palestine to preach the new gospel to all men. Large settlements of Jews in various parts of the Roman Empire helped to foster the hostile feelings that soon manifested themselves in cruel persecutions both of Jews and Christians, for during the first century of Christianity, no distinction was made by the Romans between Jews who had accepted Jesus and those who refused to recognise him as the Messiah. In the eyes of the world both parties were Jews.

---

[1] See, for many examples, Reinach's valuable *Textes d'Auteurs Grecs et Romains relatifs au Judaisme,* Paris, 1895.

Once master of the situation, Christianity accepts as a legacy from Rome the ideal and theory of a world-empire, and since, by the logic of the situation, the single empire was to be ruled by the precepts and rites of a single religion, the Roman spirit of pride develops naturally into a spirit of intolerance towards all forms of religion other than Christianity. Rome could view with complacence the various cults practised in her empire, so long as those preaching them confined themselves to their habitations and did not interfere with Roman authority. A Roman emperor could even go so far as to place the statues of Moses and Apollo in a temple dedicated to Jupiter; but to the zealous Christian such tolerance was impossible— impossible in even a stronger degree than to the Hebrew prophets. It is one of the curious phenomena in the history of religions, that only in those more advanced do we meet with the proselytising spirit, and concomitant with this, an attitude of bitter intolerance towards other forms of faith. Christianity solved the religious "problem" in a simple manner. God having revealed himself to but one people, there could be only one form of religious truth. All others were due either to the inspiration of evil forces or to benighted ignorance. The latter was to be overcome by preaching to all the only true religion, and persuasion, when ineffectual, was followed by severer measures, while in the prolonged conflict with the evil forces—of which obstinacy was regarded as a manifestation—violence in some form or other constituted the only feasible weapon. With such a spirit prevailing, there was, to be sure, plenty of interest in the religious phenomena of the world. Christian theologians devoted much of their efforts to the study

of religion, and included in their scope all forms of
religion known to them, but the frame of mind in
which they conducted these studies was fatal to any
real progress in fathoming the problems with which
they dealt.   This state of affairs prevailed throughout
the so-called Middle Ages, and when, in addition to
continuing her attempt to stamp out heathenism and
to crush Judaism, Christianity had to defend herself
against the encroachments of a new, and in many
respects more formidable foe, Islamism, she abandoned
humane feelings altogether, cast aside all ideals of
peace and good-will, and entered upon a prolonged
period of bitter warfare in the name of religion,
diversified only by a policy of cruel persecution of all
"infidels" and heretics.   The Renaissance and Reformation furnished but little relief.   Luther is as severe
in his attacks upon Islam as were his predecessors.
For him Mohammed is an incarnation of the Devil.
The revival in the study of Hebrew did not change the
general attitude of scholars or the masses towards the
Jews as a "stiff-necked" people whose hearts were
hardened against the approach of a gospel of love,
preached to them by means of pillage and *autos-de-
fé.*   It would have been better if with the sentiments
prevailing till the middle of the eighteenth century,
less attention had been given to the study of religions,
for such study, inspired by hatred and carried on with
bitter prejudice, merely furnished additional fuel for
the fires of religious fanaticism.

III.

The natural and inevitable reaction against this
policy, dictated by the spirit of intolerance, sets in

about the middle of the eighteenth century. Scepticism is the corollary of fanaticism. The glaring inconsistency of a religion preaching love, and everlastingly brandishing the sword, led men to the other extreme of questioning whether there was any logical basis for religious belief in any form.

The independence of a few thinkers in the seventeenth century was followed in the eighteenth by a revolt against the authority of religion which threatened to assume large proportions. Under the leadership of France, writers in various countries vied with one another in the boldness of their attacks upon the representatives of religious faith, who were held up as deceivers prompted by sordid motives, who had cunningly foisted superstitious rites and doctrines upon the masses with a view of frightening them into permanent subjection. Religious faith was viewed as a mere fantasy, a survival from the childhood of the race, artificially maintained by priests. All religious rites were the deliberate invention of a body of men, and could have neither sanction nor authority in the eyes of people who exercised their reason. The evolution of religious thought was a phrase utterly devoid of meaning to the superficial rationalists who mark the so-called *Auf-Klärungsperiode*. The attitude of intolerance was succeeded by a hostile attitude towards religion, which was as little able to deal in a just manner with religious phenomena as had been the previous attitude of indifference, pride, and intolerance. In some respects this attitude of hostility towards all religion was more disastrous than other false attitudes, for so long as it was held that one religion was true, or that all had a justification, the confidence in the lofty destiny of the human race was maintained, whereas the hostile attitude towards religion was inseparable from a general contempt for a hopelessly weak humanity that had permitted itself to be deceived for so many thousands of years. If it may be said of Christian theologians of the Middle Ages that they had too much religion of their own to appreciate the general phenomena of the religious life of mankind, the charge of having too little religion, which must be brought against the French encyclopædists in the eighteenth century, is at least equally serious.

Voltaire and Luther[1] both agree, for example, in making Mohammed a deceiver and a monster of cruelty, and they differ only in the associates which they would give this monster. Voltaire would not hesitate to place Luther in the same general category of "deceivers" with Mohammed, while Luther would denounce Voltaire equally with Mohammed as a wicked infidel, and each would make an exception in favour of himself, and of those who shared his beliefs or his scepticism on religious questions. Until the threshold of the nineteenth century, we have these two attitudes—the attitude of intolerance, and the hostile attitude—practically occupying the whole field, and contending with each other for supremacy; and, it should be added, numerous representatives of each attitude are to be found at the present day. On the one side we find arrayed those who, while they call forth our profound admiration (if not envy) for the strength with which they held to their religious convictions, yet shock the softened sensibilities of a later age by the severity of their religious temper. Shrinking from no conclusion to which an inexorable

[1] See below, pp. 13 *et seq.*

logic applied to their beliefs, drove them, they condemned—in some cases with a heavy heart, but often
cheerfully—to eternal misery those who were not
disposed to agree with them.   It is doubtful whether
people in such a frame of mind were qualified to form
an intelligent judgment even as to their own religion,
but certainly with such an attitude, the development
of a proper method in the study of religion was out of
the question.   Indeed, so far as the study of religion
involves a search for truth, the pursuit was superfluous
to those who already believed themselves to be in
possession of the absolute truth, and who naturally
look upon such a pursuit either with contempt or
suspicion; and it may be added, that when the
general criterion for distinguishing between the true
and the false in religion hinged upon the position
occupied by those who set themselves up as judges,
it was just as well that people did not concern
themselves very seriously with the religion of their
fellows.

IV.

But equally fatal to the development of a proper
method was the attitude of those who, in a natural
reaction against the acerbity of a dogmatic theology,
lost sight entirely of the ideas controlling the course
of events in human history, and, either bereft of all
faith in the virtues of mankind, or misled in their
judgment by regarding the abuses to which religion
was put as its essential ingredients, came to hold
theories respecting the origin and nature of religion
which, in addition to being most crude and unjust,
rendered their expounders unfit for approaching its
study in a proper frame of mind.   Gifted with no

historical discrimination, such persons saw everywhere the machinations of evilly-disposed priests,
and were totally blind to the great part played by
religious ideas and religious organisations in the
progress of the human race.   This hostile attitude,
precluding that broad and impartial investigation
of religious phenomena which alone makes a study
fertile in results, may be combined with the exclusive
attitude under the caption—dogmatic ; for whether
we start with a definition that limits true religion to
a given circle, or with a theory that there is no truth
at all, in either case we are prejudicing the results
of any investigation we may undertake, by giving
theory the precedence over facts, whereas it is in just
the reversed relation in giving facts the precedence over
theory, that we must seek for the key-note to what, in
contradistinction to the dogmatic attitude, may be
called the historical position.

While it is not surprising that in the age preceding
the Renaissance and the Reformation the exclusive
attitude towards religion should have been the prevailing one, it is rather strange that, during the sway
of the Renaissance movement, men's minds should
not have been led to a broadened view of the course
of the religious development in the world. We
should have supposed that, with a revival of interest
in classic learning, with an increased knowledge of
the world through travel and exploration, revealing
cultures that had flourished anterior to the rise of
occidental civilisation, and that had never come under
the influence of Judaism, Christianity, or Islam, a
widening of the mental horizon, at least among the
leaders of thought, would have resulted; but we
search in vain for any indication that this was the

case. Despite even important discoveries in the natural sciences, the spell of mediæval intolerance still held Europe captive, nor was it possible even for so towering an intellect as Luther to free himself from its thraldom. Indeed, in many respects Luther may be taken as the best representative of the exclusive attitude towards other religions than his own, resulting from the general spirit of intolerance of the age, which he shared in a conspicuous degree. Throughout all his writings, which abound in flashes of genius that betray a far-seeing and acute mind, there is not a single utterance from which we might conclude that the thought of accounting in some rational way for the great variety of religious phenomena in the world ever entered his mind or disturbed his soul. In illustration, we need not confine ourselves to the severity, and even cruelty, of his polemics against the Roman Catholic Church, for which there was abundant reason in the special circumstances of Luther's career, nor to his position towards the Jews, for it is quite as much as we have reason to expect, if we find that Luther treated the Jews with his pen, just a trifle better than he did the Pope. Luther knew of the existence of Islam, and at one time appeared to have paid some attention to it. In 1542 he published a refutation of the Koran, furnishing some translations from the work. The titles of the chapters indicate the spirit of the work. One of these titles reads: "That the Koran of Mohammed is brutish and hoggish;" another, "About the coarse lies in the Koran." Mohammed he describes as "the devil's worshipper," and elsewhere he declares that "Antichrist is the Pope and Turk together. A beast full of life must have a body and

a soul.   The spirit or soul of Antichrist is the Pope;
his flesh or body is the Turk."   One of Luther's
hymns begins—

> " Lord, shield us with thy word and hope,
> And smite the Moslem and the Pope."

With the leaders of thought maintaining such an
attitude towards a faith to which many millions of
earnest and intelligent men and women had pinned
their salvation, what was to be expected from those
who looked to their leaders for guidance?

Turning to the philosophers who revolted from the
sway of scholasticism and ecclesiastical authority, it is
not until we reach Spinoza that we find an attempt
at setting up a system of religious philosophy which
is broad and inclusive, and takes into account the
general growth of religious ideas in various parts of
the world.   In consequence, no doubt, of the peculiar
religious evolution which he himself experienced,
Spinoza is led to formulate in his *Tractatus Theologico-Politicus* (1670) certain leading principles in
the ancient Hebrew faith, and he makes an attempt
to show how these principles, passing on from age to
age, are modified and elaborated until they reach
their culmination in Christianity.   His treatise is
remarkably suggestive, and time has not deprived it
of its freshness as a study of religious ideas, but the
range of Spinoza's observations is after all narrow.
Outside of Judaism and Christianity, he does not
appear to recognise the sway of religious ideas.   His
religious system, so far as formulated in this work, is
built upon the basis of Christianity alone, for Judaism
is from Spinoza's point of view merely an earlier
stage of Christianity.   Still, in his attitude towards

religious phenomena, Spinoza represents a great advance over his predecessors, and indeed over his age, and his treatise will always retain a unique position as having been largely instrumental in suggesting to later thinkers, the historical attitude in the study of religion.

The age of Spinoza is, however, precisely the one in which the tendency becomes marked among thinkers who rejected the current theology, to regard the religions of civilised nations as mere human fabrications, and mischievous fabrications at that, devised by priests, for the purpose of securing a firm control over men's minds. The rites of these religions are adaptations of superstitions practised in early days when man lived in a state of rudeness and ignorance, and to which as a matter of course no divine or rational sanction can be attached, while the beliefs are a fabric ingeniously devised with a view of terrorising people into subjection, and of providing the needed semblance of authority for a continuation of the rites of the church. Such a theory results naturally in engendering a distinctly hostile attitude towards religion in general. It is to the English school of philosophy, represented chiefly by Toland, Collins, Hume, that this hostile attitude is in the first instance due. John Toland, in his famous work, *Christianity not Mysterious* (1696), appears to have been the first to propound the astounding proposition that all religions except those of savages are the fabrications of priests introduced in a spirit of selfish greed for power over the masses, or inspired by even more sordid motives. For a hundred years and more, "priestcraft" became the watchword of a succession of thinkers in England and France.

It is drummed incessantly into our ears until we
weary of it, and the echoes may still be heard occasionally in our days. This distorted view colours
the thought and shapes the systems devised by the
philosophers of the eighteenth century. For all that,
we must recognise the valuable services rendered
by these men, who were prompted by a correct instinct of revolt against a species of ecclesiastical
authority which had checked free discussion and
independent thought. The better knowledge of the
laws of nature had produced the firm conviction, that
all phenomena were to be explained by the natural
workings of universal law. Applying the principle
to religion, there arose a necessary contrast between
religious views based upon the observation of natural
laws and those which rested upon a different order of
things, upon a special dispensation and revelation of
the Divine will accorded to certain favoured individuals. Hume, as the greatest apostle of natural
religion,[1] puts the problem concisely when he declares,
in agreement with his predecessors, that only such
parts of a religion could be true which agreed with
the postulates of reason. Whatever in Revealed
Religion contradicts "Natural Religion," or is not
in full accord with the latter, represents an addition
of human origin for which no authority could be
claimed. A lack of historical sense prevented these
"Naturalists" from advancing to the real problem
involved in this contrast between Natural and Revealed religion. To assume wilful deceit as the
source of revealed religion was to ignore the fact
that the development of revealed religion follows

[1] *The Natural History of Religion* (1757), in vol. ii. of Green and
Grose's edition of Hume's essays, London, 1882.

regular laws as much as does so-called "Natural Religion." In consequence of this error, the revolt against ecclesiastical authority, instead of leading to a more profound attempt to account for the phenomena of religion among mankind, has its outcome in the superficial cynicism of such French thinkers as La Mettrie and D'Alembert, until in Voltaire the hostile attitude towards religion reached its culminating point. It seems strange that one possessed of the keen sense of justice which led Voltaire to enlist his services in behalf of the wronged and oppressed,[1] of the courage which prompted him to expose ruthlessly the foibles of his age, and of a personal nobility, which kept him singularly free from contamination by the degraded moral standards that were current,—strange that such a man should have been ready to attribute so large a share in the shaping of man's destiny to injustice, cowardice, and deceit. Nothing can be finer than Voltaire's definition of a Theist as "one who says to God, 'I worship and serve Thee,' and who says to all mankind, 'I love you,'" and yet he can see nothing more in the religious sects of the world than "a combination of doubt and error." Voltaire, the author of the noble article on "Toleration" in the famous *Dictionnaire Philosophique*, which contains so many valuable things that are not at all philosophical, is also the author of a wretched tragedy, *Mahomet*, which Lessing must have had in mind when in his proposed epitaph for Voltaire he says—

---

[1] His long struggle to secure justice for the persecuted Protestant family Calas forms an interesting parallel to Zola's heroic efforts to force upon the French courts, and upon public opinion, the recognition of the innocence of Dreyfus.

"Der liebe Gott verzeih aus Gnade
ihm seine Henriade
und seine Trauerspiele." [1]

The alternative title of the tragedy, "The Fanatic," prepares us in a measure for the view of Mohammed which Voltaire unfolds. The point of interest in the composition is the strikingly close resemblance of Voltaire's portrait of Mohammed to the conception which Luther formed of him. Voltaire's Mahomet, like Luther's, is a cunning and passionate villain who stops short at no crime to accomplish detestable ends. Both from a dramatic and a historical point of view, Voltaire's drama is to be condemned, for such a character as he depicts never did exist, and never could have existed. Voltaire's weakness, like that of the entire school of thought in which he appears as the culmination, consisted in a lack of historical sense and historical perspective. The hostile attitude towards religion, with its crude theory of priestly villainy as the mainstay of religion among mankind, presented human history as an endless succession of tragic pantomimes enacted by puppets, and showed itself as little capable of penetrating the problems of religious history, as the attitude of intolerance in a former generation. The broader range of vision which characterised many of the thinkers who, as Deists or Pantheists, gave strength to the cause of "Natural Religion," proved of little avail because of the distorted light in which the facts of history were viewed. A fundamental error of the school, which saw the evil workings of priestcraft everywhere, was a total misapprehension of the *rôle* of

[1] Lessing's *Ges. Werke* (ed. Kurz, Leipzig), vol. i., p. 48. ("May God in His mercy pardon him for his 'Henriade' and his tragedies.")

the priest in the drama of history. The priest is held up primarily as an originator, whereas his real *rôle* is that of a conservator. The priest uses what he finds existing among the people for good or evil purposes, as the case may be, and what the English and French philosophers mistook for fabrications were merely the moulds in which human thoughts, fears, and aspirations took shape. Indeed, the historical treatment of religions shows that there is no such thing as deliberate invention in religion—there is only natural or nurtured growth.

V.

The reconciliation between the exclusive (or intolerant) and the hostile attitude is the historical attitude; and while the honour of having procured general recognition for this attitude belongs to the nineteenth century, its beginnings are to be found in the same eighteenth century in which the hostile attitude acquired its greatest strength. Before proceeding to trace its rise, it may be well to characterise briefly the salient features of a historical treatment of religion. In the first place, as already indicated, the fundamental principle of this method is the careful and impartial accumulation of facts, and what is more, the facts of religion everywhere. Starting out without bias or preconceived theory, the historical method aims at determining as accurately as possible what are the beliefs, what the rites, what the aspirations of any particular religion or system of religious thought. In this work of gathering the facts of religion, it is essential not to assume at the outset a distinction between important and relatively unimportant facts. Nothing for the time being must be neglected. Pass-

ing to the arrangement and systematisation of the
facts, the historical treatment demands an exclusion
of all dogmatic schemes.   It does not follow that the
facts can in every case be ranged in the same order.
It is just here that the peculiarities of each religion
enter into play, and unless due account is taken of
these peculiarities, it is a hopeless task to endeavour
to present the facts of the religion in question in their
proper light.   In close contact with the arrangement
of the facts is their interpretation; and it is in the
interpretation that the historical attitude is put to
the severest test.   It is obvious that, for the time
being, all such factors as special dispensation and
miraculous intervention must be excluded.   Not that
the historical attitude involves disbelief in a supernatural order, but it protests against the encroachment
of this order into a foreign domain.   Unless human
history is to be explained by a thorough study of
causes and results, and by an exclusive regard to
human conditions, no explanation in the real sense
of the word is possible.   To have recourse to super-
naturalism is to confess our inability to solve the
problem on which we are engaged.   It may well be
that certain or many problems in the religious life of
man cannot be solved by mere investigation of facts,
but when this stage is reached, the frank confession
should be made that historical science has reached
its limitations.   To introduce factors with which
history can have nothing to do, is to obscure the
problems submitted for investigation.   On the other
hand, it must not be supposed that the historical
attitude towards religion excludes the introduction of
what may be called the psychological factor.   On the
contrary, as will be more fully shown in a separate

chapter,[1] a knowledge of the peculiar workings of the human emotions under certain circumstances, an insight into human nature, which forces us to acknowledge the existence of a religious faculty as an essential part of that nature, is most necessary to an interpretation of the facts of religion. The satisfaction of the emotional needs of man is not only fully as important, but quite as worthy an aim as the catering to the intellectual and physical needs; and in so far as religion responds to a certain phase of man's nature, that phase must be studied in connection with the facts of religion. But to take into account a religious instinct as part of man's constitution does not mean a desertion of the solid ground of reasoning, and is quite different from taking airy flights into the regions of the unreal. The salient feature of the historical treatment of religions consists in the endeavour to treat facts in connection with the conditions under which they are produced, and likewise to trace the origin of religious phenomena to the conditions appropriate for their production.

The comparative study of religions follows as a natural corollary from the historical treatment of particular religions. Its proper place in the scientific study of religions will be indicated further on. Here it is sufficient to point out that its chief value consists in enabling us to determine the essential elements of religion, and to formulate the laws of the development of religion. As such the comparative study of religion forms the only secure basis for the philosophy of religion, but only secure so long as in the comparative study itself, the historical method is adhered to.

[1] Chapter IX.

VI.

The direct impulse to a historical study of religions was given by the further widening of mankind's mental horizon through the exploits of intrepid voyagers and travellers, who, in the sixteenth and seventeenth centuries, *forced* upon occidental Christianity a recognition of the great variety of religious systems in the world, the significant character of some of which could not be disregarded. Mohammedan culture had by this time expended its force. Fettered to a narrow theology, Islam was no longer capable of being stirred by contact with other civilisations. It had retired into privacy after a short period of intellectual supremacy, but the Christian civilisation of Western Europe, aroused by the revival of the fine arts, and by an awakening of intense interest in Greek culture, was in a favourable position for yielding to new influences. The lack of a historical method, however, in scientific pursuits, prevented these influences from making themselves felt in the domain of religious thought for some time to come. Through the lack of the historical spirit, the reaction against the attitude of exclusion or intolerance produces the hostile attitude towards religion which we have already characterised. Still, even in the seventeenth and eighteenth centuries, while the exclusive attitude held sway, or shared the field with the hostile attitude, signs were not wanting of the coming of a new spirit. The strong interest felt by scholars in the religions of the world, past and present, is in itself the most noticeable of these signs; and, what is particularly noteworthy, this interest did not spring altogether from a controversial tendency, but rather from a desire to connect with one another the manifestations of religion in various quarters, and among different peoples. In the year 1653, there appeared in England a work by Alexander Ross on "The Religions of the World."[1] Ross still represents in his book the intolerant attitude, repeats the absurd tales of travellers about the religious customs of distant nations, is most unjust towards Islamism, and shows little kindness towards Judaism; but despite his lack of sympathy with religions other than Christianity, he recognises some merits in many of the religions which he treats, and the apologetic tone which he feels obliged to adopt in his Preface— devoted to a justification of engaging in the study of "false" religions—is a significant concession to the dawning liberality of the times. Ross represents the intolerant attitude in its decline. His tone is less severe and cruel than that adopted by Luther, and at times the thought penetrates his mind that the true and the false in religion cannot be so sharply separated as the theologians of an earlier generation imagined. Ross's work was published in the middle of the seventeenth century. At the beginning of the eighteenth century appeared the encyclopædic compilation of Bernard Picart and J. F. Bernard on the *Ceremonies and Religious Customs of the World*, which marks a great advance over Ross. This work, which in its completed form embraced eleven folio volumes, attracted much attention, and was translated into English.[2] Despite its imperfections, the material

---

[1] *Pansebeia, or a View of all Religions in the World*, London, 1653.

[2] "The Ceremonies and Religious Customs of the Various Nations of the Known World, together with Historical Annotations and Various Discourses equally instructive and entertaining, . . . by Bernard

it contains retains much of its value, and it may still, in a measure, be regarded as a basis for modern studies of religious rites. Treating in succession the religion of the Jews,[1] of Roman Catholics and of the various Christian sects, as well as of Islam, the religions of China, India, and even of Armenia, Bernard, who wrote the text accompanying Picart's illustrations, shows a marked desire to be accurate in the information he furnishes, and has recourse to the best sources at his disposal. The fairness of the author towards the Jews and Mohammedans would be most commendable, were it not that this fairness is purchased at the expense of Christianity, towards which he maintains the hostility born of the reaction against ecclesiastical domination. In so far as Bernard emphasises the need of investigating all the phenomena of religion, he is the forerunner of the historical school, and he also belongs to this school by virtue of his endeavour to represent the rites of the various religions embraced in his work from the point of view of their adherents; but he has added to his elaborate compilation an essay on the general and comparative aspects of "Religious Worship," which betrays his limitations. He shares the common opinion of his age, as set forth also in Thomas Hyde's *Religion of the Persians* (Oxford, 1700), regarding the pristine purity of religious faith. Everywhere in the development of an elaborate ritual he sees evidences of the degeneration of this pure and simple faith, and he

---

Picart, and curiously engraved by most of the best Hands of Europe," London, 1733.

[1] The fourth part of this division is a translation of Leo Modena's treatise on the "Ceremonies and Customs of the Jews," first published in 1637.

has no hesitation in ascribing its degeneration to the authority, in part given by the people to priests, and in part usurped. Bernard has enough of the historical sense to recognise that in organised religious cults, the appointment of ministers for the deities becomes necessary,[1] but, unwilling to abandon his theory, he is led to draw an arbitrary distinction between priests whom God himself designated for the service of the true religion, and those "whom mankind established to propagate" that which was the false. Apart from this theory, which illustrates the dogmatism inherent in the hostile attitude towards religion, the essay abounds in misconceptions of the real purpose of religious rites, which become perfectly clear when viewed in a historical light. Bernard's learning is prodigious, and it is therefore all the more curious to find by the side of flings and sneers which are due to a superficial view of religious phenomena, exceedingly keen and suggestive remarks on the reason for the observance of certain attitudes in prayers among various peoples, and he surprises us frequently by his methodical deductions from the comparison of customs observed by nations in different parts of the world.

Bernard's essay is singularly free from the abortive attempt to trace all religions to a single source, which marks several works produced towards the close of the eighteenth century. The most curious, if not the most noteworthy, of these is Charles Dupuis' *Origin of all Cults*,[2] which is an elaborate discussion of the claims of Natural Religion as the source of all religions. Rejecting the doctrine of

[1] Vol. i., p. 5.
[2] *Origine de tous les Cultes ou Religion Universelle*, Paris, 1795.

a special Revelation vouchsafed to any particular
people, Dupuis sets forth the universal character of
nature-worship, and shows how among all nations
there are traces that the earliest powers addressed as
divine are the sun, moon, and planets—God is but
another name for Nature. Dupuis goes further, and
derives from the worship of the powers of nature, the
doctrine of good and evil beings, of immortality and
of retribution. In short, the systems of theology, as
developed in advanced religions under the guidance
of priests and philosophers, are naught but the upper
storeys built upon the universal foundations of
Natural Religion. The point of interest to us in
Dupuis' work is its wide scope. In the discussion of
his theme, he extends his horizon so as really
to embrace all the great religions of the past and
present, as well as the views prevailing among
people in a primitive state of culture, or still abiding
in a savage condition. His researches are much
more profound than those of Bernard, or of any of his
predecessors, and he also shows much greater ability
to enter sympathetically into the feelings which
inspire devotion and worship in their numerous forms.
Indeed, but for his fatal defect of giving theory the
precedence over fact, he would have merited the distinction of being the founder of the historical study
of religion. It is quite clear as one penetrates into
Dupuis' work, that he had reached his conclusions
before entering upon his investigations. He evolved
a theory of the origin of religious cults, as the result,
no doubt, of careful and independent thought, but
not as the result of careful and independent investigation. He reached his main thesis as a philosopher who, by dint of speculation, reaches a general

formula which serves him as a starting-point for an
entire system of philosophy. The facts are then
introduced as a test of the theory. Dupuis is perfectly fair and exceedingly suggestive in his manner of
presenting these facts, but he does not present them
all, or rather, in his infatuation for his thesis, he does
not see all the facts, and those which he does see, are
viewed by him from a single point of vantage. The
interpretation he proposes for the material brought
together by him is frequently far from being the only
one that could be justified, whereas in many cases his
interpretation is positively erroneous. Once on the
hunt for nature-worship, he sees evidence of it everywhere, and one of the weakest portions of his book
is the forced interpretation of all myths, and practically all ancient traditions, as symbols of the movements of sun, moon, and stars, and of such natural
phenomena as the change of seasons. His error in
this respect is one that must not be too severely
judged, for in our days the untenable theory that
there is a single key that can unlock the mysteries of
mythological lore, still has its zealous supporters. In
the days of Dupuis the favourite key was allegory,
and extravagant as his fancy at times is, he is far
from being the most extreme representative of the
school to which he belongs.[1] In another respect, too,
Dupuis falls short of the requirements for a historical
study of religions. He fails to grasp the spirit peculiar to a certain religion. Concerned as he is with

---

[1] For a contemporary criticism of this allegorising "craze,"
Priestley's remarks in the Appendix to his *Comparison of the Institutions of Moses with those of the Hindoos, etc.* (Northumberland, 1799),
pp. 365-372, "On the Allegorising Talents of M. Boulanger," are
interesting reading.

determining what religions have in common, he neglects essential differences, and is often satisfied to support his theory upon agreements in external rites. This is particularly noticeable in his treatment of Christianity. While fairer than most of his French contemporaries in his estimate of the value of Christianity, he is misled by certain resemblances in Christian ceremonies to the Mithra cult, to trace the entire Christian system, at least in its essential particulars, to Persia. It cannot be denied that the comparisons which he institutes are often ingenious and generally suggestive; but his lack of a true historical spirit prevents his perceiving the differences between accidental resemblances, or those due to direct borrowing, and such as are the result of similar currents of thought, seeking for some outward expression in religious practice.

This fondness for comparisons is a characteristic trait of the comparative method in its infancy, whereas a matured comparative method is as much concerned with determining where comparisons should not be made as with drawing conclusions from comparisons instituted. But the weakness of Dupuis is in itself a sign of progress, and in tracing the rise of the historical school in the study of religions, an honourable place must be assigned to him as one of its precursors.

VII.

The real founder of the historical school, however, is the German, Johann Gottfried von Herder. It is not by accident that German scholarship gives the impulse to viewing in the light of history the course and development of religions. The seriousness and sobriety of the German mind revolted against the hostile attitude towards religion which culminated in the cynicism of the French materialists, while the freedom of research, which had become more firmly established in Germany in the eighteenth century than in England, enabled even theologians to throw aside the bonds of tradition, where tradition conflicted with ascertained facts. A reconciliation between the hostile and the exclusive attitude towards religion was sought in treating religions as an integral part of human history, and in an endeavour to trace through the religious history of mankind the natural development of certain religious ideas common to the human race. In the year 1784 Herder published the first part of his *Ideas for a Philosophy of the History of Mankind*,[1] which was followed in 1786 by a second part, and completed in 1787 by a third instalment. The plan of the work is in itself an indication of the historical spirit which animates Herder in all his investigations. Beginning with an account of the place occupied by our globe in the planetary system, he proceeds with a characterisation of the various forms of life to be met with in the world. He points out the salient features which distinguish man from the rest of the animal world, and then comes to his main theme—an endeavour to trace in the history of mankind, the gradual unfolding of certain fundamental ideas. The general conditions of culture, which are elaborately set forth, are followed by a more rapid consideration of the significant points in the various ancient and mediæval cultures. Herder had intended adding a fourth

---

[1] *Ideen zur Philosophie der Geschichte der Menschheit*, vols. 13 and 14 of Suphan's edition, Berlin, 1889.

part in order to carry the application of his theory down to modern nations, but he died before carrying out this portion of his task.

While, as will be apparent from this brief sketch, Herder's chief object is to set forth the philosophical background in mankind's course, the acceptance of one and the same point of view for the secular and religious phases of human history makes his work the point of departure for a new method in the investigation of religious phenomena.[1]

According to Herder, the history of the human race is a continuous chain of which the fortunes of single nations are the links. Through all the past, he sees a movement forwards and upwards, and so the chain becomes for him "the golden chain of culture." "Since I have come to recognise thee, oh, golden chain of culture," he exclaims in a noble, albeit sentimental, outburst, "that encirclest the world and reachest out through all individuals to the throne of Providence . . . history has ceased to be to me a horrible spectre of devastation on holy ground." Examining in this light the religious systems of the world, he reaches a general conception of the place occupied by religion in human history, which once for all disposes of both the hostile and the exclusive attitude of French and English writers. Herder sees in rites and ceremonies not the invention of certain individuals, but the natural expression of certain religious ideas. He aims, in each case coming under his observation, to show what these ideas are, and in some measure to account for them. More than this, he shows the manner in which these ideas are unfolded, and

---

[1] See particularly the fifth chapter of the ninth book.

thanks to his broad studies, his own particular views
are no longer the criterion by which religious ideas
and phenomena are measured. The firm conviction
held by him, that the history of religion as an
integral part of the fortunes of the human race
represents a steady upward movement, enables him
to be just in his criticism of the shortcomings and
defects of the various religious systems with which
he deals, and he does not refuse to apply the
scalpel of criticism to Christianity, equally with
others. The way to truth, Herder sadly admits, lies
across error, but he is also assured that truth and not
error is the goal of mankind. Of course, there is
much in Herder's work which no longer satisfies us.
Much appears trite because we have absorbed it,
much false because our knowledge has increased ;
but while he is too fond of dealing in generalisations
based on insufficient data, still his method is distinctly historical. He sinks his personality in the
subject that engages his attention ; he seeks to explain the actions of nations through an understanding
of traits peculiar to them, and, above all, he is catholic
in his spirit.

But while assigning to Herder the distinction of
being the founder of the historical treatment of
religion, we must not lose sight of the fact that he
does not stand alone in his attitude. To a large
extent he but gave expression to sentiments which
constituted a natural reaction against the extremes to
which English and French writers on religion went,
and among his contemporaries, Lessing stands out
prominently as sharing Herder's spirit. Indeed as
early as 1780, some years therefore before the publication of Herder's great work, Lessing foreshadows

the historical attitude towards religion. In the closing paragraph of the preface to his *Education of the Human Race*[1] he propounds the question "whether it is not wiser to see in all positive religions the course taken by the human intellect in its unfolding, rather than to make sport of, or to denounce any particular religion." In these words there is contained the essence of the historical method, but in the work itself, Lessing confines the application of the principle to the religion of the Old and New Testament. In so far his range is narrow as compared with Herder, who extends the principle to all nations, ancient and modern. The famous parable of the three rings in Lessing's drama, *Nathan the Wise*, might be adduced as a proof that Lessing does not fall short of Herder in his appreciation of all religions and in his ability to enter sympathetically into their spirit, but the historical attitude towards religion must not be confounded with the mere spirit of general tolerance which that parable reveals. A tolerant spirit, to be sure, is a necessary condition to a historical study of religions, but it by no means follows that this study levels all religions to merely varying expressions of truth. Carried to an extreme, the attitude of toleration blinds us as effectively to the real purpose served by religion as does the intolerant attitude, and it may become as mischievous in its consequences as the hostile attitude. Indeed, Lessing betrays to a strong extent the influence of the supposed pre-eminence of "priestcraft" in shaping the cause of religion, which belongs to the age in which he lived, and although Herder is not altogether free from this influence, he does not permit it to colour

---

[1] *Die Erziehung des Menschengeschlechts*, Berlin, 1780.

his general conception of religion, as it occasionally colours the views of Lessing, who shares with Samuel Reimarus, the author of the *Wolfenbütteler Fragmente*, a strong feeling of hostility towards priests and the clergy in general.

Again, while Herder does not publish his *Ideas* till 1784, his previous writings already foreshadowed his philosophical system, and as Julian Schmidt, in an admirable introduction to Herder's work,[1] well says, "the Ideas constitute the culmination of his thought, to which everything that preceded them acted merely as a preparation, while what follows falls under the caption of supplementary elaboration." As early as 1768 Herder had prepared an essay on the "Origin and Development of the earliest Religious Ideas," the title of which sufficiently indicates the line of thought taken by him. There are others besides Lessing among the contemporaries of Herder, in whom the thought of a purely historical treatment of religions had taken shape, but it was Herder who, by virtue of his encyclopædic grasp of human history, proved to be the inspiration of subsequent students of religion, and whose method became a model for the generation that succeeded him.

Before passing on, it will be necessary to notice a work which appeared simultaneously with Herder's *Ideas,* and showed the direction which the historical study of religion was taking. In 1785 there was published a voluminous work by Meiners[2] on the general history of religions, which is marked by its broad spirit and its large historical grasp. In contrast to

---

[1] Leipzig (Brockhaus), 1869, p. vi.

[2] *Grundriss der Geschichte aller Religionen*, followed in 1806 by the *Allgemeine Kritische Geschichte der Religionen.*

the superficial treatises of most of his predecessors,
Meiners, so far from supposing that religion is an
artificial product imposed upon humanity, declares
that there never existed a people devoid of religion,
and, moreover, that it is impossible to suppose mankind ever deprived of religious influence in the
shaping of its fate. He held this position in spite of
the statements of travellers, who, because they did
not encounter religious observances with which they
were familiar, returned with accounts of peoples
among whom no religion existed.

Meiners' work still retains its value, although much
of it is necessarily antiquated. Less satisfactory is the
elaborate treatise by Constant, published in 1824-31.[1]
The author, while also admitting the universality of
the religious sentiment, shows traces of the Voltairean
attitude in his specific treatment of the various
religious organisations. He is still on the scent for
traces of priestcraft, and, as a consequence, frequently
mistakes a perfectly rational process of development
for the deliberate machinations of a body of men
imposing their views upon the guileless masses. The
day, however, when the hostile attitude towards
religion could make an impression on the scholarly
world passed away with the advent of Herder's
historical method, and Constant's work therefore may
be passed over as an interesting survival, though like
"survivals" in other domains, this attitude had a
tenacious existence. Representatives of it, as already
intimated, are still to be found in our time, and
there can be no more significant illustration of the
truth of Bacon's dictum that "a little learning is

---

[1] *De la Religion considérée dans sa source, ses formes et ses developpements* (6 vols.), Paris, 1824-31.

dangerous" than the pathetic attraction which an
antiquated work like Paine's *Age of Reason* (1794-95)
—-remarkable as the production was for its own
days—still exercises upon minds which have, in a
self-deceptive spirit of supposed impartiality, secured
a superficial acquaintance with the course taken by
religion in its long and complicated process of
development.   But if this hostile attitude still
survives, the fault is in some measure at least due
to the direct opposition that still exists in certain
circles to the historical study of religions, and to
the half-heartedness with which the results of the
study are accepted in other circles.   As long as the
unfounded impression prevails that the study of
religious phenomena is in some mysterious way
detrimental to the interests of religious faith, just so
long will there be found many to suspect, either that
existing religions have something to conceal from the
gaze of the public, or that the representatives of
religious faith are not sure of their ground.

VIII.

It has already been pointed out that Herder is
primarily concerned with the general history of
culture.   In his *Ideas* he touches upon religion only
in so far as it forms a part of human culture.   It is
not until some decades later that we obtain, through
Hegel, the first systematic attempt of dealing more
specifically with the history of religion on the lines
laid down by the author of the *Ideas*.   One thinks
of Hegel chiefly as the founder of a school of meta-
physical thought, and hardly as a student of
religions from the historical point of view, and yet

his *Philosophy of Religion*[1] (1821-31), while having as its professed aim the application of his system to the facts of religion, is in reality a structural history of religions. Hegel is nothing if not historical in his attitude towards all things. One of the main propositions of his philosophy, that all being is "becoming," sufficiently shows this. The thought that as everything is the result of antecedent conditions, so at the very moment that something comes into being it is already in the state of passing on to become something else, could only have emanated from a mind accustomed to view all phenomena of nature and history in the light of their historical development. Like Herder, Hegel endeavours to seek the ideas that underlie events, and in order to find these ideas for the sphere of religion, it is necessary for him to undertake an examination of all the various forms which religion has assumed. He does this in his *Philosophy of Religion*, and from Hegel down to Pfleiderer, the most recent of the more eminent writers on the "Philosophy of Religion," this historical method has been followed as the only sound basis for a philosophical view of religion. Starting in true historical fashion with the religious notions of savages and of people living in a primitive state of culture, Hegel passes on to the religions of the Persians, Egyptians, Hebrews, Greeks and Romans, and concludes with Christianity. Rejecting, as contrary to the laws of development, the opinion of English and French Deists that the religion of primitive man was the purest, and the religions of civilised nations but corrupted forms of it, produced

---

[1] Published after his death as vols. 11 and 12 of his complete works, ed. Marheineke, Berlin, 1832.

under the agencies of evilly-disposed men, the order
of the treatment of religion which he adopts in his
work represents an order of the progressive development of what for him is *the* religious idea, or, as he
also expresses it, the religious consciousness of the
world. That the panorama which he brings before
us is incomplete—Islam and Buddhism are among
its most serious omissions—does not detract from
the truth which he establishes, that there is an *order*
in the growth of religious ideas, though one is inclined
to dissent from his conclusion (which is a part of his
general system of philosophy) that this order is
single or fixed as he declares it to be. It is not,
however, necessary to accept Hegel's system in order
to recognise the value of his *Philosophy of Religion*,
for what makes the exposition noteworthy is, firstly,
the emphasis which he lays upon the universal phenomena of religion, and, secondly, his endeavour to find
in these phenomena the rational expression of certain
leading ideas. That portion of his work which deals
with the religion of savages is particularly noteworthy
in this respect. The array of facts which he marshals
together is astonishingly large and varied, embracing
practically all that was known of savage life in
Hegel's days. At this period it is easy to point out
the defects in Hegel's method. There can be no
doubt that he sees too much in the facts of the
religious life of savages, and forces these facts in
order to strengthen his theory, but for all that, Hegel
represents an advance over Herder, who identifies
religion too closely with human culture, and leaves
out of consideration its *rôle* in the life of man at the
time when he was still without the adornments of
civilisation. In the systematisation which Hegel

attempts of the phenomena of religion he also passes
far beyond the horizon of Herder, and although here
too defects are apparent, and one revolts against what
appears to be over-systematisation, yet, as an attempt
at grouping long series of facts, this part of Hegel's
work has a permanent value. The essential point in
which Hegel and Herder agree is in the sympathetic
treatment which they accord to all religions. In the
case of Herder one feels that this sympathy is due to
a mind naturally elevated and noble, whereas with
Hegel it is the result of his mode of thought. As a
consequence, Herder's sympathy is perhaps wider,
whereas Hegel's is bounded by his system of philosophy, but for both it is strengthened by the historical
spirit in which they treat the multifarious phenomena of religion. As an illustration of the frame of
mind in which Hegel approaches this subject, one
may choose the following words from the introduction to his *Philosophy of Religion*, where, in speaking
of religion in general, he says, "All phases of human
relations, all actions and enjoyments that possess any
value for man, wherein he seeks his happiness, his
glory, his pride, have their outcome in religion." He
is led to accord a religious consciousness to all
nations, to the lowest as well as to the highest. "This
religious consciousness," he says, "has always been to
all nations the badge of their true dignity. . . . In
this domain of the soul, there flow streams from which
the soul drinks oblivion of all her pains and trans-
forms all hardships of time to a brilliant vision of the
night, illumined by the halo of eternity." Hegel,
like Herder, sees in the religious history of mankind
a continuous attempt to reach the truth, and while we
may differ from him in the manner in which he

characterises the various forms that truth assumes, the atmosphere into which he transports us is pure, and free from that cynicism which sees only knavery everywhere, and equally far removed from that exclusiveness which sees nothing but falsehood outside of a narrowly prescribed circle.

We may regard the work of Herder as supplemented by the philosophical treatment accorded to the unfolding process of religion by Hegel, but there is lacking in the great German philosopher an element which is essential to a historical attitude towards religion, and that is, simplicity. His metaphysics generally get the better of him, and while one has the conviction that his system of religious philosophy did not take shape in his mind until he had proceeded far in the investigation of the facts of religion, there are strong grounds for believing that, before he had brought his studies to a *conclusion*, theory obtained the mastery, and led him to construe his facts in accord with his general system of thought. The main objection to that system is that it plays too much with certain formulas. Hegel may be said to see at times too much in facts, which is almost as bad as seeing too little in them. So strongly is he himself fettered by his peculiar dialectics[1] that he seems unable to regard phenomena in a purely historical light, but resolves them into illustrations of certain formulas.

This element of simplicity is supplied by a thinker who arises in England about the same time that Hegel completes his great historical system of philosophy—Thomas Carlyle. Carlyle was steeped

[1] See McTaggart, *Studies in the Hegelian Dialectics*, Cambridge, 1896.

in German thought. He loathed the superficial
frame of mind in which English and French Deists
discussed religious problems, and while it is difficult
to say just how far he was influenced by Herder and
Hegel, he holds the same attitude towards religion
which characterises these German thinkers. He is
profounder than Herder, penetrating deeper into the
essential nature of the religious emotion or instinct
in man, and his utterances are free from the meta-
physical speculations which obscure Hegel's thought.
Unlike Hegel, he lays no claim to having a key that
can unlock all the mysteries of the universe. In
1841 Carlyle published his remarkable lectures on
Hero Worship. The second of these on " The Hero
as Priest," in which he uses as the illustration for his
theme the career of Mohammed, is a profound
analysis of the character of the Arabic prophet.
As a study in religious history it takes rank with
the best that has been written on Islamism. Carlyle attempts to show from the results achieved
by Mohammed what Mohammed *must* have been.
He reasons that one whose word has been the " life
guidance for twelve millions of souls these twelve
hundred years " could not have been an impostor, as
the writers of Europe had made him out to be, nor
could a cunning fanatic have accomplished what
Mohammed did. Only a man possessing faith can
communicate faith to others. He must have been
born to be a leader of men, or men would not have
followed him. Above all, he must have been true
to himself and to his ideals. " A false man," says
Carlyle, " cannot build a brick house — much less
found a religion." Reasoning in this way, he gives
us, on the basis of what was at the time known of

Mohammed, a portrait which is psychologically correct, and its faithfulness to history is all the more remarkable because of the comparative scantiness of trustworthy material about Mohammed that was accessible to Carlyle.   Guided by a correct historical insight, Carlyle set aside the absurd anecdotes and baseless stories in which his narrow-minded predecessors had placed implicit credence.   For the first time the prophet's career is set forth in a historical light, and an attempt made to account for his strength and his defects by the conditions under which he laboured.   As a biography of Mohammed, Carlyle's essay is of very little value at the present time.   It is full of errors which modern scholarship, through the publication of important sources of Arabic history, is enabled to correct, but as a historical conception of Mohammed the essay retains its significance, and remains as a lasting monument to the keenness of Carlyle's historical sense, as well as a justification of the historical and sympathetic treatment of religious phenomena.   In order to bring clearly before us the varying results to which one is led, according as he adopts the intolerant, the hostile, or the historical attitude towards religion, we cannot do better than place side by side Luther's bigoted denunciation of the Koran, Voltaire's cruel tragedy of *Mahomet*, and Carlyle's noble essay on the " Hero as Priest."

IX.

It has already been intimated that in accounting for the rise of the historical attitude towards religion, the general growth of the historical spirit, which

becomes marked after the French Revolution, must
be reckoned as a factor.   Under the influence of this
spirit, the study of ancient cultures as well as of
Christian civilisation was attacked with a vigour
which gave to these studies an impulse that is still
felt.   The young school of comparative philology
widened the historical horizon.   With the discovery
that the languages current in Europe could be traced
back to two or three groups, and that these groups
were related to others in the distant East; and
what was even more astonishing, that some parts
of one and the same group had become separated
in the course of time by a distance of thousands
of miles, an unprecedented interest in the history
of the mysterious East arose.   Activity in the
domains of history and philology thus led to researches that revolutionised our views of the state
of ancient culture.   The publication of Sanscrit
texts revealed the existence of a rich religious literature that appeared worthy to receive a place by the
side of the Old and New Testament.   A French
traveller, Anquetil Du Perron,[1] brought from Persia
authentic accounts of the history and present state of
Zoroastrianism.   The era of excavations began.   Out
of the soil the remains of Egyptian, Assyrian, and
Babylonian cities were dug up, and everywhere, with
added historical material, the sources for studying
the religious thoughts of the ancient world were
largely increased.   The strong impulse thus given to
the historical study of religions was still further
strengthened by travellers who penetrated into

---

[1] He published his great work on the Zend-Avesta in 1771, embodying a translation, together with an account of his voyages and a life of
Zoroaster.

regions, of which little had hitherto been known. The account of the religious conditions prevailing in these regions formed in almost every case the most interesting and noteworthy result of these expeditions. The extension of classical and biblical studies through the interest manifested in Sanscrit, Egyptian, Babylonian, Assyrian, Phœnician, and Persian researches, resulted in producing a comparative method for the study of religions which forms a parallel to the rise of the school of comparative philology.

By the middle of the nineteenth century, the historical attitude towards religion was so thoroughly established as to have successfully set aside all competitors. It had become the dominant one, and the results were seen, not only in the production of important researches, but in the perfection of a sound method in conducting these researches. In Germany, Austria, France, England, Holland, Italy, and America, scholars arose who devoted themselves to the methodical study of ancient religious literatures, to the investigation of religious customs, and to utilising the various sources that had been opened up for tracing the progress and course of religious ideas. It is but proper to mention some of those who have been instrumental in bringing about the adoption of the historical method in the treatment of religions.

X.

Foremost among these, by virtue of his works as well as by virtue of his services as a pioneer, stands the late Professor F. Max Müller, of Oxford. Early in his career his efforts were directed towards the elucidation of the various religious systems that

flourished at one time or another in India. His
publication of the Rig Veda,[1] with an elaborate
native commentary, stands out as a monumental
work which marks an epoch in Vedic studies, while
his numerous volumes embodying results of researches in the field of comparative philology,[2]
apart from their intrinsic value and their importance
for the specialist, have been the means of making
the general reading public familiar with the methods
and achievements of modern scholarship.   Though
primarily a philologist, Professor Müller's interest in
linguistic studies was at all times closely associated
with the mental phenomena represented by language.
He saw in language a means of ascertaining the unfolding of human thought, and as in this process the
religious side of man's nature plays perhaps the most
prominent part, he was naturally led to the study of
religious phenomena, more particularly as manifested
in Eastern literatures.   He himself succinctly expresses the main purpose of his career to have been
to discover "the thread that connects the origin of
thought and languages with the origin of mythology
and religion."[3]   In a series of lectures on the
Science of Religion delivered at the Royal Institution
in London in 1870,[4] he laid down in a lucid manner
the principles governing the historical study of

---

[1] *Rig Veda Sanhitâ, the Sacred Hymns of the Brahmans* (6 vols.),
London, 1849-74.

[2] *Chips from a German Workshop* (4 vols.), London, 1867-75; *The
Science of Thought*, London, 1887.

[3] *Autobiography* (London and New York, 1901), p. 3.   In this same
autobiography, p. 10, he recommends Montcalm's *L'Origine de la
Pensée et de la Parole* (Paris, 1900), as furnishing a clear and complete
abstract of his own writings.

[4] *Lectures on the Science of Religion*, London, 1872.

religions, and at the same time furnished an illustration of these principles by a discussion of some of the more important phases of the religious ideas embodied in branches of the subject so far apart as the teachings of the Vedas and Polynesian mythology. Some years later, he was instrumental in the establishment of the Hibbert Lectures on the Origin and Growth of Religion, with a view of initiating the general public into a proper appreciation of the subject. The first course was delivered by Professor Müller himself in 1878, and his plan in choosing a particular religion, as an illustration of the general theme of the series, was followed by those who succeeded him.[1] During the years 1878 to 1897, thirteen courses of lectures were delivered by eminent scholars, covering the religions of Egypt, Mexico, and Peru, of the Babylonians and Assyrians, Celtic Heathenism, Judaism, as well as various periods of Christianity, and such general themes as Universal and National Religions, and the Evolution of the Idea of God.

By far the most important of Professor Müller's achievements, however, was the publication of an extensive series of " Sacred Books of the East." Begun in 1879, no less than forty-four volumes have been issued, with the co-operation of a numerous band of scholars. The copious sacred literature of India occupies the most prominent place in this series, but in addition, the Koran, the Zend-Avesta, miscellaneous Pahlavi Texts, and some of the Sacred Books of China have up to the present been included. The

---

[1] For an account of the Hibbert foundation see the Preface in Professor Max Müller's volume, *On the Origin and Growth of Religion, as illustrated by the Religions of India*, London, 1880.

editing of this series assures for Max Müller the lasting gratitude of all students of religion. Moreover, by thus placing within reach of all the sources for the study of the various religions of the ancient and modern world, a fatal blow was given to the dilettantists to whom the history of religion at all times offered unusual attractions. For, as the project of the series arose in Max Müller's mind from a profound conviction that through a study of its sources alone could correct views as to the contents and significance of any given religion be found, so the great weakness of scholarship previous to this century lay in the lack or neglect of these sources. Abstract speculation had free scope when it was uncontrolled by a knowledge of the actual facts. As a consequence old prejudices were strengthened and new ones engendered. A broad mind like Herder's, in conjunction with an unusual degree of sympathetic interest in the struggles and heartaches of mankind, could break through these prejudices, but his work would have failed of permanent effect but for the zeal with which philologists pursued the search for the literary remains of Babylonia, Egypt, China, and Japan, and rescued from oblivion the records of mankind's efforts to satisfy its religious emotions and to interpret the divine. The importance, therefore, of the "Sacred Books of the East" series can hardly be over-estimated. The fruits of the undertaking were soon apparent in the greater interest that in Europe and in America began to be taken in the historical study of religions, but above all in the recognition that the subject began to receive in scientific circles, as a legitimately constituted and exceedingly important branch of serious research.

To Holland belongs the distinction of having been the first country to make adequate provision for the study of the subject in her higher schools. A decree was passed in 1876, by which the theological faculties of the four Dutch universities—Leiden, Amsterdam, Utrecht, and Groningen—were changed from mere training schools for ministers of a certain denomination into purely scientific bodies of the same order as the philosophical, law, and medical faculties. All the subjects represented—Old and New Testament, Church History, Dogmatics—were henceforth to be taught as purely historical disciplines and from a purely scientific point of view, the specific training for the service of the Church being left to supplemental courses provided for by each denomination, or relegated to non-official separate seminaries. At the same time the important step was taken of adding to each of the four faculties a chair for the general and comparative History of Religions. The most distinguished representative of the subject at the Dutch universities is Professor C. P. Tiele, whose contributions to the elucidation of the religious history of mankind have secured for him the place of honour by the side of Max Müller. Like the latter, Tiele is endowed with rich literary gifts, so that whatever issues from his pen has the charm of style in combination with the widest possible range of scholarship. While Max Müller betrayed in all that he wrote the scholar who views religious thought from the point of view of the student of language, Tiele's frame of mind is essentially that of the philosopher. Max Müller and Tiele thus complement each other. Both are distinguished by the accuracy of their scientific method, and it is unusual to find in a single generation two scholars, working within the same field, who possess such rare and yet divergent qualifications for their task. Professor Tiele's studies cover both Semitic and Aryan religions. He has published *Outlines of the History of Religion*,[1] which is by far the best that has been done in this line. His work on *The Comparative History of the Ancient Religions of Egypt and of the Semitic Peoples*[2] (1872) is a most valuable exposition. Besides numerous monographs and articles, two of his recent works call for special mention. In 1896 he began the publication of a *General History of Religion in Antiquity till the days of Alexander the Great.* Two volumes have appeared,[3] covering the religions of Egypt, Babylonia and Assyria, and Persia, and two more are promised. His work has been recognised far beyond the confines of his country. Various of his books and monographs have appeared in French, English, and German translations. He was selected to write the general article on "Religion" for the *Encyclopædia Britannica*, and what may be called the crowning work of his career was undertaken at the solicitation of the Gifford Trustees, who twice called Professor Tiele to Edinburgh to deliver courses of lectures on the general aspects of religion. These lectures have been published in two volumes, under the title *Elements of the Science of Religion*.[4] They furnish an exhaustive study of the morphological and ontological phases of the subject. No other work so well

---

[1] English translation by J. E. Carpenter (London, 1877).

[2] French translation, revised by the author (Paris, 1882).

[3] In Dutch and German.

[4] Edinburgh, 1897 and 1899. See a review by the writer in *The New World*, June 1899, and also a biographical sketch of Tiele in the *Open Court* for December 1900.

illustrates the present high grade reached by the science of religion in modern times.

XI.

By the side of Max Müller and Tiele, Professor Albert Réville merits a special mention. In 1880 France followed the example of Holland by establishing a chair for the history of religions at the Collège de France. Professor Réville was elected to fill it. He inaugurated his career by a general introductory course, which was subsequently published.[1] In 1884 he was elected Hibbert lecturer, and chose as his subject *The Native Religions of Mexico and Peru* (London and New York, 1884), but his chief work is an elaborate exposition of *The Religion of Non-Civilised Peoples*,[2] in which he greatly advances our understanding of the religious conceptions formed by man in the early stages of his development. Starting as a Protestant theologian, Réville is particularly to be commended for his courage in applying the same scientific methods to the study of Christianity which he applies to other religions. His elaborate *Jesus de Nazareth* (Paris, 1897) may be instanced, together with a volume of *Essais de Critique Religieuse* (Paris, 1869), as models for the manner in which problems of living moment can be treated by the application of this method.

A distinguished writer of modern times who has made valuable contributions towards establishing the historical study of religions on a sound basis is Ernest Renan. While the charge has often been brought

---

[1] *Prolégomènes de l'Histoire des Religions*, Paris, 1881 ; English translation by B. S. Squire, London, 1884.

[2] *Religion des Peuples Non-civilisés* (2 vols.), Paris, 1883.

against Renan that he allows his poetic fancy to
obtain the mastery over his sober scholarship, yet
even those to whom the peculiar spirit in which
Renan treats religious themes is distasteful will not
deny him a psychological insight as to the profound
mysteries of soul life. If Max Müller is essentially the student of religious literatures, and Tiele
the philosophical student, Renan may be designated
as the psychological expert.[1] While not a strict
adherent of any school, or even method, Renan is
perhaps the most distinguished exponent of two
of the leading principles in the historical study of
religions—sympathy with all religious manifestations,
and a conscientious study of the sources for the
various religious epochs embraced in his numerous
works. Confining himself more particularly to Semitic
religions, his essay on Mohammed,[2] together with his
profound work on *Averroes and Averroism* (1852), his
seven volumes on *The Origins of Christianity* (1863-
81), and his five volumes on the *History of Israel*
(1887-94), have done more perhaps than any other
publication to popularise the results of modern scholarship within these fields. To mention all those who
have enriched the literature of the subject in hand lies
beyond the scope of this chapter. Such names as
Professor E. B. Tylor of Oxford, the late Professor
W. Robertson Smith, Professor C. H. Toy of Harvard,
J. G. Frazer of Cambridge, F. B. Jevons of Durham
College, Professor Chantepie de la Saussaye, recently
elected to a chair in the University of Leiden,
occur to one as distinguished in this regard, and

---

[1] For an appreciative sketch of Renan, see James Darmesteter's
Selected Essays, pp. 178-248, Boston, 1895.

[2] In the first series of his *Études d'Histoire Religieuse*, Paris, 1857.

who have made noteworthy contributions to this important branch of research. Tylor's volumes on *Primitive Culture* (1871) and *The Early History of Mankind* (1878) mark the opening of new fields of inquiry. He has gathered together a large array of facts to illustrate the views that men living under primitive conditions are led to take of the nature by which they are surrounded, of animals, of trees, and stones, and plants. The theory of animism, which assumes that man attributed life and a living spirit to all the phenomena of animate and inanimate life, is associated with Tylor's researches. Robertson Smith, following in the lines of Sir Henry Sumner Maine and F. McLennan, devoted himself chiefly to tracing the development of religious institutions among the Semites.[1] Professor Toy, who is the most distinguished of American scholars within this field, has made valuable contributions to the more general problems connected with the unfolding of religious thought; while J. G. Frazer and F. B. Jevons have by their ingenious interpretations placed religious rites and customs in an entirely new light. Frazer's great work more particularly, *The Golden Bough*, marks an epoch in the study of religious rites. To Professor de la Saussaye belongs the credit of having produced, in collaboration with several scholars, a most serviceable manual for the History of Religions, which is marred only by its exclusion of Christianity and post-Biblical Judaism.[2] Reference has already been made to the Hibbert lectures established in 1878, which have done so

---

[1] His chief work, of which, however, only the first part was completed, is his *Religion of the Semites*, 1889.

[2] *Lehrbuch der Religionsgeschichte*, 2 vols., 2nd ed., Freiburg, 1898.

much to awaken general interest in the historical
study of religions among the general public. An
even more notable foundation for the direct advance-
ment of the scientific study of religion is that established by the will of the late Adam Gifford, one of
the Senators of the College of Justice of Scotland.
By this will, which became operative in 1888, a
sum of £80,000 was bequeathed to the four Scotch
universities, Edinburgh, Glasgow, Aberdeen, and St.
Andrews, for "Promoting, Advancing, Teaching, and
Diffusing the Study of Natural Theology—in the
widest sense of the term." By natural theology Lord
Gifford meant the search for the explanation of the
universe, or, as he put it, "the Knowledge of
God . . . of the Relations which men and the whole
universe bear to Him, the Knowledge of the Nature
and Foundation of Ethics and Morals," independent
of the question of a special revelation or dispensation.
Setting aside the mere history of specific religions,
lecturers were to be called under this will who should
treat of the most fundamental problems involved in
man's contemplation of the universe. The provisions
of the will are characterised by their broad spirit.
Among other things, Lord Gifford stipulated that in
the choice of lecturers no religious test of any kind
is to be prescribed. "They may be of any religion
or way of thinking, or, as is sometimes said, they may
be of no religion, or they may be so-called sceptics,
or agnostics, or free-thinkers." All that Gifford desired
to secure was "sincere love of, and earnest inquiries
after, truth." The subjects chosen, moreover, were
to be treated in the fashion of a "strictly natural
science." Natural theology was to be considered "just
as astronomy or chemistry," and to be investigated

"without reference to or reliance upon any supposed special, exceptional, or so-called miraculous revelation."[1] At Glasgow the series of lectures was opened by Professor Max Müller, who in four successive seasons, 1889-92, treated exhaustively Natural Religion, Physical Religion, Anthropological Religion, and Psychological Religion. The opportunity was thus afforded him of summing up his views on the various aspects of religion as embodied in the systems of ancient and modern times. Similarly, Professor Tiele, in his two courses before the Edinburgh University, gave the fruits of his life-long studies on the permanent and transient elements in religion.[2] Among other eminent lecturers on the Gifford foundation may be mentioned Professor Edward Caird on "The Evolution of Religion;" Sir G. G. Stokes on "Natural Theology" from the point of view of the physicist; Professor Otto Pfleiderer, of Berlin, on "Philosophy and Development of Religion." The Trustees of the fund, it will thus be seen, have been catholic in their choice, and it may be noted that two American scholars, Professor William James and Professor Josiah Royce, both of Harvard University, have recently been appointed as Gifford lecturers.[3] England is pre-eminently a country of lecture foundations, and while such as the "Bampton," "Congregational," "Burnett," and "Croall" have for

[1] See for a full account of the Gifford foundation an article by Professor R. M. Henley in the *Open Court*, xiii., pp. 72-84; also, Professor Max Müller's first lecture in the volume of Gifford Lectures on *Natural Religion* (London, 1889). The full text of Lord Gifford's will appears in the Preface to this volume.

[2] See above, p. 48.

[3] The first series of Royce's lectures has been published, *The World and the Individual*, London, 1900.

their more specific purpose the treatment of Christian theology, yet the subjects chosen by the lecturers necessarily overlap into the general field of religion, and some valuable contributions have thus been produced bearing on the historical study of religions in general.

XII.

In the United States there are also indications of awakening interest in the study. In 1891 an American committee for Lectures on the History of Religions was formed, and under its auspices four courses of lectures have been given by European and American scholars, and published.[1] At several universities the subject has been introduced into the curriculum, and as another sign of the times may be mentioned the series of Handbooks on the History of Religions now being published by Ginn & Co., Boston.[2] In 1897 the American Oriental Society established a "Section for the Historical Study of Religions," and decided to devote one of its annual sessions to papers bearing on the subject. A volume, embodying a selection of the papers read, is issued annually.

[1] For an account of the organisation of the Committee see the prefatory notice to the volumes published as follows, by G. P. Putnam's Sons, New York:—Rhys Davids, *Buddhism: Its History and Literature* (1896); D. G. Brinton, *Religions of Primitive Peoples* (1896); T. K. Cheyne, *Jewish Religious Life after the Exile* (1898); Karl Budde, *Religion of Israel to the Exile* (1899).

[2] Edited by Morris Jastrow, Jun. Two volumes have appeared— Hopkins, *Religions of India* (1895), and Jastrow, *Religion of Babylonia and Assyria* (1898); a third, Chantepie de la Saussaye, *Religion of the Teutons*, is in the press, and five others are in preparation.

An event of great importance was the establishment in 1886 of a special section for the Historical Study of Religion at the École des Hautes Études in Paris, with a faculty of about twenty members.[1]   In this way the entire field can be covered, extending from the religious notions and customs of primitive peoples to the latest phases of existing religions.   In addition to the courses, the section publishes volumes from time to time, embodying the researches of the professors and advanced students.   Two journals now exist specially devoted to promoting researches in the History of Religions.   The older of these is the *Revue de l'Histoire des Religions*, published since 1880 under the auspices of the Musée Guimet, and ably edited by Jean Réville and Leon Marillier ; the other, the *Archiv für Religionswissenschaft*, established in 1898, and published by Dr. Th. Achelis of Bremen.

Lastly, provision has also been made for that important adjunct to all historical studies — the Museum.   A public-spirited citizen of Lyons, M. Emile Guimet, after devoting many years to the collection of objects illustrative of the religions of the world, presented to the city of Paris the result of his labours, and a handsome building was erected in which the precious collections were housed.[2] Besides the endowment of the Museum, M. Guimet has also provided amply for publications of researches. Some thirty magnificent volumes have been issued under the title, *Annales du Musée Guimet*, and if it be borne in mind that, in addition to this, M. Guimet

[1] See Appendix.
[2] See the *Guide Illustré* of the Museum, by the Director, M. Milloue, and also Chapter XV. of this book.

also established the *Revue de l'Histoire des Religions*, it will be recognised what a profound debt scholarship owes to this munificent example of public-spirited interest in advancing an important branch of research. With special chairs, a well-organised school, journals and publication resources, and an elaborate museum, the outlook for the further progress of the historical study of religions in France is more favourable than in any other country.

One cannot close this chapter without expressing surprise that so little has been done to secure official recognition for the subject at German universities. The late Professor Roth, of Tübingen, was in the habit of giving courses on the history of Religions, and, sporadically, elsewhere the subject has received the attention of German scholars—generally as a part of the theological curriculum, but nowhere has there been established a special chair for such instruction at any of the twenty German universities. This rather strange omission is no doubt due in part to the prejudice prevailing in a country in which scholarship insists upon strictly scientific method, against a branch of study so frequently invaded by the dilettante ; but in order to drive the latter out of the field, there is no more effectual method than to encourage earnest and properly-trained scholars to take up the investigation of the problems in this branch of research, and to this end chairs must be established at institutions of learning, where scholars may be trained. What applies to Germany also holds good for England. Courses of lectures are not sufficient. If permanent results are to be secured, provision must be made for systematic instruction at English universities ; and similarly in the United States, where but little has been done by universities to encourage the subject, the example set by Holland and France needs to be more largely followed.[1]

[1] See a paper by the writer on " The Historical Study of Religions at American Colleges and Universities " in the *Journal of the American Oriental Society*, vol. xx., pp. 317-325.

CHAPTER II.

THE CLASSIFICATION OF RELIGIONS.

I.

THE question as to the proper classification of religions is manifestly one of great importance. Before the rise of the historical study of religion the problem was solved in a very simple fashion. A particular religion was set down as true and the balance were designated as false, though within the pale of the false religions, certain distinctions were drawn. Thus, Christian theology, which after the decline of the Mohammedan power swayed men's minds completely, started from the assumption that a special revelation was vouchsafed to ancient Israel, and that the covenant made between God and his chosen people, and recorded in the Old Testament, was abrogated by the advent of the Messiah—Jesus. The New Testament was viewed as the sole depository of religious truth. This theory was defended and elaborated with great learning and acumen. Viewed merely as intellectual achievements, the writings of the Christian scholastics merit profound respect; nor must it be supposed that facts were wanting which appeared to justify, beyond reasonable doubt, the system of religious philosophy that was reared upon the theory in question. The necessity, for example, of a Divine Revelation to man rested upon com-

paratively solid foundations.   Even to this day, the
problem of how a being with definite limitations in
all directions could conceive the idea of the Infinite,
is one for which it is difficult to find a satisfactory
solution.   As a working hypothesis, the supposition
that the Deity had of His own will communicated to
man a certain knowledge of Infinite Power, answered
many of the questions that otherwise appeared hopeless conundrums.   Scholastic theology, moreover, had
certain broad aspects which in a superficial estimate
of it are frequently overlooked.   While drawing
the lines of demarcation sharply between the true
and the false in Religion, it yet accorded even to the
false religions a semblance of truth.   On the basis of
the Old Testament a primitive revelation was vouchsafed to all mankind.   It was held that even the most
degraded forms of religion prevailing among savages
showed traces of this revelation.   The theory of the
original purity of the human race, which was also an
inherent part of the Christian theology of the Middle
Ages, imparted at all events to the position of mankind a dignity which is lacking in the views held by
many modern scholars.   The evolution of religion
according to the older view, was a devolution ; and
though modern scholarship has demonstrated the
improbability of this view, the theory that false
religions were not inherently wrong, but resulted
through a series of degradations from a pristine condition of purity, prevented a one-sided view from
degenerating into a condemnation of the history of
the human race.

As for the special revelation accorded to the
Jewish people, the facts of history clearly pointed
out that the specific mission set aside for this people

was to proclaim to mankind a particular view of
religion differing totally from beliefs developed
among other nations. However one might account
for the facts, the lesson taught by them was clear.
And again, the spread of Christianity, and its ultimate
triumph over Greek and Roman heathenism—over
both the legitimate cults and the unofficial mysteries
—its ability to secure a foothold wherever civilisation
penetrated,—all this lent a strong support to the
doctrine that the advent of Jesus marked a further
stage in the divine process of Revelation.

Considerations such as these should prevent us
from condemning too hastily the classification of
religions into true and false. Even from the historical
point of view such a classification has a certain value,
inasmuch as it admits a development of religious
thought—an upward and a retrograde movement.
Its chief weakness becomes manifest only when we
come to consider the advanced religions—Judaism,
Christianity, Islamism, Buddhism, and Zoroastrianism
—for the theory fails on the one side to do justice to
such forms of faith as Buddhism and Zoroastrianism,
which arose independently of the assumed special
Revelation recorded in the Old and New Testaments, and on the other it does not place the relationship existing between the three religions that emanate
from the Bible in a proper historical light. To either
ignore the further development of Judaism after the
advent of Jesus, or to look upon it as a survival due
to deficient faith or to obstinacy, is manifestly unfair
and unscientific; while to treat Islamism as due
to the inspiration of the Devil, or as an aberration
prompted by ignorance and supported by fanaticism,
is bound to block the way to a fair estimate of a

religion that has not only swayed the lives of millions, but has produced a theological literature that merits an honourable place by the side of Christian theology. But even within the pale of Christianity, the assumption of a true standard in opposition to a false one fails to offer a satisfactory solution of the course taken by the Christian religion itself. Such a view of necessity leads to admitting only one line of development as a legitimate evolution of the Christian idea ; and yet the formation of sects within a religion, while in one sense a disintegrating process, is in another a manifestation of vitality and of healthful growth, quite as much as the growth of a city is indicated by the opening up of new streets and byways. A religion without sects is necessarily limited in its range ; and so long as racial differences among nations exist, with variations in temperament, the same religion in different geographical centres is bound to take on various forms.

It is not necessary to plead in addition the human impossibility of being absolutely certain of possessing religious truth, in order to demonstrate the fatal weakness of a classification of religions into true and false. Even the mischief, misery, and crime produced by such a classification would not necessarily constitute a vital objection to it, for it may be maintained that such mischief, misery, and crime are factors as essential in the development of religion, as destructive rains are necessary to vegetation. The final and supreme test of a theory is its ability to explain the facts, and it is just in this respect that the theory under discussion fails.

It must not be supposed that the Christian theologians of the Middle Ages stand alone in maintain-

ing the twofold classification of religions into true
and false.   The position of Jewish and Islamic
theology is practically the same.   While the general
spirit of the Talmud, which may be taken as representative of Jewish thought, is remarkably broad,
going to the length of admitting that the righteous
of all nations will have a share in the world to come,
yet, the assumption throughout is that "the nations"
will sooner or later recognise the error of their ways
and acknowledge the Old Testament as the sole
standard of religious truth.   The grand hope of
Judaism is the inauguration of the time when all
nations will stream towards Jerusalem as the one
centre of religious truth.   Again, we must beware of
condemning this theory on insufficient grounds.   It
unfolds an ideal of the future condition of mankind
which cannot fail to prove an inspiration to those
who cling to it.   The looked-for Messiah is to
inaugurate an era of peace and general happiness,
when virtue will reign supreme and all violence and
injustice disappear, but this era can be brought about
only on one condition—the recognition of Judaism
as the sole true religion.   Islam starts out as a
religion militant.   Its professed aim is to eventually
force the world to the acknowledgment of Mohammed as the last and greatest of the prophets.
Islam has this advantage over Judaism and Christianity, that inasmuch as it is later than these, it
could acknowledge both Judaism and Christianity as
embodying the revelation of religious truth, with,
however, this proviso, that in Islam the special
revelation of God reached its culmination.   As a
sequence, the Islamic theory fails to account for the
development of religion after a certain period, while,

like Judaism and Christianity, it leaves out of account the rise of religions which are in no way connected with it.

II.

Among theories brought into prominence in modern times, none has proved more fruitful in various directions than that of "evolution." First applied to the natural sciences, it was extended to history and philology, and the attempt was made to determine the laws by which nations develop the powers peculiar to them, by which the varieties of human speech are produced, and by which the complicated machinery of modern society is brought into action. As the most elaborate presentation of the application of the idea of evolution to the whole panorama of human culture, we may instance the System of Philosophy of Herbert Spencer, divided into various branches—First Principles, or Philosophy Proper, Sociology, Psychology, Biology, and Ethics.

The same theory has also been applied to religion, and scholars are pretty generally agreed on two points —that the religious development of mankind proceeds in accordance with definite laws, and that this development is on the whole an upward movement from crude ideas and primitive forms of worship to a philosophic conception of the universe, accompanied by a ceremonial correspondingly elaborated and refined. It is true that there are still a few scholars, notably Andrew Lang, who in one form or another cling to the belief in a pristine purity of religions and a subsequent degradation, but the evidence on the other side is so overwhelmingly strong that the burden of proof now rests with those who oppose the theory of an evolution of religion from a crude to a refined state. The opposition to this "evolution" theory arises frequently from the superficial manner in which the theory is defended and illustrated. A crude or primitive form of religious belief or of doctrine does not necessarily involve a low view, as the evolutionists would sometimes have us believe, any more than primitive civilisation of necessity means a general degradation of the moral sense. Primitive culture as well as modern civilisation has its code of honour, its standard of virtue, and even its science. The belief in the progress of mankind does not involve the corollary that man begins his career in total degradation. Because the air on the top of the mountain is pure, it does not follow that the valleys are full of malignant miasma. No more fatal mistake can be made than to suppose that we must reach dirt and filth before we get to the foundations of culture. Jevons has well set forth[1] that, so far as religious conceptions are concerned, the advance of modern over primitive ideas is due largely to a single factor—the wider range of experience that comes with advancing civilisation. Indeed, the evolution theory applied to religion establishes a close bond between the primitive and the advanced forms of faith. The elements found in the latter are present in the former, and the large part played by "survivals"—frequently in the form of so-called superstitions—in all forms of faith is an admirable illustration and proof of this bond. The evolution theory, thus interpreted, in no way injures the dignity of the religious sentiment, but on the contrary, by proving the inseparable connection

[1] Jevons, *Introduction to the History of Religions*, chap. iv.

between religion and culture, holds up religion in the light of an integral part of man's nature.

III.

It would seem natural to propose a classification of religions in accordance with the various phases through which religion passes, on the supposition of the evolution theory. Various attempts of this kind have indeed been made, the most satisfactory being the classification proposed by the distinguished Professor Tiele. In his article on "Religions" in the *Encyclopædia Britannica* he sets up this successive scale— Primitive Naturalism, Animism, National Polytheistic Religions, Nomistic Religions,[1] and Universal Religions. Serious objections have, however, been urged against this division.[2] In the first place, Animism, as a distinct evolutionary phase of religion, has recently fallen into disrepute. The personification of such powers of nature as directly affect, or seem to affect, the well-being of man seems natural at a certain stage of culture, but it may be questioned whether we are justified in designating Animism as a distinct religion or phase of religion. Animism is in a measure the philosophical substratum of an early form of religion, but it is not a specific form of religion. Animism alone would not lead to worship, and it will be admitted that a religion must contain the two elements—a doctrine and a cult. Again, the distinction between national polytheistic religions and nomistic religions seems arbitrary. Accepted forms

---

[1] *I.e.*, religions possessing codes for the regulation of the cult, and of life in general.

[2] See, *e.g.*, Maurice Vernes, *L'Histoire des Religions*, pp. 40-48.

of worship shade imperceptibly into practically legal enactments, and it matters little whether these enactments are embodied in a written code, or definitely fixed by unbending tradition in combination with actual practice.   As a consequence, national polytheistic religions may also be grouped in the category of nomistic religions.   The existence of a priesthood is all that is required to bring about this combination, and workers of magic who have the secret of certain formulas are as effective in this respect as the priests of an elaborately organised temple service.   Lastly, the term universal religion is devoid of real meaning as long as there are several religions disputing the claim.   Tiele's system provides for three universal religions—Christianity, Islamism, and Buddhism, but so far as purely religious doctrines go, Judaism and Zoroastrianism might with equal justice or injustice be included. Both of these religions maintain the belief in a deity who is supreme over the whole world, whose jurisdiction is neither limited to a particular district nor to a particular people, and the fact that this deity has singled out a single people for special favours, or a special dispensation, in no way affects the universal character of the religion, inasmuch as the three other religions named also involve the doctrine of a revelation made to certain favoured individuals.   But granting the full force of the argument that Christianity, Buddhism, and Islamism find adherents among various nations, yet the extension of each of these encounters definite limitations.   Neither Buddhism nor Islamism have succeeded in forcing their entrance to any noticeable extent into centres of European culture.   Buddhism, to be sure, has exerted a certain philosophical influence upon European thought, but beyond this we have only sporadic outbursts of so-called "occultism," which, by the testimony of competent scholars, is a travesty of genuine Buddhism.[1] As for Christianity, while it has obtained a foothold in all parts of the world, its impress upon lands in which Islamism or Buddhism holds sway cannot be called profound, despite the missionary efforts of the past fifty years. Moreover, in the case of Christianity, a distinction must be drawn between the doctrinal elements and what may be called the culture element. Christianity is so closely bound up with modern civilisation that its perpetuity is assured even against the inroads of current thought.   But for this very reason its claim to universality rests largely upon this compound character ; it is manifestly unfair to call the religion universal, so long as the civilisation with which it is united has the lion's share in the process of steady extension.

In his most recent work, Professor Tiele recedes somewhat from the position[2] that he previously maintained. He emphasises the difficulties involved in drawing sharp lines of demarcation in any scheme of classification based upon a supposed order of evolution.   While not altogether abandoning his former scheme, he appears to lay more stress now upon the two main types of religion recognised by him, which he designates as nature-religions and ethical religions.[3]   Within the nature-religions he

[1] See Hopkins, *Religions of India*, pp. 562-569.

[2] *Elements of the Science of Religion*, vol. i. (Edinburgh, 1897), Lectures ii.-v.

[3] Already proposed by him in his article "Religions," in the *Encyclopædia Britannica* (9th ed.).

distinguishes again between the Lowest and the Highest stages. Such a division impresses one as much more satisfactory. The line of demarcation between non-ethical and ethical religions is, as Tiele conclusively shows, one of the sharpest that can be drawn in a comprehensive review of all historical and existing religions, and it is also true that the advance in religious development comes not so much from a change of doctrine as from the infusion of the ethical spirit into the doctrines themselves. Not that notions of right and wrong are totally wanting in even the most primitive of nature-religions, but gods, spirits, and demons are not looked upon as acting in accordance with ethical considerations. The chief and distinguishing attribute of the beings to whom primitive peoples pay adoration is—power. It is because of their power that they attract the notice of man and engage his thoughts. They wield this power as they see fit. Man is helpless against it, and his only hope lies in an endeavour to turn this power to his advantage or to ward off its evil effects. The means that he employs to bring about one of these two contingencies do not concern us here. These means are sometimes direct by acts of conciliation, but more frequently indirect, through the medium of privileged individuals, who, opposing power to power, are able to control the actions of the beings in whose hands human fate, to so large an extent, lies.

A difficulty however arises, when we come to those religions which Tiele places in the category of the Higher forms of nature-religions.[1] He finds the distinguishing mark of these higher nature-religions in the establishment of an organised polytheism, as

---

[1] *Elements, etc.* Lecture iv.

against the unorganised polydæmonism of the earlier period. Corresponding to this, in the lower nature-religions, the period of myth-formation is succeeded by the period of mythology. It may be admitted that there is a natural tendency in primitive religions towards a classification of the beings upon whose whims man feels himself to be dependent, and towards drawing distinctions among the beings themselves; but for the very reason that the tendency is natural, the carrying out of the process is not indicative of progress. Whether some Beings are called gods and others spirits, or whether all are vaguely grouped together as demons, is a mere matter of nomenclature, and of no moment so long as the character of all is essentially alike.

Similarly, the period of mythology represents no advance over that of myth-formation, and it is more than doubtful whether the distinction proposed can be maintained. The moment that myths are formed we have mythology, and the classification and transfiguration of myths goes on simultaneously with the production of new ones, or with borrowing those produced by peoples with whom a nation comes into contact. Professor Tiele admits that in the higher nature-religions the ethical element is already present, though it has not yet obtained perfect control. But the question may be asked whether it is not arbitrary to draw the line between nature and ethical religions, *after* the period where the ethical spirit makes its manifestation. According to Tiele, the religions of the Greeks and Romans still fall within the category of nature-religions. He is led to this view because of the universal attributes given to some of the gods

in the mythology of these two nations. But, after all,
a fairer test of a religion lies in the ethics which it
strives to impress upon its followers. Viewed from
this position, the Greek and Roman religions certainly
deserve to be counted among the ethical religions.

Proceeding in this way, other religions which
are grouped with the nature-religions could be
shown to have claims which warrant us in placing
them in the other class of ethical religions. The fact
is that the ethical spirit makes its appearance in a
religion the moment that the attempt is made to
regulate the relationship between men, so as to avoid
the undue oppression of certain groups or individuals
by others. This process goes on quite independently
of the moral or immoral character of the myths.
Advancing refinement finds a method of giving to
these myths a meaning from which the offensive
phases are removed. There is, in reality, no inherent
contradiction between a cult based upon conceptions
that belong to nature-religions, and the infusion of an
ethical spirit. It follows, therefore, that, while the
distinction between non-ethical and ethical religions
is a valuable one, it cannot be used as the basis for a
satisfactory scheme of classification. The introduction of the ethical spirit is but one factor in the
evolution of religion, and but a single index ; whereas
a classification can be satisfactory only if it takes
into account all important features and indexes.
Before proceeding to point out what these are, it will
be well to consider other classifications proposed.

IV.

Classifications which proceed from the purely
philosophical point of view need not detain us long.

The most notable of these is the one proposed by Hegel.[1] Starting from a philosophical determination of the idea and nature of religion, Hegel regards the actual course taken by religious development as the attempt to realise this idea. He, too, places at the beginning of the scale nature-religions, but for him such forms represent merely the spontaneous manifestations of the religious idea. The progress of religion consists in the change from this spontaneous immediate realisation to a deliberate realisation. In contrast therefore to nature-religions, he places the religion of spiritual individuality which takes its rise when thought begins to obtain control of the natural emotions. Within this second category he distinguishes several forms : firstly, the religion of majesty, in which the reflecting mind is overwhelmed by the contemplation of the manifestation of the Divine Being ; secondly, the religion of beauty, the characteristic feature of which consists in the combination of the natural and spiritual. The thought of the Deity is materialised, so to speak, combined with personality, in consequence of which the spiritual conception of the universe involves the thinking subject as well as the subject of thought. A third form appears when the idea of religion, deliberately determined by human thought, comes to include the recognition of the purpose served by the powers of nature and by the personal deities that form part of the doctrine of the religion of beauty. Hegel compares these four types to the four ages of man, childhood corresponding to the natural spontaneous manifestation of the religious ideas ; youth to the form of religion when contem-

---

[1] *Philosophie der Religion,* see especially vol. II, pp. 183-188 (ed. Marheineke, Berlin, 1832). See above, p. 36.

plation begins, without however recognising a purpose ; manhood to the devotion towards a definite
aim, but combined with the inclusion of self as part
of the aim ; while old age, setting aside all subject-
ivity, comes to realise the absolute goal of the
universe.

The manifest objection to such a scheme, which
may be regarded as typical for a philosophical
classification, is its unhistorical character. We may
distinguish in the various forms assumed by religion
certain leading ideas of which the religions in
question form the expression, but such ideas can
never be regarded as constituting the *essence* of a
religion without doing violence to the general purpose served by all religions, which is essentially
practical. Moreover, the phases which Hegel distinguishes are not so distinct from one another as to
prevent the combination of two or more of them in a
religion. To take a single example, the religion of
the Greeks is, according to Hegel himself, one of the
religions of beauty, and yet it also contains elements
which would warrant us in classing it with the
religion of majesty, while from another point of view
it also belongs to the highest form of religion. The
same reasoning applied to other religions will show
with equal force the arbitrary character of the lines of
demarcation drawn by a philosophical classification.

It may confidently be asserted that no religion
stands as the representative of a *single* idea. A
certain idea may be more strongly emphasised in a
particular religion than in another, but the religion
will upon examination be found to contain much
more than this idea. Thus, in Islam we find the
idea of fate prominently brought forward. Islamic

theology is largely based upon the impossibility for man to control his own lot, but we should miss the mark entirely were we to regard Islam from this point of view alone.   Buddhism and Christianity have been called religions of redemption, because in those religions the idea of personal salvation plays an important part, but both Buddhism and Christianity are too complicated phenomena, their history is too closely bound up with numerous other factors, to justify a description or definition of them in terms of a single philosophical idea or doctrine.   The emphasis, then, placed by a religion upon a specific idea must not be interpreted as involving an exclusion of other ideas ; and even though we are able to distinguish between various types of religion, yet in every religion, so long as it constitutes a vital part of the life of a people, there are two sides—a theoretical and a practical side—which are not necessarily in harmony.   The distinctions set up by Hegel, however, apply chiefly if not entirely to the theoretical substratum of a particular religion, and his theory leaves out of consideration the practical aims of religion as manifested by popular rites and even popular superstitions, which cannot be neglected in any comprehensive view of the subject.

But above all, Hegel's classification does not accord with the actual facts as presented by the historical evolution of religion.   While, as already pointed out, there is general agreement among students of religion that there is, on the whole, an upward tendency in religion from crude to more refined ideas, and corresponding to this tendency, an evolution from crude and even cruel rites to such as more worthily express spiritual aspirations and emotions, still the line followed by religion is far from being a straight one. The track it leaves is marked by deviations and windings, and the course taken by religion among a people is so closely bound up with changes in political and social conditions, that it is the height of arbitrariness to study the manifestations of religion as isolated phenomena—expressive merely of certain abstract ideas.

In explanation of the system set up by Hegel, it must be remembered that his own mental growth falls in the period when the historical horizon of the intellectual world had indeed been extended, but before the time when a method of investigation adequate to this widened horizon had been perfected. Had he written his *Philosophy of Religion* some twenty years later, it seems safe to assert that he would no longer have attempted to force the complex manifestations of the religious spirit into so narrow a compass. However this may be, the reaction against the Hegelian manner of thought came with the growth of the strictly historical method in what may be broadly termed anthropological research. The careful study of facts, independent of preconceived themes, swept away many scientific superstitions to which men had clung for a long time, and the way was prepared for a classification of religions, based primarily upon an inclusive survey of the actual facts.

V.

M. Réville, the distinguished Professor of the History of Religions at the Collège de France, has proposed a classification which may be designated as the combination of the historical and philosophical point of view.[1] Retaining the familiar division between polytheistic and monotheistic, he begins by distinguishing between (1) the primitive religion of nature, and (2) animist and fetichist religions. The former he defines as the naïve cult of natural objects represented as possessing life, and influencing by their supposed power the destiny of man ; the latter represent a further development of the former, the advance being signalled by the beginnings of a mythology. A third division he designates as the national mythologies, based on the dramatisation of nature. To this class belong the religions of China, Egypt, Babylonia, as well as the religion of the Teutons, Gauls, Greeks, and Romans. A fourth stage begins with the introduction of the legal factor. Brahmanism, Mazdeism, and the two philosophical religions of China, Kong-fu-tzu and Lao-tsu, make up the polytheistic-legalistic religions. The highest stage of the polytheistic religions is marked by Buddhism, which he designates as the religion of salvation, and which, while opposed in principle to polytheism, rests in its practice upon the local polytheistic faiths. The monotheistic religions are three in number—Judaism, Islamism, and Christianity, the difference between these being that, while Judaism is legalistic and national, Islamism is legalistic and international, and Christianity, the religion of salvation, is international.

The objections to be urged against this classification are of much the same order as those advanced when considering Tiele's earlier views. In the first

[1] *Prolegomena of the History of Religions* (London, 1884, English translation), pp. 100-101.

place, to set up a division between polytheistic and monotheistic religions is so exceedingly unsatisfactory, and has so often been shown to be so, that it is a matter of surprise to find so eminent a thinker as Réville retaining it, even as a matter of convenience. The monotheistic tendency exists among all peoples after they have reached a certain level of culture. There is a difference in the degree in which this tendency is emphasised, but whether we turn to Babylonia, Egypt, India, China, or Greece, there are distinct traces of a trend towards concentrating the varied manifestations of divine powers in a single source. Upon reflection, it will be found that this tendency is quite natural—suggested indeed by the growing complications of social organisation in a people on the high road to advanced culture, and which depend for their satisfactory workings upon gradations of powers deriving their authority from a single source. Natural logical processes come to the aid of such a tendency, adding strength to it, and prompting to greater (though not absolute) consistency in the form taken on by a monotheistic conception of the universe. National pride may be instanced as a third factor in contributing to the growth of the monotheistic spirit in matters of religion. When a nation places at the head of its pantheon a deity supreme over all others, endowed with unique powers which likewise mark him off from others, fidelity to this god, added to that innate sense of its own importance which a people possesses, will easily lead to the conclusion, either that the supreme gods of other nations cannot for an instant be compared to this supreme god, or that other gods are but variant forms of this one Supreme Being. The former is the popular view; the latter that to which the philosophical minds among a people are inclined. For the Hebrews, Chemosh, the chief god of the Moabites, was not at all a god to be compared to the national Hebrew deity, Jahweh, while the Greek philosophers had no difficulty in seeing in the Egyptian god Ammon a form of their own Zeus.

It is needless to carry this argument any further, beyond pointing out .that the supposed opposition between polytheism and monotheism which such a classification assumes is likewise fallacious. There is, from the practical point of view by which popular conceptions are guided, no inherent inconsistency between the belief in many gods and the decided tendency to place one in supreme control with attributes which practically differentiate this god, in the quality as well as in the quantity of his powers, from all others. Henotheism,[1] a term which Professor Max Müller has proposed in order to describe the disposition to attribute to a particular god, on certain occasions, the powers of all others, is but an illustration of the way in which polytheism may shade into practical monotheism, without, however, losing much of its real force; and when monotheistic conceptions in a more complete form come to prevail, angels and evil spirits, including the supreme evil spirit, the Devil—belief in whom is not looked upon as inconsistent with monotheistic faith—are merely thinly-disguised substitutes for the pantheon of polytheistic religions surrounding the supreme god. The popular notion which makes the Hebrews the originators of

[1] *Lectures on the Origin and Growth of Religion, as illustrated by the Religions of India,* Lecture v. ; see Chantepie de la Saussaye, *Lehrbuch der Religionsgeschichte,* 2nd ed., p. 16.

monotheism is erroneous. The distinctive contribution of the Hebrews to religion is not the belief in one
god, but the investing of that god with ethical
attributes, which separated him gradually from the
deities in which the other nations believed, and
eventually brought about his triumphant survival in
the great crash which befell the ancient world, and
swept away the faiths of Egypt, Babylonia, Phœnicia,
Greece, and Rome. Still more serious is the objection
to be urged against Réville's classification, because of
his assumption of a sharp demarcation between
animism, fetichism, and mythology. These features
do not represent successive stages in religious
development. Whatever method be adopted for the
interpretation of myths, the tendency towards myth-
formation certainly appears at a stage when animism
and fetichism—using these terms in their ordinary
acceptation—are controlling factors, and so far as
animism and fetichism are concerned, it cannot by any
process of reasoning be shown that the one shades off
into the other. Animism in some of its forms passes
over into the higher and indeed into the highest forms
of religion, and so fetichism, which after all is but an
attitude of the mind rather than a form of religious
belief, never loses its hold upon the masses, no matter
what the particular religion is which they profess. A
valuable feature in Réville's classification, and one
which must be taken into consideration in any scheme
based upon the historical study of religions, is the
emphasis he lays upon the appearance of the legal
factor as marking a distinct stage. Whether a nation
produces a literature or not may be a matter of
accident, and the Phœnicians are at least one example
of a people reaching a high stage of culture without

possessing a literature, while the literary productions of ancient Egypt are without great merit, and certainly do not form the basis of Egypt's claim to immortal glory.

When, however, in addition to a religious literature, we find the ordinances of religion set forth as part of the legal constitution of a people, the ritual regulated, not by incrustated custom or tradition, but by stipulations in legal form deduced from certain principles, the ceremonies becoming legal institutions, the priesthood performing its functions with the minutiæ of legal procedure—in short, when religion, instead of symbolising the emotional life of a people, is itself a symbol of the legal spirit which has found its way into the national life, a form of religion is produced which is indeed distinct in its character, and can without difficulty be separated from other forms.   The further development of a religion into which the legal factor has been introduced, will be in a totally different direction from its former course. The most complete illustration of this thesis is furnished by the history of the Hebrew religion. Among the Hebrews, the prophetical movement of the eighth century, which definitely gave an ethical flavour to the conception of the national deity, and thus paved the way for a distinctive form of monotheism, resulted in the creation of an elaborate legal code, in which all the rites of the religion and the functions of the priesthood are brought into accord with the principles of ethical monotheism as preached by the prophets.[1]   While many of the regulations

---

[1] For an elaboration of this thesis, see the recent histories of Israel by Renan, Stade, Wellhausen, Piepenbring, Guthe, etc., or Montefiore's Hibbert Lectures on the *Origin and Growth of Religion as illustrated by the Religion of the Hebrews*, London, 1893.

in these codes antedate the prophetical movement, and some indeed belong to a high antiquity, the novel feature in the codes is the creation of a bond between religion and law, which was destined to be permanent. Henceforth, with all the further refinement of the monotheistic idea, and despite the growth of universalistic tendencies in Judaism, legalism continues to make steady encroachments until it becomes the controlling factor in the religious life of the people. The various prophetical codes are welded together into a fictitious unity. The history of the nation is viewed merely as an incident in the promulgation of the law, or as an illustration of its workings, but the chief goal of the national existence is the law itself. As a result we have the Pentateuch in its present form, in which history occupies precisely this subsidiary position, and the historical books— Joshua, Judges, Samuel, and Kings—in which the entire history of the nation, from the period of the supposed promulgation of the law, is reviewed in the light of this law and its obligations. The process, which reaches a definite shape after the return of the Jews from Babylonia, is continued, and leads finally to that enlarged Pentateuch, known as the Talmud, in which the principle of regulating religious life by law is carried to an even more complete issue.

The entire departure of the Hebrew religion from lines common to the Semites is thus marked at the point where the legal spirit is introduced as a controlling factor; and whatever the modern view may be as to the extent to which legalism should enter into religious life, there can be no doubt that its appearance in the Hebrew religion betokens a distinct advance over antecedent conditions. Hinduism,

Zoroastrianism, and Islamism will serve as further illustrations of the same theme, and, though it does not of course follow that the legal factor manifests itself in the same way in all the more advanced forms of religion, or in the same degree, it will be found that in all, the appearance of legalism results in a new direction henceforth given to the unfolding of religious faith among a people.

VI.

A classification differing from the philosophical and the philosophical-historical systems which we have so far discussed is the one, proposed by Professor Max Müller many years ago[1] and to which he clung to the last, on the basis of the linguistic branches into which the human race may be divided. Max Müller contented himself with recognising three main divisions —the Indo-Germanic, the Semitic, and the Turanian. It is rather surprising that so acute a thinker as Max Müller should have been led to such an arbitrary system of classification. One might have expected such a scheme from one who was "merely" a philologist, who might be pardoned for looking at all phenomena through the spectacles of linguistics, but not from a scholar of Max Müller's remarkably broad range, combining in his person the poet, historian, philosopher, and linguist. Professor Tiele in his article on Religions[2] has pointed out the weakness of any classification of religions based upon linguistic groups, and indeed it is but necessary to follow Max Müller's argument, brilliant though it is, to recognise

[1] *Lectures on the Science of Religion* (3rd lecture), London and New York, 1872.

[2] *Encyclopædia Britannica* (9th ed.).

the untenability of his position.   Max Müller aims to
show that each one of the three groups of languages
corresponds to a certain type of religion.   Among
the Aryans, he finds the leading religious idea to be
the manifestation of "god in Nature," whereas among
the Semites worship resolves itself largely into the
adoration of "god in history."   The gods of the
Aryan pantheon, he says,[1] assume an individuality so
strongly marked and permanent that with the Aryans
a transition to monotheism required a powerful
struggle, and seldom took effect without iconoclastic
revolutions and philosophical despair.   On the other
hand, among the Semites, the divine powers are
viewed as affecting the destinies of individuals and
races and nations rather than manifesting themselves
in nature.   When he comes to the Turanians, he
experiences some difficulty in finding a single characteristic trait, but finally settles upon ancestor-worship
as more prominently dwelt upon in the religion of the
Turanians than in that of the other groups.

In 1870, when Max Müller delivered his lectures,
the unsatisfactory character of the appellation
"Turanian" was not as clearly recognised as it
is to-day, but even he does not disguise the difficulties involved in assuming an inherent relationship
between all these nations and races whose language
is neither Semitic nor Aryan.   Instead of the two
branches of Turanian which he recognises, scholars
now assume four or more, and, indeed, the term
"Turanian" has fallen into such discredit that it can
hardly be introduced now in a linguistic discussion
without an apology or an explanation.   Max Müller's
attempt to find a common religious type among

[1] *Science of Religion*, 3rd lecture, p. 63 (New York ed., 1872).

nations so far apart as the Lapplanders and the Chinese is exceedingly strained.   Not only are magic rites and ancestral worship not peculiar to the branches of the Turanians, but they represent stages in religious development to be found among all nations, and, similarly, the distinction between a recognition of "god in nature" and "god in history" is not borne out by the facts.   Applying this criterion, it would be easy to make out the Babylonians to have been Aryans, since the starting-point of religious growth among the Babylonians is the recognition of the gods as manifestations of the powers of nature, while among nations undoubtedly to be classed among the Aryans, as for example the ancient Teutons, the divine powers are certainly viewed as primarily affecting human destinies.   This conception is prominent also in certain phases of Greek religion.[1]   In short, the features which Max Müller points out in his scheme of classification are *phases* of religion to be met with at different times among all peoples, independent of racial origins and linguistic peculiarities, and not at all *types* of different religious faiths.

Another manifest objection to Max Müller's classification is the non-differentiation, or at all events the insufficient differentiation between race and language. He speaks of Semites, Aryans, and Turanians as though each group represented a racial and linguistic unity, whereas the Semites include at least two races, among the Aryans at least four are to be distinguished,[2] while the nondescript designation Turanian embraces a still larger number.   An ultimate linguistic unity of the languages spoken by the Aryan group is thus

---

[1] Campbell, *Greek Religion in Greek Literature*, pp. 56, 69.
[2] Isaac Taylor, *Origin of the Aryans*, chap. iv.

quite independent of the racial types to be distinguished in this group, and in view therefore of the
racial complexity of each of the three groups, it
follows that the factor of linguistic unity is to be
regarded more in the nature of an accident, due to
geographical proximity and other causes which in no
way involve the question of ethnic type. Languages
extend their scope through success in war, or through
the mental superiority of those who speak them. A
nation emigrates and adopts the language of the
country into which it comes, and thus language becomes a variable factor and manifests a tendency
to separate itself more and more from the factor of
race. To be sure, the racial type too is subject to
change. A mixture of races is constantly going on,
and has been ever since the process (whatever it was)
which led to the formation of separate races was
completed, but these racial changes, though not
wholly dissevered from linguistic considerations, are
conditioned by causes which in themselves have
nothing to do with the factor of language. It is
essential, if we would avoid confusion, to keep these
two elements—race and language—apart; certainly
much further apart than any scheme of classification
of religions does which takes linguistic unity as a
basis of division.

Bearing this in mind, we may of course admit, with
Professor Max Müller, that the religion of a people is
conditioned upon racial peculiarities, and that, so far
as these peculiarities are also reflected in language,
the latter comes in for some share of consideration.
In a subsequent chapter, when we come to deal with
the relationship existing between religion and psychology, we shall have occasion to discuss this question

more fully. Here we may content ourselves with sounding a note of warning against the present tendency in ethnological science to give undue weight to the factor of race in producing mental traits, that on the surface appear to distinguish one people from another. It is the merit of the late James Darmesteter[1] to have pointed out in one of his lucid and suggestive essays that many of the so-called national traits which may be observed among a people are due not to the accident of race, but to a totally different factor, which he calls "tradition." Common surroundings, common aims, common struggles develop common mental traits, and more effectively than descent from the same ancestors. People of different racial origin who are thrown together will grow to be alike, and the proof of this thesis is furnished by the great nations of antiquity and of the present time, who represent the result, not of racial isolation, but of racial intermingling. National aspirations, and the sense of national unity, are produced in groups of people, no matter of how diverse an origin, compelled by force of circumstances to pursue common aims. The proportion of racial intermingling varies with every people and with every age. Some periods are more favourable to the process, others less so; but if the strength of a people is to be measured by achievement, it will be found that national strength is developed in a direct ratio to the variety of different racial elements found among a people. The social conditions prevailing in the United States may be regarded as an extreme instance of the extent to which the process of racial intermingling may be carried. Celts, Teutons, Anglo-

[1] *Selected Essays* (Boston, 1895), p. 155.

Saxons, Semites, and Romanic nations have been combined to produce a nation possessing as strong a sense of unity as has ever existed, and inspired by purely national aims, to such an extent indeed as to lose sight, in the zeal to advance the national power and influence, of what were until recently regarded as the traditions of the American republic.

Under such circumstances, it is manifestly misleading to emphasise race as a very decided and influential factor in determining forms of religious belief. The facts of history are all against the supposition that there can be such a thing as a Semitic form of religion, and that there is another type peculiar to the Aryans, and a third which expresses the aspirations of the Turanian race or races. The religion of the Hebrews produced among a people who belong to the Semitic race certainly takes on a colour from the mental traits peculiar to the Hebrews, but these traits are not due to racial origin, and even if they were, this would not make the religion a type of Semitic belief. Several factors being admittedly involved in the production of any form of belief, it is manifestly unjust to single out one of these factors and make it the determining force. Again, the religion of the Greeks is not fairly described as Aryan, merely because the head of the pantheon bears the same name in Greek as in Sanscrit, or because the conceptions connected with Zeus are allied to those held of Dyaus. Greek Culture, Art, Philosophy, Literature, Politics—all enter as factors in giving a direction to the religion of the Greeks, which separates it sharply even from the religion of a people with whom the Greeks had so much in common as the Romans. We miss the point of a genuine classification by leaving out of account the distinctive traits of an important religion, and by dwelling only upon vague and general points—points so vague and general as to become merely phases in the development of religious ideas and customs which are practically universal.

VII.

A classification which commends itself for its simplicity is into National and Universal Religions. In recent times it has found a powerful advocate in the late Abraham Kuenen, the distinguished theologian of Leiden, who chose as the subject of his Hibbert Lectures *National and Universal Religions.*[1] The main purpose of Kuenen was to show why certain religions had passed beyond national bonds, while others remained confined to the people among which they originated. In so far as Kuenen's investigation of the reasons which led to the remarkable course of such religions as Buddhism, Christianity, and Islam is concerned, his exposition is by far the best work that has been produced on the subject, but his book is also a condemnation of the classification upon which it rests. Kuenen himself recognises that the term universalism is a misnomer, and proposes instead "international."[2] Apart from the objection, upon which we shall have occasion to dwell further on, that there is no such thing as a universal religion, the phenomenon of a religion independent of nationality is characteristic of primitive religions as well as of the most advanced. The beliefs and rites of people

[1] Published under this title in London, 1882. [2] Page 6.

living in a primitive state of culture have scarcely any
bonds at all with the national life. Religions at this
stage are practically alike, the differences having no
more significance than those which separate the sects
within one of the universal religions. It is only when
we come to a people in which, by virtue of its political
organisation and social condition, the national spirit
becomes accentuated, that the chief deity becomes
a distinctly national god, and the religious worship
affiliated with national aspirations. It is the advance
in religious thought that again leads to the gradual
separation of religion from nationality, though the
bond is never entirely broken between the two.
Judaism and Zoroastrianism are unique only in the
degree to which they are racially limited, despite the
universal character of their doctrines, but there are
also limitations of a racial or national character to
Buddhism, Christianity, and Islam. It is inconceivable that Buddhism should ever spread to northern
countries with populations marked by great intellectual activity. No form of it could flourish in a
community which sets up as one of life's ideals the
satisfaction of personal ambitions, resting upon the
axiom that life without activity is spiritual death.
On the other hand, the failure of Christian missionary
efforts in many parts of the world is a proof of the
non-adaptability of this religion to peoples with
different habits of thought from those prevailing in
occidental Europe. But more than this, it is to a
large extent purely conventional usage which groups
all the varieties of Christian sects under one head,
and the equally numerous divisions into which Buddhism is split up under another. There is sometimes
more resemblance in one of the sects of Christianity

to another of Buddhism than between one of these sects and any other of the group among which it is classed.   Can there exist a wider gap than that which prevails between Greek Catholicism and the extreme Unitarian position?   And the latter is manifestly closer to Reformed Judaism than to any of the sects connected with Christianity.

What therefore appear to be universal religions are in reality religions the doctrines of which have no direct relation to national ideals, and this position is merely a phase of religious development reached at a certain period by peoples everywhere. But, on the other hand, the theoretical severing of the bond between religious doctrine and nationality is not necessarily followed by the practical division. Tradition and custom, and the heritage of common experiences prompt people to hold together in their manner of worship long after the justification for such clannishness in religion has passed away; and again, differences of temperament, often mistaken for racial traits and due to different experiences through which people pass, act as a barrier against bringing those closer together who intellectually, and in the nature of their religious beliefs, can hardly be distinguished from one another.   There are other factors, then, besides doctrine and cult which keep religions from overstepping national bonds, and the supposed distinction between national and universal religions thus resolves itself into a question as to the extent to which these factors can be overcome, while so far as the actual experiences of mankind are concerned, they have never yet been entirely overcome.

There is even less to be said in favour of another classification, which has still found advocates in our day,[1] into such religions as have been founded by individuals, and such as are a natural growth. As Ehni has pointed out,[2] the more prominent position accorded to the individual in a religion is due to the growth of the sense of human dignity. When this stage of intellectual development is reached, we have in all religions, leaders coming to the front, men who by virtue of special penetration into the mysteries of existence impress their personalities upon their surroundings. It is purely from conventional usage that we speak of founders of religion. All religions are a natural growth, and personages like Buddha, Zoroaster, and even Moses, Jesus, and Mohammed, merely mark certain important epochs in the evolution of religions, either bringing to a focus a movement which may have started long before the appearance of the great personality, or directing by the force of their personality the existing religion into new channels. But, in the second place, to set up founded religions as a special class is to draw important conclusions from insufficient premises, for we know too little of most of the religions of antiquity to determine the share taken by individuals in their development. Only a few names survive in history, of the large number who continue to produce the order of events, and it is therefore quite within the sphere of possibility that Babylonia and Egypt had their religious "founders" as well as Judæa and Persia.

The strongest argument against this classification

---

[1] *E.g.*, the late Professor W. D. Whitney. See his article in the *Princeton Review*, May 1881.

[2] "Ursprung und Entwickelung der Religion," *Theologische Studien und Kritiken*, 1898, p. 636.

has been brought forward by Professor Tiele, who in his Gifford Lectures takes occasion to restate it in a concise and forcible manner. The so-called "founders" of religion generally start out with a determination to make a sharp break between the new and the old, but their appearance is invariably followed by a reaction in which much that they hoped to do away with reappears. As Tiele puts it, "The ancient faith has only bowed before the mighty storm; but as soon as calm is restored it raises its head again, either unchanged in the old form, or in modified shape, and under new names, while preserving its former substance."[1] In view of this, it becomes manifest that a really new religion is never produced through the efforts of an individual; and significant as the *rôle* of the religious leader is in the history of religions—and more particularly in the more advanced religions—the form which this influence assumes, and the circumstances under which it is exercised, both illustrate the limitations of the individual factor, limitations which in themselves are sufficient to prevent this factor from being taken as the basis of a satisfactory classification.

VIII.

Finally, we must consider, briefly, an elaborate scheme of classification, based on the study of religion approached from the philosophical side, and proposed by one of the profoundest thinkers of the century—Eduard v. Hartmann.[2] Its superiority over

---

[1] *Elements of the Science of Religion*, vol. i., pp. 43-45.

[2] "Das Religiöse Bewusstsein der Menschheit," forming the first part of Hartmann's *Religionsphilosophie*.

Hegel's classification is unquestioned, due in part to the manner in which Hartmann has utilised the important investigations of the past decades in the field of religious history, and in part to his introduction of a larger number of factors in the development of what he calls "the religious consciousness of mankind."

Starting out with a broad twofold division into "Naturalism" and "Supranaturalism," Hartmann places in the former category the religion of savages, of people living in a state of primitive culture, as well as the religion of the Greeks, Romans, Teutons, Egyptians, and Persians (to follow his order of enumeration), while in the second division belong Brahmanism, Buddhism, the monotheism of the Hebrew Prophets, Judaism, Islam, and Christianity. Within each division, he distinguishes of course several sub-divisions. After showing that as the starting-point of the religious consciousness, we must take man's observation of the phenomena of nature independently of their connection with his welfare—for which reason Hartmann denies a religious sense to animals—he designates as the lowest stage of religion "naturalistic henotheism." Accepting the term introduced into the science of religion by Max Müller,[1] Hartmann interprets it in a much larger sense than Max Müller was inclined to do, and discusses this tendency as prominent already in the earliest stage of religious belief. The religions of the Greeks, Romans, Teutons, Egyptians, and Persians represent merely so many phases of the dissolution of henotheism with a view of solving the contradiction inherent in the disposition to attribute the concentrated powers

[1] See above, p. 77.

of all gods to a particular one in turn. If each god possesses the attributes of all others, then the existence of all is practically denied. There are two alternate solutions of the problem—either the assumption of positive polytheism, or the practical assertion of monotheism. The Greeks, Romans, and Teutons, accepting the former solution, are yet differentiated in their religion from one another through the specific character of their polytheism, which reflects in each case the peculiar mental disposition of each people. In the Greek religion, Hartmann recognises the æsthetic refinement of henotheism; in the Roman, the utilitarian secularisation ; and in the religion of the Teutons, the tragical and ethical transformation of henotheism. In the case of the Egyptians and Persians, the process of theological systematisation led, in the one case to a naturalistic monism, and in the other to a semi-naturalism.

The bold step of cutting loose from naturalism altogether and recognising the pre-eminence of spirit in control of the universe was reserved for only a few religions. Hartmann denominates this step as supranaturalism, because the religious conceptions connected with the Divine manifestations are freed from all material representations. Here again the thought assumes different phases. In the case of people endowed with speculative tendencies of a dreamy character, the outcome is an abstract monism, of which Brahmanism represents the partially completed process, and Buddhism, with the emphasis laid on "absolute illusion and self-abnegation," the final word. In the case of the Hebrews, on the other hand, a positive theism is evolved through the influence of the prophets, culminating in the legal religion of Judaism. Islam represents an attempt at refining this religion, whereas Christianity, as the last step in the evolution of theism, emphasises the realistic salvation of the individual, as Buddhism illustrates the idealistic salvation.

As the last stage in the religious evolution of mankind, Hartmann assumes a concrete monism in which the absolute spirit no longer possesses a super-human and extra-mundane personality (which is theism), but is a unity constituting the absolute source and absolute being of the universe. One cannot withhold one's admiration from this scheme, conceived on a magnificently large scale, and carried out into the smallest detail with wonderful perspicuity and acumen. It may well be questioned whether, taken as a philosophical classification of religions, it will ever be surpassed, but it suffers from the inherent weakness of all classifications which necessarily take into account only the salient features of a religion. Not only will opinions as to what constitute the salient features differ among those who approach the subject from different points of view, but the estimate of a religion is bound to be one-sided which does not take into account all its phases. After all, the Greek religion is something more than the esthetic refine-ment of "naturalistic henotheism," although it may be admitted that this is one of its features; and so to group all primitive religions under "naturalistic henotheism" is to pick out one element and arbi-trarily assign to it a predominating position. The life of man, and more particularly his religious life, is too complicated to be reduced to the simple pro-portions of representing the evolution of a *single* idea; and even though we admit numerous ramifications of this idea, the mistake consists in starting from a single one instead of the great variety which combine to produce the manifestation of religion even in a primitive form. Nevertheless, Hartmann's analyses of the various religions which he examines retain their value. He has penetrated deeper into the spirit of both ancient and modern religious movements than most philosophers, perhaps deeper than any of his compeers, and in addition to this, his analysis of the way in which the religious consciousness awakens and gradually grows, is a contribution to the psychology of religion which it is safe to declare has a permanent value.

IX.

The most recent discussion of the classification of religions is by Raoul de la Grasserie,[1] who summarises the various propositions made for distinguishing religions from one another. The list, comprising no less than twenty-two classifications, is of value as illustrating the large number of attempts that have been made to obtain a satisfactory classification, and commends itself as the result of a study of the subject. The first classification is into human and divine religions, by which, however, De la Grasserie does not mean to enter upon the question of the supposed origin of the religions involved, but upon the objects of worship—whether addressed to human beings deified or to gods humanised, so to speak. The second is into revealed and non-revealed religions, according as the

[1] *Des Religions Comparées au Point de Vue Sociologique*, chap. xii. (Paris, 1899).

claim of a special revelation is or is not set up. The third has reference to the scope of the religion—whether limited to individuals and families, or extended to the nation and then to all mankind. Then follow (4) a classification into legalistic and non-legalistic religions, according as the religious rites and duties are or are not regulated by formal codes; (5) concrete and abstract religions; and (6) anthropomorphic or non-anthropomorphic. These three sub-divisions may be grouped together, for they represent phases through which religion passes in the course of progressive development. The seventh division, into pantheism and theism, has a certain philosophic value; and the eighth, into polytheistic and monotheistic religions, is of importance when we enter upon the detailed study of a particular religion, but such a division again represents a phase of development, rather than a genuine classification. Most unsatisfactory is (9) the division into egoistic and altruistic religions, as though in anything which concerns man so deeply as his own welfare, it is possible for altruism to become a determining factor. The tenth division into mythical and non-mythical, and the eleventh, representing the extent to which morality enters as a factor, are again certain phases of development. Several of the following sub-divisions have reference to peculiar conditions existing within a particular religion; thus (12) the distinction between open and occult forms of worship, closely allied with which is (13) a division among a people between the religion practised by the educated and that followed by the ignorant. Of a most general character, but without practical value, is the broad division (14) into the religion of civilised and non-civilised peoples, and peculiar conditions again determine (15) whether a religion has a political character or not, and whether the intellectual and social differences among the sexes is such that (16) there is a special religion for men as distinguished from the cult observed by women. Important criteria to be observed in studying religions are furnished by the classification (17) into religions of natural origin and such as are founded by individuals, and (18) into religions of a pure type and such as are the result of syncretism of religious ideas derived from widely different sources. The classification (19) into indigenous and imported religions is historical rather than theoretical, while the two following (20), the distinction between religions producing literature and such as have none, and (21) religions which present a sacerdotal character and such as do not, again represent phases of religious development everywhere, and do not therefore furnish a basis for a scheme of classification. Lastly (22), the division into the individualistic or socialistic character of a religion is dependent upon the mental calibre of those to whom a particular religion aims to appeal. I have given the enumeration in the order followed by De la Grasserie. It is possible to group them under five heads.

(1.) Classifications which represent natural phases of development through which religion, by virtue of the laws of its being, must necessarily pass.[1]

(2.) Classifications which reflect peculiar conditions prevailing in certain religions, but by no means common to all.[2]

[1] Nos. 4, 5, 6, 10, 11.
[2] Nos. 12, 13, 15, 16, 20, 21.

(3.) Classifications based upon specific doctrines.[1]

(4.) Classifications based upon special events or the historical growth of religions.[2]

(5.) Classifications dependent upon temperament and intellectual grade of individuals and peoples.[3]

De la Grasserie gives the preference to a classification of religions into theistic and deistic, the former assuming an extra-mundane personal deity, the latter a god immanent in the world; but it is hardly necessary to point out how unsatisfactory a scheme is which picks out a specific doctrine, such as the relationship of God to the world that can be clearly grasped by only a small minority, and which makes it the basis for a division of a subject, whose peculiar province it is to appeal to all classes of mankind—to the most educated as well as to the most ignorant.

X.

Having considered various schemes of classification proposed by representative scholars and thinkers, we are in a position to advance to a classification which will accord with the facts of religious history as ascertained by actual research, making due allowance for the historical point of view in the study of religions, which, we have seen, furnishes the most satisfactory means of reaching sound conclusions. From the discussion of the questions involved in classification, it will have become evident, firstly, that there are certain phases through which religions pass everywhere among peoples who have entered upon the road leading to advanced civilisation, and secondly,

---

[1] Nos. 1, 2, 7, 8.　　[2] Nos. 3, 17, 18, 19.　　[3] Nos. 9, 14, 22.

that there are several factors involved in the growth of religious ideas and the development of religious rites.

A broad division is thus suggested between the forms assumed by religion among peoples while in a primitive state of culture, and those which appear after a certain stage of culture has been reached. It may at once be admitted that we know little of the religion of savages, and that our means of ascertaining what the religious ideas of the human race were in the lowest stage of mental development are totally inadequate to the subject. Now that we know that in ancient times communication between various parts of the world was much closer than was surmised by scholars until a short time ago, it is an open question whether the "savages" encountered by the travellers of the last few centuries in the remote regions of America, Asia, and Africa, had not at some time come under the partial influence of civilisation. Certainly neither the Indian tribes of North and South America, the natives of Borneo, nor even the aborigines of Australia and the inhabitants of the interior parts of Africa, had remained entirely free from contact with some forms of ancient or mediæval culture, as little as had the Germans at the time when, in the eyes of Tacitus, they were mere "barbarians." Moreover, the moment that so-called "savages" enter into a discussion on religious questions, as we so frequently find them doing in the accounts of travellers, it is preposterous to suppose that we are in the presence of people who stand upon the lowest level of human culture. When a "savage," pointing to the sky, says that the "great father" dwells there, he is perforce many stages removed from the starting-point of civilisation. Indeed, the ability to communicate his views to a stranger already stamps an individual as having passed beyond the borders of "savage" existence.

We are thus thrown back largely upon such uncertain means as conjectures, popular traditions, and speculation from imperfect observations of savage life, to determine what constitute the earliest manifestations of religious life among the human race. The material at hand appears to justify at least the assumption, that in a vague way the powers of nature were by a sort of reasoning from analogy personified, or, perhaps, it would be safer to say that the savage does not differentiate between such an object of nature as the sun and its personification as a power possessing life in some form. Whether the savage made any attempt to dispose this power and others which fell under his observation favourably towards himself cannot be stated as certain, but seems a likely conclusion.

That fear also played a prominent part in the earliest religious rites may be concluded from the prominence which this emotion receives in comparatively advanced cults ; and hence the further conclusion is justified that the mystery of death led to the according of some form of adoration to those who had passed beyond the ken and control of the living. Meagre as these conclusions are, they are sufficient to set up the religion of savages as a hypothetical category by itself—sharply differentiated from the religion of primitive culture. Fortunately for the practical purposes of the study of religion, our ignorance as to the religion of pure savages is not a serious matter. The certainty that the religious instinct is, so far as the evidence goes, innate in man, suffices as a starting-point for a satisfactory classification, and more than a starting-point is not needed.

Coming to the manifestations of religion among people living in a state of primitive culture, there are naturally several stages that may be distinguished within this rather indefinite region. The organisation of the religious cult may be more or less advanced; the relationship of the various powers recognised may be more or less determined, but there are certain features which are common to all these stages. These are in the main three—(1) animism, in the domain of belief, (2) magic, in the domain of practice, and (3) ancestor-worship. It is the merit of E. B. Tylor[1] to have been the first to make an elaborate investigation into the various phases presented by Animism—which, briefly put, is the belief which ascribes conscious life in some form to whatever in nature manifests vitality or force. The great value of Tylor's researches are recognised by all, but in the interpretation of the facts adduced by him, there is at present wide divergence among scholars. He has gathered his material from various sources, but inasmuch as the nations among whom he finds evidences for a belief in Animism represent various stages of culture, doubts have been raised as to the trustworthiness of the conclusions drawn by Tylor and his followers.

But however much scholars still differ as to the scope of Animism in the religions of primitive peoples, it is generally admitted that at a certain stage of culture the theory which differentiates between the manifestation of life or power, and the source of that life or power, forms the basis of religious belief. The con-

[1] *Primitive Culture*, chaps. xi.-xvii.

nection between the manifestation and the source
may be variously expressed. The spirit residing in
the tree, which produces the life manifest in the tree,
may take its abode there voluntarily or be bound to
it ; so long as the view is held which attributes a form
of life to the tree similar to that which a man is
conscious of possessing in himself, Animism remains
as the characteristic trait of a people's religion. What
is essential to bear in mind for our purposes is that
Animism, even in its lowest stage, is more than a mere
personification of the powers of nature. It is an
actual theory, which attempts to account for the
phenomena that man notes in the world around
him, and since he is particularly concerned with
phenomena affecting his being and welfare, the
theory has a direct bearing upon his life. Inasmuch
as it leads him in certain directions in regulating his
conduct, the theory acquires also a religious aspect.
From this it will be clear that it is a mistake to co-
ordinate Animism with the lowest stage of civilisation.
As a religious system Animism belongs to a much
higher grade than what is ordinarily understood by
savage life. It belongs properly to cultures which,
while they may be designated as primitive, reach far
beyond the borderland of the lowest intellectual
life. A people which understands the uses to which
fire can be put, which builds shelters, which trusts itself
to the waters with contrivances devised by its own in-
genuity, is no longer in a state of savagery. Yet it is
among those whose life is characterised by the traits
just mentioned that the animistic theory flourishes.
Animism, accordingly, is the basis of religious
belief for those who have taken more than the first
steps of civilisation, who have done much to pave the

way for the higher forms of culture which we call
civilisation.   This view is borne out by the nature of
the cult which corresponds to the animistic theory
and which centres around magic rites.

Magic may in a general way be defined as the
attempt either to propitiate the spirits behind the
phenomena of vitality and force, capable of manifesting their power for good or evil, or to secure
control of those spirits.   Jevons has shown[1] in how
thoroughly logical a manner people proceed who
pin their faith to magic rites.   So far from being
due to caprice or accident, magic represents a primitive form of real science, based as is modern science
upon experience and observation.   Its fallacy or its
weakness is due merely to the limited scope of the
observation and experience upon which it rests ; and
the greater value of modern science results, primarily,
from the infinitely wider scope of our experience and
observation.

The method, however, involved in trusting the
efficacy of magic rites is precisely the same which we
follow in placing supreme confidence in the corollaries
of modern science.   Noting that certain misfortunes
when they come are coincident with certain natural
phenomena, people of limited experience naturally
drew the conclusion of a connection between the
accompanying phenomena and the misfortune.   They
naturally strove to avoid at certain times an exposure
to the danger of again encountering this misfortune.
In this way man, in the course of time, developed a
more or less extended series of precautionary measures
to avoid unpleasant experiences, and correspondingly,
by noting the circumstances which accompany favour-

[1] *Introduction to the History of Religion*, chap. iv.

able incidents in life, he endeavoured to bring about a repetition of them by repeating at the proper time the activity in which he was engaged when some good fortune befell him.

The further application of this principle will prompt him to endeavour to bring about phenomena which he regards as favourable. He will, in various ways, try to attract the attention of spirits whose aid he needs in certain emergencies; or in other ways, again, he will try to divert this attention from him when he wishes to avoid their presence. The various forms of nature-worship, adoration of certain trees, plants, and stones, all rest upon this primitive form of science,[1] and, similarly, the rites of taboo and of sacrifice[2] are the natural outcome of one and the same principle.

A somewhat peculiar position is occupied in early religious practice by ancestor-worship. We have seen that in the period of savage life it was natural for man to pay some sort of adoration to those who have passed into the mysterious domain of death. In this case it is the profound mystery of death, leading naturally to a fear of the dead, which prompts the savage to a crude form of religious worship. In the higher stage of religious belief, represented by Animism, ancestor-worship continues in force, primarily, as a survival which in no way conflicts with other rites that now arise. The contradiction between a theory of religious belief which makes manifestation of power (for good or evil) depend upon the assumption of vitality, and a cult which attributes power to such beings as no longer possess vitality, does not present itself to

---

[1] See Jevons, *ib.*, chaps. xvi.-xvii.   [2] *Ib.*, chaps. vi. to xii.

peoples who are overwhelmed by the mystery of death.   Indeed, this very theory of Animism leads to a partial solution of the mystery by predicating vitality even of those who to all appearances are deprived of it, only that this vitality is of a different kind from that which is attributed to the living.   Seeing life everywhere, the theory of animism is unable to account for the extinction of life, as little as it can account for its rise.   Life becomes the synonym for whatever is, and the thought of "not being" far transcends the intellectual limits of those who are held fast in the clutches of Animism.

As a consequence, ancestor-worship, while not arising from the theory of Animism, is taken over into religion at this stage and brought into accord with it. In this process it undergoes profound modifications. It no longer occupies that prominent place which we may reasonably predicate it to have occupied in the religion of savages.   Magic in its various manifestations becomes the chief element in the cult.   Secondly, the element of fear in ancestor-worship, while far from disappearing, is counteracted by the strong belief in the efficacy of the ever-growing scope of magic rites, and in this way the natural sentiments of affection for the dead have a better chance of asserting themselves.   In the accounts of travellers among nations who belong to the higher grade of primitive culture, this factor of regard and love for ancestors is noticeable, not only in the funeral rites of such a people, but in the adoration paid to the dead at stated intervals, long after they have been removed from the sight of the living.   Again, it would appear as a natural consequence of the different position assumed by ancestor-worship in the animistic stage of religious

belief that it should be relegated more to the domain
of the family. A differentiation thus arises between
an official and an unofficial cult, which in the next
stages of religious development leads to important
consequences.

The religions from this point of view falling under
the division Animism are numerous, and include such
as are compatible with a tolerably advanced state of
culture. The ancient Teutons, the religions of ancient
Mexico and Peru, as well as the religion of many of
the sub-divisions among the North American Indians,
belong to this category. It is a question also whether
the religion of the Polynesians, with its rather elaborate mythology, and the religion of the Finno-Tartaric
peoples, are not to be removed from the category of
"non-civilised" religions in which Réville[1] places
them, and accorded a higher position in the scale.
Naturally, a sharp dividing line between the religion
of savages and the religion corresponding to the
period of primitive culture cannot be drawn, since,
in the nature of things, the religious growth is
as gradual as mental unfolding, and one stage of
religious belief passes almost imperceptibly into
another.

This difficulty, which is inherent in every system
of classification, is particularly noticeable when we
come to the third division of religions—the religion
of peoples who have advanced to that degree of
mentality which warrants us in placing them within
the category of higher culture. We have in mind
the religions—firstly, of ancient India, the religions of
Babylonia and Egypt, with their offshoots; secondly,
the religions of China, of Greece, and of Rome.

[1] In his work, *Religion des Peuples Non-civilisés*, vol. ii., 4e Partie.

Attempts to find points of resemblance between these religions are apt to be arbitrary, and, on the other hand, to pick out certain traits in each as particularly characteristic is a procedure which may easily lead us astray. Thus, for example, it might seem that the mythological features in the Greek religion are the predominant elements, and yet from what we already know of the religion of Babylonia, the mythology developed in the Euphrates valley is scarcely less rich and varied,[1] while, to go still further, even among the Polynesians we encounter a mythological element, which, while not as varied as that found among the Greeks, is yet remarkably elaborate.

Again, from a superficial point of view, one might be tempted to designate the religion of China as one in which ancestor-worship assumes such proportions as to constitute its characteristic trait, and yet in ancient Egypt the care of the dead, with its elaborate ceremonial, acquires equal prominence,[2] and at the same time illustrates that external symbols alone do not necessarily touch the core of a religion. If, again, we have regard to the elaborateness of the ritual, it will be difficult to decide between the mass of detailed ordinances found in the Vedic literature, in dealing with methods of preparing sacrifices, and with the interpretation of omens, and the extensive material of this character to be met with in the remains of Babylonian literature.

The considerations which warrant us in placing the religions named in the same class are of a different order, and must be sought in the relationships established between religion and culture at the stage

[1] See Jastrow, *Religion of Babylonia and Assyria*, chap. xxiv.
[2] Budge, *The Mummy*, Cambridge, 1893.

reached by nations who have developed an advanced form of civilisation. Characteristic of religions corresponding to this stage of mental evolution is the close bond existing between religion and morality, and the accentuation of the legal factor in the regulation of the cult and of religious duties. In a subsequent chapter[1] we shall have occasion to deal more fully with the relationship existing between religion and morality, and it will be shown that in the earlier forms of religion there is no direct bond between belief and right living. Even in the higher stage, when Animism forms the basis of religion, religion as such does not sanctify certain lines of conduct and condemn others; but when we come to the domain of civilisation proper, where the entire fabric of society rests upon the recognition of certain moral principles, it is to religion that people turn for the ultimate justification of these principles. The gods regulate standards of right and wrong, and we soon reach the position that things are right and wrong because the gods will it so, or if you choose, because the religion so ordains it. Religion and morality thus tend to approach each other until they become inseparable. The strength of the bond naturally differs in the religions under consideration, but in all of them we shall find the ultimate justification of conduct to rest in religious doctrines.

In order to bring about this union between religion and morality, the regulation of religious duties by the solidification of vacillating practice into unchangeable routine, appears to be essential. But here, again, the extent to which religious codes are effectual in determining individual conduct varies considerably,

[1] Chap. VI., " Religion and Ethics."

though the general tendency everywhere is towards the extension of the scope of religious control so as gradually to co-ordinate religion with the entire range of common occurrences and practices. The natural result is that what once were popular customs become religious precepts, and, when recognised by religion, become binding and obligatory instead of fleeting and voluntary. To funeral rites, of which religion always had a control by virtue of the beliefs connected with the mystery of death, are added "birth" rites, and other momentous events in the life of the individual, such as marriage; and they are given a religious significance that was originally foreign to them. Seasons of merry-making become religious festivals, and country fairs are transformed into religious pilgrimages. Some of the religions falling within this category go to even greater extremes in this respect. The elaborate rituals of the religions of India and Babylonia embrace many more details than the older Hebraic codes, and yet the latter appear complicated by the side of the simpler procedures in the religious practices of the Greeks.

What, however, is common to all religions at this stage is the tendency of the cult to embrace all phases of life and to give to religious regulations a permanent and fixed form, determined by the influence of the official representatives of religion— the priests. It is at this stage in religious development that the position of the priesthood becomes prominent. In earlier periods the *rôle* of the priest is essentially that of a "go-between" between the deity and the worshipper. Singled out for the purpose because of the supposed possession of peculiar powers, the priest presided over magic rites

and brought the petitions of the worshippers in
proper form before the deity invoked ; but here his
function ended. On such occasions when he was
approached, his power was undisputed and his
authority supreme, but he exercised little influence
over the daily lives of the people. When popular
practice, however, extending gradually over the entire
range of human experience, changed into religious
law, the more efficient organisation of the priesthood
became essential, and with this organisation the scope
of priestly prerogative was extended.   All law—in so
far as it concerned conduct—having a religious aspect,
the priest became the physician for the physically
sound, in addition to having been the judge who
ordains the conduct of those who seek healing from
disease, or are overwhelmed by existing or impend-
ing disaster.   He becomes the law-giver as well as
the medicine-man.   Instead of being a more or less
passive factor in the affairs of ordinary life, the priest
becomes the most active influence at work in regulating the conduct of the populace.

Consistently carried out, the process leads to
theocracy as the natural form of government, with
the prerogatives of priest and king united in the
same person.   If, as a matter of fact, the process
was not carried to this extreme in all the religions
of the ancient world, it is simply because of the
gap which continued to exist between an official
and an unofficial religious cult. Not all popular
customs could be carried over into the province of
religious precept.   Some were totally unsuited to
such a purpose, others did not sufficiently coincide
with the religious precepts and conceptions of the
gods which had meanwhile developed.   But popular

practices die hard, if they die at all, and what was "refused" the sanction of religious obligation, nevertheless continued in vogue, though degraded to the rank of popular superstitions. There thus remained a section of life into which religion not only did not enter, but which was in a measure hostile to the officially recognised forms of the cult, in the widest sense of that term. As a general thing, however, this hostility is not recognised in ancient religions, and the official cult—under the superintendence of the priesthood—proceeds on its course, having at best a contempt for the unofficial cult, even though popular superstitions continue to maintain a strong hold upon the people.

When, however, the conflict between the scope of official religion, regulated by codes, and popular forms of worship, regulated by tradition, does break out, we reach a new stage in religious development, and indeed the highest. Historically the first, and in many respects the most significant, instance of this conflict takes place among a small people settled in a section of Palestine—a people which had never played any great political part, but which under peculiar circumstances was destined to revolutionise the aspect of religion in various parts of the world. In the eighth century before this era, a movement arises among this people boldly aiming at an overthrow of all forms of worship and of all practices which are inconsistent with the stage reached by the growth of religious doctrine. The fact that the chief element in this doctrine is a belief in the superiority of the national deity of Israel over the gods of other nations, is of less moment than the conception which makes the deity intolerant of any controlling power save himself. Only what Jahweh ordains can be right, and what is not sanctioned by him must be for ever set aside. From this point of view no place is left for the unofficial cult, and, accordingly, the leaders of the movement have no hesitation in rudely and unmercifully denouncing the traditional customs to which the people had clung from time immemorial (as it seemed), as the enactments of gods with which Jahweh could have nothing in common.

True, the ethical conception of the national deity plays a most significant part in this movement, but it is an error to suppose that ethical monotheism constitutes the *quintessence* of the religion—Judaism —which results from the triumph of this movement. In other countries, notably Babylonia and Egypt, the gods were invested with ethical attributes, and at the time when Judaism arose, the religions of Greece and China had already become the mediums of ethical aspirations. The significant and unique feature of the prophetical movement—as it is called in Israel—is the attempt to make religion consistently *coextensive* with life itself—to wipe out all distinctions between an official and an unofficial cult, to set up a *single* standard for all conduct, public and private, and to bring religious doctrine and religious practice into absolutely consistent accord. It is natural that in the course of this movement the doctrine itself should have been submitted to a process of purification, and as a consequence, a remarkable advance is signalled in religious thought, but the rise of absolute monotheism in Israel is only a consequence of the central idea of the prophetical movement, which is the identification of religion with life. A curious feature in this movement is that while paving the way for the most perfect possible control of religious belief over the individual, it is not taken in hand by the official representatives of a religion, but by those who, without being hostile to priestly prerogatives of the legitimate sort, yet stand outside the priestly circles.

The priest is averse to sudden changes. His own position is conditioned upon permitting the process of gradual growth to proceed without violent breaks. While not opposed to progress, he frequently fails to recognise that a forward step can, under certain conditions, be brought about only by an apparent break with the past, and hence he is found in history but too often on the side which puts obstacles in the path of religious advance. The great religious movements in the world—movements which ultimately redound to the benefit of the representatives of religion as well as of religion itself—have by a strange contradiction been generally inaugurated and carried on in apparent opposition to religion itself, as represented by the exponents of the official cult. The prophetical movement in Israel forms no exception, and it will be found upon examination that the religious movements which led to Buddhism in India, and to Zoroastrianism in Persia, are characterised by the same feature, inasmuch as they are taken in hand by those who are not officially connected with the cult.

Buddha, as is quite evident, represents a reaction against the predominance of the priesthood, precisely as the prophetical movement in Israel appears in this light, though he manifests an equal opposition to the secular authorities. His plea is like that of the prophets for absolute consistency between religious doctrine and religious practice. So far, therefore, from restricting the scope

S

of religious influence, his leading purpose is to make religion coextensive with life ; only, like the prophets in this respect also, he lays the chief stress upon the purification of religious doctrine, and from the doctrine derives a practice both religious and secular, which should be in harmony with the conceptions formed of the universe and of the relationship of man to the world around him.

Obscure as the origin of Zoroastrianism is, one feature of it at least is clear, its strong emphasis of the tendency to bring religion and life into consistent accord, to wipe out all distinctions between an official and an unofficial cult, to regulate the entire field of conduct by deductions from certain leading religious principles. Judaism, Buddhism, and Zoroastrianism are therefore to be placed in the same category, representing as they do the same stage in religious development, characterised by the purpose to so extend the scope of religious influence as to make religion, instead of an incident in life, its controlling factor.

The history of these religions, when once the decisive step has been taken, represents merely the swing of the pendulum from one side to the other in an endeavour to realise practically the high ideals of the religious leaders. In all three a reaction sets in, which, while apparently throwing the religions back to the earlier stage, yet does not obscure the fundamental principle of the highest form of religious faith —the union between religion and life. Prophetical Judaism is followed by Talmudical Judaism, Buddhism by Jainism, and in the further development of Zoroastrianism there is a departure from the high plane on which Zoroaster endeavoured to place religion; but in all the forms assumed by these religions, the doctrinal purity is only affected to a minor degree, whereas it is a misconception of the relationship of religion to cult that leads in the case of all to a predominance of the element of law in the regulation of religious duties.

Attempts to resist this natural tendency are not lacking. Christianity, at its origin, represents such an attempt to throw off the yoke of legal ordinances and to bring about a correspondence between religion and life through the intellectual force of the religious doctrines of Judaism, but Christianity, too, in the course of its development, falls short of this ideal, and a few centuries after its appearance a compromise is effected between its Judaic phases and the ancient cult of Rome, which conditions its history, until at the time of the Reformation another attempt is made to realise the ideal relationship between religion and life. In our own days we have witnessed in Unitarianism—which appears in different countries under various names—and in Reformed Judaism still another attempt in the same direction, and the Ethical Culture[1] movement is but one symptom among many, of this constant endeavour among people who have reached higher conceptions of the scope of religion, to realise an ideal which appears indeed to demand an intellectual grasp of the meaning of life, for which the masses never have been, and perhaps never will be, entirely fitted.

Finally, Islam is but the illustration of the growth of the religious ideal among the Arabs,

---

[1] For a general view of these modern movements see Goblet D'Alviella's *Contemporary Evolution of Religious Thought in England, America, and India* (London, 1885), tr. by J. Moden.

modified in an adaptation to peculiar conditions.
At the time when Mohammed appeared, his people,
the Arabs, were still in the second stage of religious
development, the one which we have found to accord
with primitive culture.   The cult was largely made
up of magic rites, and the deities worshipped were
personifications of nature, or the outcome of animistic
conceptions.   The influence of Judaism and Christianity had, however, begun to make itself felt several
centuries before the appearance of Mohammed.   As
a consequence, the faith in the old gods was dying
out, and the great work of Mohammed consisted in
leading his people immediately to the position occupied by the higher form of faith, without their taking
the intermediate step.   Naturally, the conception
of Judaism and Christianity which he preached was
quite crude, but crude as it was, the Arabs were
still less prepared than was Mohammed himself to
abide by the ideal of religious conduct and faith
advanced by Judaism and Christianity.   As a consequence—but for the assertion of the monotheistic
principle—the religion of Islam during the centuries
following Mohammed, resembles more the third stage
of religious development, that represented by the
religions of India and Greece, or Babylonia and
Egypt, than it does the faiths of the next stage—
Buddhism or Christianity.

However, even at its lowest ebb, Islamism maintains
the theoretical relationship between religion and life
as emphasised in the highest religions ; so that despite
the large scope given to popular practices which
were carried over from the period of "ignorance," or
"crudeness,"[1] as Islamic writers called the time before

[1] Goldziher, *Muhammedanische Studien*, i., pp. 219-228.

Mohammed, Islamism nevertheless, by virtue of its theological superiority, belongs to the highest category of religions. Islamism, like Judaism, Buddhism, Zoroastrianism, and Christianity, has witnessed various attempts to come closer to the religious ideal—attempts which are followed again by periods of reaction, just as in the case of the religions named.

The classification which we would thus propose for religion is fourfold, corresponding to four stages of intellectual culture and moral development:—

 I. The Religions of Savages;

 II. The Religions of Primitive Culture;

 III. The Religions of Advanced Culture;

 IV. The Religions which emphasise as an ideal the coextensiveness of religion with life, and which aim at a consistent accord between religious doctrine and religious practice.

XI.

This classification will upon examination be found to rest upon a single principle which presides over the development of religion itself, namely, the relation of religion to life.

In the earliest stage the bond between religion and the experiences of everyday life is loose. In the life of the savage, religion plays a comparatively small part. On the occasions of unusual phenomena in nature, or when overwhelmed by disaster, he may seek to avert the hostility of the Power or Powers of which he stands in mortal dread; or he will in some way endeavour to elude the grasp of those whose actions he can no longer control—his dead ancestors. The religious cult at this stage being as meagre as

the doctrine, it is not surprising that unobservant
travellers should so frequently have returned with
the statement that the savages whom they have
encountered have no religion whatever. So faint is
the relationship between religion and life that one
must indeed search for traces of it.

In the second stage the bond is much closer.
The man of primitive culture has approached nearer
to the mystery of the universe and of life itself.
Having worked out a theory which recognises life
throughout the universe, and life of a kind similar
to the one of which he is conscious in himself, he
naturally endeavours to put himself in touch with
the various manifestations of the life about him.
The savage is chiefly conscious of his helplessness
in the midst of the accidents of life; the man of
primitive culture, conscious of his power by virtue
of achievements which already are his, makes a
bold attempt to obtain the mastery over the forces
of nature—partly by rites which are to conciliate
them, but in part also by acts which are to terrify
them. He plays off one power against the other,
secures the favour of some, and with these on his side,
threatens the hostile ones.   It is therefore the growing
power of man, as he advances in intellectual strength,
which prompts a closer union between religion and
life. Yet, there are large sections within the territory
of existence which are not at all occupied by religion.
Marriage in this stage has no contact as yet with
religion. Certain precautions are observed at the
birth of a child to secure it against the encroachment
of hostile or jealous powers, but there is as yet no dedication of children to the service of a deity.   Funeral
rites assume larger dimensions, and ancestor-worship

becomes more prominent, but there are no regular periods at which the Powers are invoked. No elaborate or permanent structures are reared in their honour to remind the worshipper of their presence, there is no organised priesthood to constantly suggest by their presence the activity and scope of religious faith, and much of life passes along without any contact with religion.

In the third stage, the period of civilisation in the proper sense—marked by the still larger scope of religion—the relationship between religion and life becomes correspondingly closer. The establishment of the bond between religion and morality is of course an important factor in bringing about this closer union. The sanction for conduct being found in religious doctrine, it follows that a larger proportion of the acts of life enter into direct contact with religion; and the regulation of religious duties thus acquiring a fixed and permanent character by the growth of religious codes, the relationship between religion and life likewise assumes a permanent character. The growing complications of social conditions lead to the elaboration of forms of government, religious as well as secular, and when once an organised priesthood is established, the tendency becomes marked to make the presence of religion felt on all possible occasions. Important acts of life, such as marriage, setting out on a journey, reaping the fruits of the soil, are given a religious aspect. The Powers of nature themselves are organised through systems of theology which now arise, and fixed times are set apart for approaching the various Powers.

Yet, despite the growing influence of the priest-hood, religion at this stage does not become the

controlling factor in the life of the individual.
Numerous popular practices are maintained, which
while not officially recognised in the cult, yet
have a religious bearing. The significance attached
by the masses to these practices—which being
unofficial, are regarded by those in priestly control
as superstitions—acts as a deterrent force, and helps
to maintain a gap between religion and life; and
again, the development of religious codes tends to
accentuate religious rites, which become more and
more minute, to a preponderating degree, as against
religious doctrines. The popular religion does not
keep pace with the intellectual advance, which, through
the pressure of mysterious forces making for progress,
goes steadily on; and this condition continues until
the time is ripe for advancing towards the highest
stage of religious development—the absolute union
between religion and life, accompanied by a consistent
accord between religious doctrine and religious
practice.   Some ancient cultures, as Egypt and
Babylonia, pass away without advancing to this stage;
others, as Greece and Rome, are in a stage of decay
when the step is taken, whereas others, like the
Hebraic and the Indian, are accorded a new and
increased vitality, by movements in their midst which
lead to the establishment of a sublime religious ideal.
Be it emphasised once more, that through natural
causes the ideal, though set up, is never fully attained,
and that the religious history of those nations who
once set up the ideal represents a constant succession
of attempts to reach it, followed by movements which
throw them further away from the goal; yet in these
forward and backward movements there is never a
complete reversion to a lower stage, and the principle

is never lost sight of, that religion, morality, civilisation, and life itself, stand and fall together.

The objections may be urged against this scheme of classification that in its last stage there is no recognition of the advance towards the monotheistic conception of the universe, and that, in addition, no account is taken of the universalistic tendencies of such religions as belong to the highest divisions. Important, however, as the doctrine of monotheism is, the tendency towards the recognition of one supreme Power in the world is manifested at a comparatively early stage in the development of man. Be it emphasised once more that so far from being peculiarly Hebraic, as is commonly supposed, many nations that belong to the category of primitive culture have an inkling of such a Power. So noticeable is this, that, as already indicated,[1] until this century the common belief among religious thinkers was that a primitive revelation of the one god had been vouchsafed to man, and that so-called polytheism marked a subsequent departure from a once higher level. This view, however, is not tenable, and we must perforce assume that the tendency towards a monotheistic conception of the universe is due to reflection, and in part suggested by the fact, obvious to man the moment that he begins to reflect upon the universe, that inequalities exist among the Powers themselves, and that hence there must be one Power above all others. Political developments, such as the union of states in the Euphrates Valley,[2] further lead towards according a superior place to the deity of the district which acquires supremacy; and while such a belief is as

[1] See above, p. 59.
[2] Jastrow, *Religion of Babylonia and Assyria*, pp. 116-121.

yet far removed from absolute monotheism, it must
be remembered that even in the Old Testament the
conception of Jahweh is not supposed to be inconsistent with the supposition that there are other gods,
albeit inferior ones, and unworthy of notice. Again,
the influence of the doctrine of monotheism is by no
means as powerful as is frequently taken for granted.
It was not this doctrine which led to the triumph
of the prophetical movement. Christianity spread
throughout the world, while interpreting this
doctrine in a way that permitted placing by the
side of the one God, Powers which could only be
united to Him by the assumption of a mystery.
Buddhism attracted millions, and held sway for
centuries without a doctrine of monotheism. Zoroastrianism never admitted it in its pure form, and
the strength of Islam lies in its capacity to attract
masses by virtue of the promises it holds out to the
" believer," rather than by insistence upon what is,
after all, a philosophical abstraction.

XII.

As for the supposed universalism of certain religions,
the difference of opinion which exists with reference
to the religions which merit this distinction, makes
it advisable to leave this factor out of consideration
entirely. Strictly speaking, there is no such thing
as a universal religion, since there is no religion
universally professed. There are a number which
aim to be universal—as Buddhism, Islamism, and
Christianity,—and there are others—as Judaism and
Zoroastrianism—which contain elements that might
under given conditions become the universal property

of mankind, but it is manifestly unjust to place tendencies and aspirations on a par with reality. The fact that the doctrines of a religion do not set up national or racial distinctions, does not make that religion universal; and while due allowance should be made for the remarkable scope attained by such religions as Christianity and Islam—accepted by a larger variety of races than any others—it is not proper to allow personal pride in achievement to get the better of one's judgment, and to proclaim a certain religion as containing the elements which are destined to make it universal. It is natural and proper for those who profess Christianity, or Islam, or Judaism, or Buddhism, to hold to this belief, and it is the duty of those so professing to do all in their power towards realising that ideal; but when we come to the study of facts in religion, the circumstance must be reckoned with that a universal religion, up to the present, remains an ideal which has not been realised by any religion.

I regard it as an advantage of the scheme of classification here proposed, that it can consistently and properly leave out of consideration an ideal that may so readily warp our judgment as to facts. The universal religion can come only when intellectual and social conditions in all parts of the world become alike. The spread of a certain form of culture—which in our pride we are fond of calling "occidental"—may, if the process continues, succeed in bringing the various nations of the world to an intellectual level; but this culture itself, in the course of this process, may expend its force long before the universal sway is attained. Even if this danger could be averted, it is not reasonable to suppose that the nations which become the teachers and guides to others will be contented to stand still, until those in a lower grade are brought up to their level. Inequality appears to be not only a law illustrated in the domain of nature, but, so far as mankind is concerned, the condition underlying human effort and presiding over human achievement. But why, it may furthermore be asked, need a particular religion be universal, in order to demonstrate its efficacy? Taking as the test the relation of religion to life, we conclude that that religion belongs to the highest category which establishes the strongest bond between itself and the lives of its adherents, and which induces the latter to lead lives as nearly perfect as an imperfectly constituted humanity can hope to reach. If there are several religions which claim this prerogative, we may feel sure that, provided the claim be justifiable, they will all be marked by similar ethical ideals and substantially similar aspirations.

The various ways in which these ideals and aspirations are expressed—taking shape in varying doctrines and in more or less profound differences in the cult—are due not only to the inequalities in existing social and political conditions, but to the inequalities of the human mind, as the result of the totally different directions followed by mankind in the slow and tedious process of intellectual and moral growth. But, above all, the religions belonging to what we have designated as the fourth stage, will all be characterised by the conception of religion which makes its scope and ambition coextensive with life itself. The question may be asked whether within this category further sub-divisions may not be made, and what the direction is which religious progress takes when once the higher conception of its relationship to life has been reached? To the first part of this question an affirmative answer may be given, and it is not difficult to set up a criterion by means of which the progress of further religious development is to be measured. While in the third division of religions, the relationship of religion to life is marked chiefly by ceremonial observances, which have a steady tendency to increase in number, and which, introduced into the incidents of daily life, serve as a reminder of the all-absorbing nature of religious influences, the higher stage is marked by the direct appeal to the *character* of the individual, by imbuing him with a religious spirit to such an extent as to shape, not merely his conduct, but his attitude of mind.

How far external observances of religious rites may act as a factor in bringing about this result depends largely upon the intellectual qualities of the individual. These qualities being unequal, more importance will be attached to religious ceremonials among groups of people less capable of abstract thought than among such as are prepared to come under the influence of religious ideas by an effort of the will. Again, the emotional side of religions will be more accentuated in sects which aim to reach large masses than in those which, in the nature of things, can be attractive only to a limited number. In general, then, it may be said that as individuals or groups become more intellectual, the influence of religion upon life will manifest itself more in producing a certain attitude of mind, either without the aid of religious observances at all, or with such observances reduced to a minimum. But such individuals or groups will necessarily, at all times, form a small minority. The great bulk of mankind, no matter how much further human progress may extend, will, so far as can be foreseen, always feel the need of props—in the shape of religious ceremonies—to maintain and strengthen the religious spirit within them; and these ceremonies, again, will present practically infinite varieties of form, corresponding to the differences in intellectual and social conditions among mankind.

A marked feature, however, of the sub-divisions to be noted in the highest stage of religious evolution is that these sub-divisions are to be found not in a comparison of the religions themselves that come within this category, but in each, with perhaps the single exception of Zoroastrianism. Judaism, Buddhism, Christianity, and Islam,—all have shown in the sects into which they are split up, precisely those variations which we have delineated. The question of further sub-divisions in the classification here proposed becomes of importance only when we approach the detailed study of any of these religions. It is within this narrow field that we are permitted to institute comparisons, and note how a specific religious idea or doctrine manifests itself with special force in an offshoot of one or the other of these religions; how in one sect the intellectual side of religious belief is more prominent, while in another there is a stronger appeal to the emotions.

XIII.

From the point of view here maintained, it will be apparent that the common practice of playing off one religion against another, and of setting up a category which places at the end of a series that religion to which we are particularly attracted, is totally misleading.   To maintain the superiority of one religion over another, because, forsooth, it controls the lives of larger numbers of individuals, is manifestly absurd; and, on the other hand, to claim a superiority for the doctrines of one, except on the supposition of a specially vouchsafed revelation to which all lay claim, is a proceeding that cannot be justified in a scientific treatment.   Lastly, with all the religions that belong to the highest category (and even many of those that belong to a lower division), teaching a lofty system of ethics, and laying *equal* stress upon conduct as the index of religious control, a further possibility of declaring one of the religions involved superior to the others, disappears.

It is one of the merits of the application of the historical method to the classification of religions that it thus fosters a spirit of appreciation of the aims and achievements of all religions, no matter to what category they belong; and while setting up the four sub-divisions which we have discussed, it exposes the fallacious attitude of those who would make their own religious predilections the criterion of religious truth.   The historical study of religions by no means undervalues the importance of this factor of "truth" in religious doctrines, but, recognising the impossibility of a scientific inquiry which starts out with a preconceived conclusion, it sounds a note of warning against falling into the serious error of mistaking opinions for sound argument.   The highest aim of the study of religions is to *understand* the meaning and purpose of religion in its varied manifestations.

Corresponding to this aim in proposing a system of classification of religions, we must have in mind, not the formation of a scale starting with the religions of our opponents and ending with our own, but such a grouping of religions past and present that the arrangement may illustrate the various ways in which the purposes of religion are realised.

CHAPTER III.

CHARACTER AND DEFINITIONS OF RELIGION.

I.

THE definitions proposed for religion are almost as varied in character, and as numerous, as are the schemes of classification. One reason for this variation is to be found in the twofold aspect presented by religion, its theoretical and practical side, so that according as the one or the other phase is foremost in the mind of a writer, the characterisation of religion will naturally assume a different aspect. Clemen, in a suggestive article dealing with different definitions proposed by recent German theologians and philosophers, well characterises these two aspects by defining the one as having reference to the belief in a deity and the conception formed of Him, while the practical aspect may be summarised in the attempt to lift oneself up to God or to come into communion with Him.[1] In the form which Clemen adopts, the distinction is applicable only to monotheistic religion, and more particularly to the monotheistic religion which Clemen has in view—Protestant Christianity; but the form can easily be so altered as to be of universal application. For whether we turn to those religions which occupy the lowest scale, or to

[1] "Der Begriff Religion u. seine verschiedene Auffassungen," *Theologische Studien und Kritiken*, 1896, pp. 472-505.

9

those which belong to the fourth category, according
to the classification proposed in the preceding chapter,
religion invariably has a practical aspect, and at the
same time involves of necessity theoretical questions
of belief in some form or other.

The apathy of the ancients towards the investigation of religious phenomena has been dwelt upon in
the first chapter.[1] In view of this, it is not surprising
to find that among ancient thinkers but few furnish a
definition of religion based upon a serious study of
the facts.   We have not yet encountered in Egyptian
or Babylonian literature a term which corresponds to
our word "religion."   The ancient Hebrews certainly
did not possess one, and when, in post-Biblical times,
it became necessary to devise one for philosophical
and theological nomenclature, the one chosen was
a word which simply indicated "faith."   The question
of the life after death, the relationship of the gods
to one another, and even the problem of evil and
injustice, engaged the attention of the theologians of
the Nile,[2] the Euphrates valleys,[3] and Judæa,[4] but
the suggestion that it was necessary to define the
nature and scope of religion does not occur to any of
them.

Coming to the Greeks, it is significant that neither
in Aristotle nor in Plato do we meet with any attempt
at a philosophical analysis of religion.   Among all
these peoples religion is simply a fact, taken for

---

[1] Page 3.

[2] See Wiedemann's recent monograph, *Die Toten und ihre Reich
im Glauben der alten Ægypter*, Leipzig, 1900.

[3] Jastrow, *Religion of Babylonia and Assyria*, chap. xxv.

[4] Books of Job and Ecclesiastes.   See Charles, *Critical History
of the Doctrine of a future Life in Israel, in Judaism and in Christian'ty*, London, 1899.

granted, and requiring no explanation. If, however, any of the thinkers of antiquity had been asked to define religion, the same answer would have been given by each one—the worship of the gods, and this is practically the force of the first definition of religion known to us, namely, the one given by Cicero. This writer, in his *De Natura Deorum*,[1] professes to divide the word into two elements, *re*-legere, "having a care" for the gods ; nor is there much difference in the counter-proposition made by another Roman writer, Lactantius,[2] who advocates as the etymology of the word the division into *re*-ligare, "bind to," forging a link between mankind and the gods.[3] The latter etymology became more generally accepted, and through the influence of Augustine, who adopted it, dominated the theology of the Middle Ages.

Until the sufficiency of Christianity was questioned by the sceptical philosophers of the seventeenth century, the thought that it was necessary to define religion beyond what was involved in an exposition of Christian theology, did not occur to those who concerned themselves with the study of religious phenomena. There lay on one side the large but well-defined field of the only true religion revealed by God himself, and on the other, separated by a wide gulf from the former, the still larger and undefined territory of false religions. The intensely practical interests of the one religion to which the theologians of the Middle Ages were attached made them necessarily

[1] II., 28, 72.

[2] *Divinarum Institutionum Libri Septem*, iv. 28.

[3] See the discussion of these definitions by Max Müller, *Natural Reiigion*, pp. 33-36.

oblivious of any need for investigating the general character of religion. True religion was Revelation; other religions than the true one were either creations of the Devil, or preliminary and provisional dispensations vouchsafed to mankind before they were prepared for the one genuine revelation of religious truth. Unsympathetic as this view may appear to us, there was at least one redeeming feature in the theory. It was quite generally held that the Divine Source of the Universe had never left mankind entirely without a witness of His being and power. In accordance with this, it was héld that already to Adam, the first man, a glimpse of the truth had been given, but that, owing to his sin, Divine favour was withdrawn, and the world, borne down by the weight of sin, languished until the time came for its redemption. The assumption of a primitive revelation, though scientifically untenable, or at least not capable of proof, yet embodies the important truth, fully borne out by the historical study of religions, that the essence of true religion is to be met with in the earliest manifestations of the spiritual side of man's nature, and that it is in his religious acts that this side is revealed.

II.

Coming to the philosophers of the seventeenth century, with whom a new epoch in the history of Philosophy begins, we find that the revolt against scholasticism had its chief result in leading to a sharp division between theology and philosophy. A fixed province was assigned to the former, and for a time at least the philosophers appeared anxious while devising their systems to avoid trespassing upon dangerous ground. Even Spinoza, who surpasses his predecessors and contemporaries in the boldness as well as in the keenness of his thought, does not question the authority of the current doctrines of the theologians so far as practical purposes of piety and morality are concerned. Whatever opinions he may have held with regard to the actual truth of these doctrines, he asserts, in common with the thinkers of his days, that the province and purpose of religion is the worship of God, summed up in obedient and pious observance of His commandments, as promulgated by a recognised authority, such as the Church.[1] The test of religious dogmas consists in their capacity to induce men to lead pious lives. It will be seen, therefore, that, according to Spinoza, religion presents merely one phase, a practical one, and his definition of religion takes into account this side alone. He is not prompted to an investigation of the origin of religion. His interest in other religions besides Judaism and Christianity is slight. Completely absorbed by the mainspring of his philosophical system—the immanence of God in the world—he is indifferent to such phases of the subject as are only brought to the front through a historical study of religious phenomena.

The attitude of Spinoza towards the practical aims served by religion is carried to its extreme logical consequence by the English Deists. Impressed by the strong mastery which the Church had obtained over the lives of the people, and which had become supreme, Herbert of Cherbury, who is generally regarded as the founder of English Deism, in an

---

[1] *Tractatus Theologico-Politicus* (1670).

endeavour to account for this state of affairs,[1] assumes
a gradual degeneration from a pure form of religion
given to man through an inner and outer revelation
of God. This theory of a pristine revelation, it will
be recalled, also formed part of the scholastic theology
of the Middle Ages, but the degeneration, instead of
being accounted for by man's sinfulness, is attributed
by Herbert to the machinations of priests, who, in pur-
suance of selfish ends, obscured the purity of religions
by forcing upon the people ceremonies and doctrines
calculated to enslave them and to make them sub-
servient to the designs of priests. The process is not
merely exemplified by the course of heathen religions,
but is illustrated by the history of Christianity as
well. In this pristine revelation five doctrines are
involved—(1) the existence of a god, (2) the duty to
worship God, (3) virtue and piety as the chief elements
in this worship, (4) repentance for sins and amend-
ment of one's course, and (5) the belief in a future
world where rewards and punishments are meted
out. These doctrines are set up as essential to
religion by virtue of the general agreement of mankind.

With the assumption of "certain" innate notions
Herbert rests content, and he does not enter
further into the question as to the means at our
command for proving the truth of the pristine
revelation. The end of religion, according to this
point of view, is to attach men to morality, and worship
is an essential means in reaching this end. It will be
seen that here again only the one phase of religion
is emphasised, and, while the theoretical basis is
recognised, no attempt is made to define religion

---

[1] *De Religione Gentilium errorumque apud eos causis* (1645).

from the combination of these two phases. The doctrine of primary revelation lies beyond the scope of philosophical investigation, and English Deism thus maintains in an even severer form than does Spinoza, the divorce between philosophy and religious doctrines. Spinoza confined the divorce to philosophy and the practical phases of religion; Herbert, with greater consistency, asserts that the theoretical substratum of religion, so far as furnished by the inner and outer revelation of God, must also be accepted without further questioning.

Hobbes,[1] starting practically from the same premises as Herbert, goes to the other extreme, and calls into question the ultimate truth of any and all religious doctrines; and while excepting from this scepticism the belief in a God, he declares that we can know nothing about Him, and that no Revelation is capable of proof. He accounts for the prevalence of religious beliefs by man's sense of fear. It was the fear of invisible powers, apparently hostile to man, which led him to acts of worship, and it is the same fear which is at the root of man's belief in divine beings, represented as spirits without bodies. The origin of forms of civil organisation is similarly sought in the union of men for mutual protection against enemies. Advancing from this position, Hobbes reaches the conclusion that authority is essential for maintaining the forms of both ecclesiastical and of civil government, and hence, so far from resenting the imposition of the priestly yoke, he maintains the necessity of investing the priests with the same absolute authority as that practised by the civil magis-

---

[1] *Leviathan, or the Matter, Form, and Power of a Commonwealth Ecclesiastical and Civil* (1651).

trates.   Religion under this view becomes merely one of the means for controlling peaceable relations among men, a factor in promoting the safety of individuals.

The ideal element still inherent in Spinoza's and Herbert's theory, which made religion of inestimable value in leading men to careers of goodness and morality, disappears from Hobbes' horizon; and society is resolved into a great police organisation, exercising authority by keeping alive the sense of fear, and by holding the masses in ignorance of truth and in complete subjection to civil and ecclesiastical magistrates.

With Spinoza emphasising the divorce between practical religion and theoretical belief, with Herbert setting up a barrier against the investigation of either the practical utility or the doctrinal substratum of primary religion, and Hobbes declaring the origin of both worship and doctrine to lie in a sense of fear, there was still another position possible—the reconciliation between religion in both its phases, and rational thought.   This position is taken by Locke,[1] who, while denying the existence of " innate notions," and declaring that all knowledge proceeds from reflection and experience, endeavours to prove that the supernatural Revelation, at least in one instance— Christianity—is not contradictory to what knowledge we acquire by the ordinary means.   In thus maintaining the necessity of bringing religious belief within the scope of investigation, Locke marks a great advance over his predecessors, and it is but a further conclusion from this position that the practical purpose of religion can only be fully carried out if

[1] *An Essay concerning the Human Understanding* (1690); *The Reasonableness of Christianity, as delivered in the Scriptures* (1695).

the theoretical substratum can be reconciled with the postulates of reason. The scope of religious Revelation thus becomes limited. Its advantage lies in communicating truths in a manner that will impress those incapable of reasoning for themselves, and it frequently anticipates the discoveries made by the subsequent exercise of reasoning powers, but the ultimate test of the truth of Revelation is its agreement with rational thought.

The result of this attempted reconciliation was to forge once more a bond between religion and the highest form of morality. Hobbes' philosophy was an endorsement of religious tyranny, and countenanced a low form of morality, if by that means order could be maintained in a state. Not so Locke, who consistently pleaded for tolerance and religious liberty, and whose ideal religion could flourish only in a pure moral atmosphere. That Locke and his followers, Toland,[1] Tindal,[2] Chubb,[3] Collins, and others, should have declared Christianity to be the only genuine form of religion, making it the "moral religion of reason," was quite natural; but the Christianity which they advocated was a diluted product, hardly to be distinguished from a non-mysterious rationalistic Theism. Christianity was but another name for the "reasonable religion of natural law." We may, therefore, take the attitude of these thinkers towards Christianity as furnishing a definition of religion that, while still laying the chief stress upon the practical aim—the morality of the individual—made worship and piety merely a means of attaining this end, and accorded a

[1] *Christianity not Mysterious* (1696). See above, p. 15.
[2] *Christianity as Old as the Creation* (1730).
[3] *The True Gospel of Jesus Christ* (1739).

higher rank to the truth and sufficiency of the beliefs taught by religion itself.

The attempt, however, to identify Christianity with "natural religion" was doomed to end in failure, and it was left to David Hume[1] to expose the weakness of the supports upon which the Christian Deists rested their claims. It argued, indeed, the possession of a perverted historical sense to set up the claim that a religion whose origins were so clear as were those of Christianity, merely represented a reversion to primitive ideas. At the base of the superficial rationalism of these Deists lay the supposition that the earliest form of religion could be of the same superior quality as the latest. Against this view Hume directs his keen criticism, and having disposed of it, he is no less incisive in his attack upon the second assumption of the Deists, that perversions of the true religion are due to the mischievous influence of priests. Hume's chief aim is to trace the development of religious beliefs and rites from the operation of perfectly natural causes. Religion begins with the personification of the powers of nature, and Hume falls back to the position of Hobbes in setting up fear as a chief factor in leading man to seek gods behind the forces of nature. The sense of dependence on these powers leads to efforts to dispose them favourably, and this is the beginning of worship. Religion thus resolves itself into a mere endeavour on the part of man to carry out his own desires and his selfish interests. In the course of its growth, Religion becomes allied to morality, but by the side of the stimulus to moral endeavour given by religion, it also

---

[1] *The Natural History of Religion* (1755); *Dialogues concerning Natural Religion* (1779).

encourages men in the delusion that, through services rendered to the Deity, they can win His favour, and in so far religion rather helps to undermine morality.   A more pessimistic conception of the character of religion can hardly be imagined, and it was natural that men were unwilling to rest content with the conclusions drawn by Hume.

III.

While the Deistic movement was going on in England, Germany was also experiencing the novelty of philosophical investigation freed from the bonds of scholastic formulas.   Leibnitz, the first eminent product of the new spirit, presents in many respects a contrast to Spinoza, noticeably in his main thought, which recognises a variety of independent substances where Spinoza saw only emanation from a single substance.   There is a close similarity, however, in the view taken by the two philosophers of the character and nature of religion.   Leibnitz, like Spinoza, lays the chief emphasis on the practical side of religion, so far as the masses are concerned.   For the masses it matters less whether the formulas of belief held by them express the full or exact truth.   Nevertheless, he does not maintain so sharp a division between theory and practice as Spinoza is inclined to do, and in his essay on " The Harmony of Faith and Reason "[1] (1710), he sets himself the task of showing the reasonableness of religious faith, even as popularly understood. He avoids the difficulties involved, by accepting

---

[1] " Discours de la conformité de la foi avec la raison "—the " Discours Preliminaire" of the *Essais de Théodicée* (ed. Gerhardt), vol. vi., pp. 89-101.

the distinction of the schoolmen between what transcends reason and what is repugnant to reason; and he allows a fuller scope than Spinoza would have accorded to views and beliefs which can neither be proved nor refuted by reason. In this category he places all the essential doctrines of Protestant theology, including the Trinity, the Incarnation, and the Resurrection, as well as miracles in general. He also accepts the necessity of a divine Revelation in the traditional sense, as the only means of communicating to man what lies beyond reason.

His conception of religion is influenced, as was Spinoza's, by the exclusive contemplation of certain religions, but he is even more exclusive, since he confines his interests to Christianity. His criterion for distinguishing between the true and the false in religious doctrines is exceedingly precarious, and the weakness of his position becomes especially manifest when he endeavours to justify views which he evidently accepted as *a priori* conclusions. Leibnitz lacks the historical sense, and his conception of religion is as one-sided as that of his contemporaries, in that it fails to account for the persistency of religious faith in mankind, entirely apart from the practical purposes served by religion.

Christian Wolff, proceeding in the path mapped out by Leibnitz, attempted[1] to set up a still more complete harmony between reason and faith. According to him, there was a complete accord between the natural revelation of God through man's reason and the historical revelation in Christianity. There was no occasion to assume a neutral territory of that which "transcended reason." "Natural theology" and

[1] *Theologia Naturalis* (1736-37).

the theology of the Scriptures balanced each other perfectly. In the latter the truths are revealed which man must otherwise acquire by a laborious process, but the results in both cases tally. Wolff's view of religion, therefore, is the one traditionally adopted by Christian theologians—with the sole difference, that it is clad in the formulas of a secular philosophy. The reaction against Wolff's position led to the same results in Germany as that brought about by the Deists in England. Reimarus, in a treatise bearing the somewhat ambiguous title of *A Defence for the Reasonable Worshippers of God*,[1] strikes a new chord in attacking the credibility of the Scriptural narratives and statements, and although his method utterly disregarded the canons of historical criticism, yet for the time being Reimarus brought into discredit the Wolffian system, and paved the way for Lessing, as well as for Kant. So thorough was the reaction against the Leibnitz-Wolffian method of reconciling theology with philosophy, that for a time philosophy appeared to be entirely neglected in the controversy that raged between the advocates and the opponents of Scriptural infallibility.

Lessing[2] is the most distinguished exponent of those who contend that the Bible is neither the sum and substance, nor the sole depository of religious truth. The Bible, as he put it, contains religion, but is not itself religion. He goes further, and shows in an elaborate argument the folly of making an uncertain tradition the basis of religious faith. The foundations of faith lie deeper than the

---

[1] *Apologie oder Schutzschrift für die Vernünftigen Verehrer Gottes* (1767).

[2] *Wolfenbütteler Beiträge* (1774-78); *Anti-Goeze* (1778).

Bible—they must be sought in the human mind and
the human heart. While all this appeared to be
merely a controversy restricted to a single religion,
Christianity, in reality it involved the entire conception of religion, and, as has been pointed out in a
previous chapter,[1] the lines laid down for the historical
development of religion in his famous essay on
"The Education of the Human Race" (1780) are
but an application of the principles which guide
Lessing in his controversy with Pastor Goeze, of
Hamburg. Looking at the various positive religions
as so many steps in the education of mankind,
he reaches the conclusion that the form which
religion assumes is to be distinguished from its
essence. This essence he finds present in "Natural
Religion," which preceded "Revealed" or "Positive
Religion."[2] The transition from the former to the
latter he conceives to have taken place, very much
as the English Deists maintained, by agreement
among a people to accept certain doctrines and ceremonies. This official "dualism" constitutes, as
Pfleiderer[3] points out, the great weakness in the
position assumed by Lessing, but he had taken a
considerable forward step in advocating that the
nature of religion was to be explained from the
course it had actually taken in history, and not from
certain speculative notions as to the character of
primary religion. While it is evident that Lessing's
view of "Natural Religion" is influenced by the
speculations of the English Deists, he discards
entirely the opinion upon which the latter laid such

---

[1] See p. 32.
[2] *Ueber die Enstehung der Geoffenbarten Religion* (1755).
[3] *The Philosophy of Religion* (English translation), vol. i., p. 141.

stress that "primitive religion" contained religion in
its purest form. According to Lessing, the tendency in
religion was steadily upward, following closely on the
track of human progress in general. The particular
form assumed by religion corresponded to the stage
reached on the road of culture. The higher the
culture the purer the religion; and in thus making
culture the index of religion, Lessing established the
proper proportions between the theoretical and practical phases of religion, between its doctrinal substratum and its external manifestations. Religion as
a factor in the education of the human race was something quite different from religion viewed merely as
a means for ensuring prompt obedience to a Divine
Power, and was equally far removed from the notion
which recognised the outcome of religion merely in
obedience and piety. In place of the theory which
looked upon religion as a police regulation to keep
people from destroying one another, Lessing held up
"Natural Religion" as the first endeavour of mankind towards the fulfilment of its mission, and maintained that the process of evolution would only then
be complete when mankind shall have reached its goal.

In a more popular form, Lessing gave expression to
his conception of the nature and character of religion in
his sublime drama, *Nathan the Wise* (1779). To look
upon this work as a mere plea for toleration in religion
is to mistake its main purpose. Lessing was no vague
sentimentalist, and in bringing the Jew and Christian
and Mohammedan together, each claiming to have in
his possession the genuine "ring," he intended to
illustrate his main thought, that the manifestations of
religion were necessarily as varied as the different
grades, and, what is equally important, as the different

varieties of culture. Hence the significant exhortation at the close of the drama, that the claimants should come again after a thousand thousand years before asking for a decision as to which of the three rings was genuine. Religion is an endless historical process—as endless as the chain of culture itself.

In thus making religion an ingredient factor of history, Lessing foreshadows the modern definitions of religion, which, in contrast to those that we have hitherto been considering, are marked by the attempt to combine the theoretical with the practical phases.

IV.

Kant may be taken as the first exponent of this conception of religion. A fundamental principle in his system of philosophy being the sharp demarcation between the realm of what he called "pure" and "practical reason," he was necessarily called upon, when touching upon the problems of religion, to view the subject from this twofold position. He takes up this theme in his work on *Religion within the Limits of Reason only*.[1] With the same earnestness which prompts him in his *Critique of Practical Reason* to set up moral duty as absolute law—"a categorical Imperative"—even at the risk of exposing himself to the charge of drawing deductions not warranted by his Critique of Pure Reason, in his work on Religion, he in characteristic fashion makes religion consist in the recognition of duty as a divine command. There is no reference in this definition to piety, with which the Deists were wont to identify religion, or to the love of God, which plays so large

---

[1] *Religion innerhalb der Grenzen der blossen Vernunft* (1793).

a part in the philosophy of Spinoza and Leibnitz; nor is it implicit obedience which is demanded. Pure Reason comes in for its share in the *recognition* of duty as a divine command, while Practical Reason suggests to individuals the importance of performing their duties as members of society, mutually dependent on one another. In religion, therefore, pure and practical Reason meet. Kant accepts the distinction between revealed and natural religion, but, much like Lessing, recognises the value of the former only in so far as it furnishes, immediately, knowledge which man subsequently obtained by the slower process of thought. There can be nothing in true revelation which is not furnished by reason.

Kant, however, is willing to go to great lengths in reconciling the tenets of revealed religion with the results of natural thought. Doctrines such as Original Sin, Justification by Faith, and the Trinity, which act as direct incentives towards eradicating evil out of the hearts of men, he readily admits, although the interpretation which he puts upon them is at variance with the view taken by Christian theology. It is also a part of Kant's view of religion to recognise the necessity of a central authority for religion. However strongly the individual may be swayed by the "categorical imperative," the supremacy of the moral principle can only be secured by its binding force upon the community. To attain this end, association in the form of a church is essential. The church, however, which Kant has in mind is an ideal institution, based upon the faith of pure reason, of which existing bodies are imperfect representatives. Still, imperfect as they are, the actual church organisations correspond to existing needs, which manifest

10

themselves in the establishment of ceremonial laws as an aid to the enforcement of moral obligations. In addition to a cult, however, the visible church also has a creed, which again bears the same relation to the creed of pure reason that ideal perfection does to practical imperfection. While, therefore, the creed of the church, according to this view, can never embody the absolute truth of religion, it is yet true if it embodies a principle by the development of which religious truth can be approximated. Kant's view of the historical religions is coloured by this single ideal which he sets up—the approach to the enforcement of morality on the basis of the faith of pure reason. He sees in Jesus the first religious teacher who set up the correct ideal of religion, but when he comes to a consideration of the details of the Christian faith and cult, he boldly rejects, as forming part of the religion of Jesus, elements—such as prayer in the ordinary acceptance, and miracles—which in his opinion do not aid in reaching the goal of pure religion. The weakness of such a position is manifest, inasmuch as it fails to account for the persistency of the belief in all religions, including Christianity, in precisely these two elements. But, as against this weakness, one must admire the courage with which Kant carries his conception of religion, which has been defined as "critical rationalism," to a logical conclusion.

The chief criticism, however, to be directed against Kant's view of religion is that whereas it takes into consideration its practical and theoretical phases, a too one-sided emphasis is placed upon the ideal, leading to a lack of appreciation of the real. Religion, after all, must be judged in connection with its applicability to man. A church that can never be realised lies outside the scope of religion, as it manifests itself in history, and hence a definition of religion which, like Kant's, divorces the religious instinct from the aim of religion, is in so far deficient as it does not recognise the actual course taken by religious development as a controlling factor.

The reaction against this purely rational conception of the character of religion is represented by Kant's younger contemporary, Herder. In the first chapter, reference was made to the great services rendered by Herder to the study of religion by the keen historical sense which he brings to bear upon the elucidation of the phenomena of religion. No less significant is the advance signalled in his writings by his view of the scope of religion in the life of man. The central idea in his great work on the "Philosophy of History"[1] is evolution. Human history is viewed by Herder as a process of development, and the course taken by development is steadily, despite appearances to the contrary, and despite reactionary movements, in the direction of progress. This process is carried out under the workings of law, and Herder recognises the same law presiding over all organic life. Religion, too, comes within the scope of this law, and hence religious history represents in its various phases the successive steps in a process of evolution. As against Kant's duality of a pure and a practical Reason, Herder maintains that if speculation leads us to deny the possibility of knowing things in themselves, we must accept the consequences and be resigned to the conclusion that our ideas do not correspond to any reality; but if it is once shown that the laws of the Universe are the

[1] *Ideen zur Philosophie der Geschichte der Menschheit* (1784-87).

expression of the highest Reason, then the conclusion is warranted that Reason presides over the Universe. This highest Reason, according to Herder, is none other than God, whose presence he recognises, with Spinoza, everywhere. The reality of God can no longer be questioned, the moment we become convinced of the reality of existing laws of nature, and recognise in addition how well these laws are adapted to serve certain ends. Herder's Pantheism, it thus appears, represents a combination of Spinozistic ideas with Leibnitzian teleology.

Coming to the place occupied by religion in the life of the individual, Herder defines this as the means of establishing his proper relationship to the divine order of things. As a part of nature, man is brought into contact with the supreme Reason which governs all things, and religion rests upon the consciousness of the fact that men are portions of the world. But by virtue of our position in the world, certain obligations are entailed upon us. What they are is clearly indicated by the course of human history. This history marking a steady upward tendency, it follows that the individual realises the purpose of existence by bringing out what is best in him. In this way Religion is brought into close touch with Ethics without being wholly covered by it. Two sources are placed at man's command for determining his duties—nature and revelation. In the earlier religions, nature was the chief guide of man. Hence the large scope assumed by myths, which are but attempts to interpret the meaning of nature and the lessons furnished by it. However, at all times this natural revelation was supplemented by the teachings of privileged persons to whom a special illumination had been accorded. Revelation from this point of view represents a guidance afforded the Human Race as an aid in its education—the ultimate goal of which is true humanity. The special feature of Christianity consists in the more perfect form in which this guidance is furnished, through the teachings of Jesus, but Jesus himself merely marks an epoch in the education of the Human Race, closely connected with preceding conditions. It is one of the merits of Herder that his historical sense did not desert him even when dealing with aspects of religion particularly dear and sacred to him as a Protestant theologian.

V.

Herder cut himself loose from Kant's philosophy by boldly asserting the reality of things; it was reserved to Fichte to accept the other alternative, and by maintaining absolutely and consistently the purely subjective character of knowledge, to reach a conception of religion in which the subjective element is so pronounced as to savour strongly of mysticism.

Pfleiderer, in his *Philosophy of Religion*,[1] has well set forth the stages in Fichte's own mental development before he reached the position set forth in his *Theory of the Sciences*.[2] Even in this work he still claims to represent the true Kantian position by declaring the "Ego," as he called it, the condition of all knowledge, all our thoughts and views and perceptions being but phenomena of the Ego. The world of the senses being but the reflection of our own mentality, it follows that belief in God cannot

---

[1] Vol. i., sect. iii., chap. i.
[2] *Ueber den Begriff der Wissenschaftslehre* (1794).

be furnished by reasoning, but by an intuitive realisation of His existence, an immediate knowledge, not derived from our senses but from the inner consciousness, and from the recognition of a moral purpose in *our* existence, patterned upon an ideal directly revealed.   This immediate knowledge forms the basis of religion, and the union between morality and religion is absolute, since both are brought home to us by knowledge not derived from reasoning or by the evidence of our senses.   Belief in God, and recognition of the stern law of duty, alike uplift man into the world of the supersensuous.   Still, Fichte does not regard religion as a prop to morality.   The former does not strengthen a man in any line of action that he would not have been led to without it, but religion reveals to him the harmony between the law of duty and the essential being of man.   The religious man has no need of recognising duty as a command— duty constitutes his very life, and as naturally as he lives his life does he observe the law of morality.

Religion, then, according to Fichte, is merely a "harmonious fundamental disposition of the soul." It is not a certain line of action, not a belief in certain doctrines; it has nothing to do with worship, but is purely and simply a certain *view* of things.   Once grasped, however, religion becomes the supreme light and guidance to the individual.

Proceeding in this direction, it was inevitable that Fichte should have been led gradually to a mystical interpretation of the religious instinct.   The religious spirit in his latest writings becomes so vague, so subtle, that one can with difficulty follow him in his attempts to define it.[1]   Distinguishing four different

---

[1] As for example, *Die Anweisungen zum seligen Leben* (1806).

views to be taken of the world—as material substance, as ruled by law, as an ethical organism, as holy and good—he regards these as successive mental stages of development leading up to religion, which furnishes the supreme truth by man's contemplation of himself as the mirror in which God is reflected. This religious view is quite sufficient for man, but by means of science, more particularly by philosophy, man also comes to see the reason for that, of the truth of which he is already assured through contemplation. It is needless for our purposes to enlarge upon the manner in which Fichte links his conception of religion to the conditions actually existing in human society. Like Kant, he recognises the value of a church organisation with all its accompaniments, and with Herder he places a high estimate upon the work of religious teachers—the religious geniuses, he calls them—whose utterances are regarded as a revelation of the Divine Will. The positive religions are the creations of the moral guides of mankind, established for the development of the religious and moral sense of humanity. The gap between the ideal and real in such a view of religion is exceedingly large; indeed so large that one must despair of ever bringing about a connection between the two.

More satisfactory in this respect is Schleiermacher's attitude towards religion, although it shares with Fichte's the element of introspection and the tendency towards mysticism. In his famous *Discourses on Religion*[1] he unfolds in a masterly manner the view that religion is essentially a state of feeling. Only by direct experience, by an introspective process, can

[1] *Ueber die Religion—Reden au die Gebildeten unter Ihren Verächtern* (1799).

we reach religious truth. Religion is neither metaphysics nor morality, but arises at the moment that
we become conscious of a contact between ourselves
and the universe. This contact he more particularly
defines as a feeling of dependence. In this specific
feeling, in the recognition that we cannot accomplish
our ends through our own efforts alone, Schleiermacher recognises at once the source and essence of
religion. The advantage of this definition over that
of Fichte is its greater simplicity. Instead of
appealing to a purely speculative idea—as that of
the Ego—Schleiermacher takes as his starting-point
a condition which may well be regarded as common
to the most ignorant and to the most highly-
developed intellect. Religion thus becomes a purely
subjective process. The question of the true and
false is relegated to a secondary place. Schleiermacher broadly assumes that every religion is true in
its kind, but the sphere being an infinite one, the
feeling of dependence may manifest itself in various
ways. Indeed, one might expect infinite variations,
but since the religious feelings have an inner connection with another, they manifest a natural tendency
to be united into a system, and the number of such
systems is naturally limited. The positive religions
represent such systems, each being characterised by
some fundamental idea, which is emphasised through
the influence of a "religious genius," who becomes,
as it were, the founder of a new religion.

It will be apparent that from Schleiermacher's
point of view the transition from this general idea
of religion to its practical manifestation is more easily
and naturally brought about; and his insistence
upon feeling as the essential factor in religion marks

his great contribution to the investigation of the subject. Others, since Schleiermacher's time, have defined the religious feeling differently, but the definite assumption of a religious instinct in man forms part of almost every definition of religion proposed since the appearance of Schleiermacher's discourses; and it may furthermore be stated as an indication of Schleiermacher's influence, that but few definitions of religion since his days have omitted as an essential element the factor of man's "dependence" upon powers over which he has no control.

VI.

In Schelling and Hegel we encounter a view of religion which endeavours, even more closely than did Schleiermacher, to connect the ideal with the real. The starting-point of both Schelling and Hegel is that the idea of religion is to be recognised in its historical manifestation, and from this the further conclusion is drawn that the actual history of religion represents a system of religious philosophy properly graded in a logical process; but whereas Hegel is led to set up a large series of grades, Schelling only recognises two forms of religion—mythology and revelation,[1] each representing an independent process. These two processes of thought correspond, however, to a reality; for Schelling solves the dualism involved in the phenomena of the mind and in things by themselves by asserting that the two worlds—the mental and the actual one—balance each other.   "Mind is invisible

---

[1] *Philosophie der Mythologie* (Abth. II., vols. 1-2), and *Philosophie der Offenbarung* (Abth. II., vols. 3-4, of Schelling's *Sämmtliche Werke*, Stuttgart, 1856-58).

Nature, Nature is mind made visible." In the domain of the former, there are three classes of phenomena— science, religion, and art; each representing, again, the development of a fundamental idea—truth, goodness, and beauty. In the idea of goodness, the two forms of religion, mythology and revelation, meet.

Religion, then, according to Schelling, serves a practical purpose—the unfolding of goodness; but he is not impelled by his peculiar manner of looking at things to proceed further, and to define the place of religion in the life of the individual. Whatever exists in thought corresponds to a reality, and hence the idea of a God from which religion starts, and to which it ultimately reverts, is of necessity the counterpart of something which has a real existence. While, therefore, Schleiermacher brings the subjective side of religion into the foreground, Schelling sets this aside in favour of the objective side, in the study of which the problems of religion all find their solution. His attitude is almost exclusively theoretical. The individual does not occupy his attention, but only the process of thought which he recognises in the historical development of religious phenomena.

Hegel, weaving into a single pattern the threads of the philosophy found in the systems of Spinoza, Leibnitz, Fichte, and Schelling, carries the fundamental principle of Schelling, the conception of phenomena as a development of certain ideas, to its consistent end.[1] In Nature and in the life of mankind he sees the same process, and religion takes its place within the life of mankind as one illustration of the process, which is essentially a mental one. Both nature religions and positive religions are viewed as

[1] *Philosophie der Religion.* See p. 36.

representing certain ideas, and the order in which religions arise corresponds to the natural growth of the ideas which they symbolise. The process is completed of necessity in Christianity, which he defines as the religion of the absolute. In the previous chapter we had occasion to discuss Hegel's classification of religions,[1] and we may, therefore, content ourselves here with mentioning his general notion of religion, which consists in the relation of the individual, as a finite spirit, to God, who is the absolute spirit. His conception is, it will be seen, purely intellectual. The subjective element is absent, as it is absent from Schelling's view, but a greater scope is given to the individual in Hegel's theory, through the admission that the starting-point of religion involves the relationship of man to some higher Power or Powers; though it should be added that for Hegel this higher Power is largely a logical deduction, and not born of any intuitive process. The great merit of both Schelling and Hegel consists in their insistence upon the study of the phenomena of religion as furnishing the key to the understanding of religion itself, but in thus remedying the defect in Fichte's and Schleiermacher's thought, which made so wide a gap between the real and ideal, they left out of consideration the subjective element—Schelling neglecting this feature altogether, and Hegel assigning to it a place not commensurate with its importance.

VII.

The definitions of religion brought forward after Hegel may all be characterised as attempts to find

[1] See p. 71.

a proper combination of these two factors—the subjective and the objective. Whether we turn to Germany, and examine the definitions of such thinkers as Feuerbach and Hartmann, or to England, and note the attitude of John Stuart Mill, Herbert Spencer, and Matthew Arnold; or examine the works of the more purely historical students of religion, as Max Müller, Tiele, and Réville, we find everywhere an agreement in regard to these points: (1) the existence of a religious sentiment; (2) the feeling of man's dependence upon a Power or Powers beyond his control as an essential factor in practical religion, whether the religion be of the lowest or of the highest type; and (3) that the development of religious ideas follows definite laws, and stands in close connection with the intellectual growth of man. This position carries with it (4) the natural origin of religion itself. According as a thinker is more concerned with the general character of religion, or with its manifestations, the one or the other of these four points is more prominently brought forward; and we may note, since the days of Hegel, at times a general tendency to lay stress upon the religious sentiment, followed again by a period which occupies itself more with the practical relation of religion to life.

Thus, in the period immediately following upon Hegel, and as a reaction against Hegelianism, there is a pronounced tendency to view religion as a subjective process. The Hegelian philosophy was put in the service of a reactionary movement in politics and religion, and, as a consequence, those who stood for freedom of thought were the religious sceptics. Among these, Ludwig Feuerbach occupies a prominent place. According to him, all religious ideas are subjective products of the human mind to which there is no corresponding reality. Man cannot go beyond his nature, and the ideas that he forms— including the idea of God—are controlled by his nature. It is man who creates God, and the God whom he forms is made in man's image. Similarly, the doctrines of religion, faith, belief in miracles, and even specific dogmas like that of mediatorship, incarnation, have all only a subjective value, and are purely subjective in origin. Feuerbach's attitude, though on the surface purely philosophical, is not unmixed with a certain hostility towards the forms of religion. He will not even admit that religious ideas have any value in raising man to the contemplation of the higher ideals of life, but regards them as practically mischievous. " Religion is the relation of man to his own being, but as a being outside of himself." The essence of religion is the identification of the human with a supposed divine nature—its outcome is the deification of man. But even Feuerbach admits the element of man's dependence upon a higher Power as active in producing the phenomena of religion, although he seems to limit the scope of this feeling to Christianity.[1] Instead, however, of regarding this factor as marking a genuine advance, Feuerbach stamps this feeling of dependence as an indication of weakness—an admission that in the struggle with nature, man has succumbed and throws himself on the mercy of a Power to which he has surrendered.

Feuerbach found many followers in Germany—

---

[1] Feuerbach's chief works are (1) *Essence of Christianity* (1841; English translation by George Eliot) ; (2) *Essence of Religion* (1845; English translation by A. Loos, New York, 1873).

notably Stirner and David Friedrich Strauss—and
the same influences which produce his attitude
towards religion are also apparent in France, where
we have as a contemporary of Feuerbach, Auguste
Comte, the kernel of whose religion is the worship
of man instead of God,[1] and in England, where a
new school of philosophy arose under the leadership
of John Stuart Mill.   Profound as are the differences
between these thinkers, they all agree in emphasising
the fact that religious beliefs are but the projection
into nature of man's own personality, and that hence
religion, in the ordinary acceptation, is to be characterised as an illusion.

The weakness of this position lies in the one-sidedness of the view taken of religion, as though it consisted solely of certain beliefs, and as though these
beliefs had been forced upon people through some
external influence, instead of being spontaneous
growths.   Among these beliefs, again, undue importance is assigned to the views held about God, as
though they constituted the very essence of religion,
whereas it is clear from the survey of the subject
afforded in this and in the preceding chapters, that
belief in a God, and beliefs in general, constitute but
one phase of religion, albeit an important one.

The movement, however, in philosophical speculation, which carries this attitude towards religion to
an even more extreme point, is the neo-pessimism
represented chiefly by Schopenhauer and Hartmann.
The former, accepting in part [2] Kant's position that we

---

[1] *Système de Politique Positive*, vol. iv. (1854).   For a summary of
present day Positivism, see Frederic Harrison's address, *The Religion of
Duty* (1901).

[2] His chief work is *The World as Will and Idea* (1818; English
translation, London, 1896).

cannot know things as they are, yet passes beyond
Kant in making the conscious will of the individual
a means of passing from a relative knowledge to the
actual knowledge of things.   This will is the essence
of the world.   There can be nothing higher, nothing
more potent.   But the will is also responsible for the
evil in the world, and since, according to Schopenhauer, evil predominates over good, there is only one
means of conquering evil, and that is by completely
repressing the will to live.   The religion which
corresponds to this ideal is one in which resigna-
tion and the looking forward to complete extinction
are the chief doctrines.   Moral conduct is a means
towards the accomplishment of the aim of the world
—the repression of the desire to live—and in so far
enters into religion; but there is no inherent bond
between religion and morality.   Schopenhauer rejects
all forms of religion which look forward to immortality, or the hope of improving the condition of
mankind while on earth.   The mystical phase of
Buddhism, with its plea for a life of retirement and
non-activity, and its doctrine of Nirvana as the goal
of existence, approaches Schopenhauer's ideal; but
except for the scope which even he grants the religious
sentiment, and his recognition of the need of morality,
it is hardly admissible to apply the term religion to
his views.   Hence when a profounder spirit, like
Hartmann, attempts to pass beyond Schopenhauer's
negations to some positive form of religion, he is
obliged to introduce in some shape the "god idea."
In doing so, he involves himself in strange contradictions; for, on the one hand, he accepts Schopenhauer's view that existence is a necessary evil, and,
on the other, he finds it necessary to assume behind

the will a power through whom redemption can be obtained. If the world is to be viewed, as Hartmann would have it regarded, there is no reason for having a religion at all, and certainly the being who represents the source of all evil can hardly be the one through whom release from pain can be expected.

VIII.

Significant as Hartmann's great works[1] are, full of suggestive thought, and replete with acute observation, it cannot be said that either he or Schopenhauer, or any of their followers, has advanced our understanding of the religious sentiment, or has added any significant element to an appreciation of the character of religion. Pessimism, as a system of philosophy, may have its justification, but pessimism is in such direct and inveterate opposition to the religious sentiment—which is essentially optimistic— that it affords no sound basis for religious faith in any form. It practically shuts out all scope for the play of the religious sentiment, even though it theoretically accords a place to this sentiment; and without such free play it is but a juggling of words to still speak of religion. Hartmann's religion of the future, to which he gives the name of "Concrete Monism," is an abstraction, the creation of a remarkable speculative spirit, but without application to the real religious needs of mankind. Pessimistic philosophy has left the problem as to the real character of religion exactly where it found it. Representing a

---

[1] Especially *The Philosophy of the Unconscious* (1868; English translation, London, 1893), and *Religionsphilosophie*, I. "Das Religiöse Bewusstsein des Menschen;" II. "Die Religion des Geistes." See above, p. 91.

hostile attitude towards religion, it practically rules religion out of the jurisdiction of serious thought. On the other hand, the anthropological, empirical, and positivist schools of thought have rendered valuable services to the study of the problem as to the real nature of religion. Thinkers like Feuerbach, Comte, and Mill brought about a healthy reaction against the dialectic gymnastics of Hegelianism on the one hand, and the sentimental and mystical tendencies of Fichte and Schleiermacher on the other. Through this reaction, the way was prepared for definitions of religion, based on the study of the history of religions. It is to these that we now turn.

The new movement is already foreshadowed by Herbert Spencer, who although generally classed with "positivists," still departs from the position of Comte and Mill in claiming that, while we are bound by the limits of actual knowledge to the relative and conditioned, it is still necessary for us to assume something beyond this limit. We cannot enter the region of the "unknowable" to the extent of determining its nature, but we can at least predicate the existence of the unknowable. Spencer was led to this position through his profound and extensive study of the facts in the development of the human race in all its ramifications. His "Sociological Charts,"[1] prepared with the collaboration of a band of assistants, constitute the material which he uses in the copious illustrations with which he justifies his views in the various sub-divisions of his encyclopædic *Synthetic Philosophy*.[2] Finding everywhere the pronounced

[1] *Descriptive Sociology*, in eight parts, London and New York, 1873-81.
[2] See especially his "First Principles" (1862).

tendency among peoples—no matter what grade of
culture they possess—to pass beyond the limits of
actual knowledge, he reaches the conclusion that
there must be at least a partial justification of this
tendency. The very recognition of "finiteness" is
a warrant for the assumption that there is something
beyond the borderland of finite knowledge. Man
everywhere instinctively revolts against making himself the measure of the universe, and this recognition
of a distinct sphere of the "unknowable" becomes for
Spencer both the source and the characteristic trait of
religion. There is involved in this recognition on
the part of man, a consciousness of his own insignificance, and with this comes naturally a feeling of
dependence upon Powers whose realm reaches out
into the "unknowable." But, after all, Spencer is
chiefly concerned with sociological phenomena, and
has comparatively little interest in the detailed history
of the great religions of the world. His facts in the
domain of religion are gathered too exclusively from
peoples living in savage state or in a condition of
primitive culture, and while such observations are of
profound value in a study of the religious sentiment,
it is the course taken by religion among cultured
races that enables us, by a recognition of it as a
permanent element in human history, to define it
more accurately.

IX.

The study of religion in its broadest scope is
represented by historical students, among whom
Max Müller, Tiele, and Réville constitute the leading trio. It will therefore be of value to see how,
as the result of their investigations, these scholars

define religion.   In his Hibbert lectures,[1] Max Müller
defines religion as "a mental faculty which independent of, nay, in spite of sense and reason, enables
man to apprehend the infinite under different names
and under varying disguises."   "We can hear in all
religions," he says, "a groaning of the spirit, a struggle
to conceive the inconceivable, to utter the unutter-
able, a longing after the Infinite, a love of God."
Recognising that such a statement laid too exclusive
stress upon the speculative side of religion, he subsequently introduced a modification into it by restricting
the apprehension of the Infinite to "such manifestations
as are able to influence the moral conduct of man."[2]
There can be no question that Max Müller hit upon
an essential element in all religions in thus bringing
into prominence the desire of man to reach out to an
appreciation of the Infinite, and he expressed this
feeling most happily when he termed it a "groaning"
and a "struggle," but it cannot be said that the
definition is improved by having tacked on to it a
reference to "the moral conduct of man."   The bond
is lacking between a speculative longing and the
determination of conduct.   No doubt Max Müller held,
with most scholars, that the connection between religion and ethics is, in the early stages of religious
development, exceedingly loose, yet there should
be included in a definition of religion an element
which enables us to see how the approach of
the religious sentiment to the ethical ideal gains
in distinctness, until they are united in inseparable
wedlock.

[1] *Lectures on the Origin and Growth of Religion, as illustrated by the
Religions of India,* p. 23, London, 1880.
[2] *Physical Religion* (Gifford Lectures, 1st series, 1891), p. 294.

This element is supplied in the definition proposed by Réville,[1] namely, "Religion is the determination of human life by the sentiment of a bond uniting the human mind to that mysterious mind whose domination of the world and of itself it recognises, and to whom it delights in feeling itself united." So far as the religion of cultured races is concerned, this definition may be said· to respond to all phases of the subject, but it is questionable whether it covers religion as it manifests itself in primitive times. Among savages religion is not a factor that can be said to "determine" human life, although it exercises an influence upon it. Again, to assume a general recognition of a "mysterious mind" dominating the world, is to attribute to entire mankind, in all its stages, a capability which is only applicable to peoples that have reached a relatively high grade of culture ; and in the third place, we are hardly justified in laying stress, in a general definition of religion, upon the feeling of "delight" at the sense of this supposed union between man and the mysterious mind. In a natural reaction against the stress which many investigators laid upon the element of "fear," in early religious sentiments, Réville has gone to the other extreme and attributed too wide a scope to the element of love, which undoubtedly is present also in the earliest religious manifestations. With the modifications suggested, which would make religion *one* of the factors determining human life by the sentiment of man's dependence upon a Power or Powers beyond his control, the definition would be acceptable.

[1] *Prolegomena of the History of Religions* (English translation, p. 25).

Professor Tiele, in the course of his Gifford Lectures,[1] took occasion to formulate anew his views on the general character of religion, and has, through his lucid presentation, made a contribution of permanent value to the problem. His distinction between "the forms in which religion is manifested" and "the constituents of religion" is an important step towards a determination of what religion really is. The forms consist of words and deeds, which are numerous and manifold. He includes under the former not merely the spontaneous utterances, prompted by man's necessity of voicing what lives within him, but the hymns and songs of praise, the epics, myths, and legends which all have their source in the actual workings of the religious emotions. Similarly, religious deeds comprise more than what is ordinarily conceived of as worship, and extend to acts of devotion and sacrifice prompted by religious fervour. Behind these words and deeds, therefore, lie the constituent elements of religion, which according to Tiele are grouped as emotions, conceptions, and sentiments. One might be disposed to question the necessity of differentiating between an emotion and a sentiment. The distinction which Tiele proposes would make the former a vague longing, while the latter would represent the more definite character assumed by the longing after it has once been clearly grasped. An emotion thus being only an undeveloped sentiment, and a sentiment a developed emotion, it would be sufficient to confine the constituent elements to emotions and conceptions, and to regard religious sentiment as the result of the combination of the two, having their outcome in

[1] *Elements of the Science of Religion,* vol. ii., lecture i.

words and deeds. However this may be, Tiele has reached the source and essence of religion, in claiming that " religion always begins with an emotion ;"[1] and he has admirably analysed this emotion as embracing three elements: (1) a predisposition in the form of certain longings and aspirations ; (2) an impression produced upon us from without, or the affection itself; (3) the fact of becoming conscious of such an affection.

The distinguishing feature of a religious emotion in contradistinction to an æsthetic, intellectual, or ethical impression, is brought about by the object which calls it forth. This object being none other than some Being revered as standing above us, and to whom we feel attracted and related, it follows that the religious emotion consists in the consciousness that we are in the power of such a Being, and in a longing to come into touch with it.

Tiele, it will be observed, does not define this Being as a " mysterious mind," nor does his description exclude the possibility of recognising more than one Being to whom man feels himself related, but a definite religious emotion can only be aroused at the time by the contemplation of one Being.

In combining the religious emotion with the definite conception, Tiele establishes the necessary bond between religion and life. While admitting that there are other factors beside religion which influence conduct, it stands to reason that since the religious emotion, in the more definite form of sentiment, leads to words and deeds, religion already on its first appearance enters into the actual circumstances accompanying the career of the indi-

[1] *Loc. cit.*, p. 15.

vidual and of a people. In our survey of the various definitions and characterisations of religion, we have necessarily limited ourselves to the most important systems of thought, and to such thinkers as have impressed their personality upon the study of religion. The list could, of course, be further extended, but it will probably be found that other definitions of religion fall under one or the other of the categories which have been taken into consideration.

X.

Summing up the discussion, we may regard as definitely established these essential points for forming a proper estimate of religion.

(1.) A connection of some kind between religion and life, vague and loose in the early stages, but with a tendency to become closer as religious thought advances, until in the highest religions the two factors are united. At the same time, we must beware of interpreting the early connection in terms of ethical conduct. Religion may conceivably influence life without necessarily giving an ethical colour to the acts of the individual, and, as will be shown in a subsequent chapter,[1] the course of ethics runs alongside of religion for a time, without being regulated by the latter. But, on the other hand, because religion does not necessarily have its outcome in ethical conduct, there is no reason for severing the bond between religion and life ; unless religion in some way manifests its presence in the life of the individual or of the people, it is bereft of all practical importance, and it is inconceivable that it should have so

[1] Chap. VI., " Religion and Ethics."

profoundly influenced the course of human history, did it not contain, in its most primitive form, the capacity to exert some influence, beneficial or noxious, upon the affairs of life.

(2.) In seeking for a bond uniting religion in its earliest manifestations with the form it assumes in the most advanced of the positive religions, the feeling of man's dependence upon a Power or Powers beyond his control appears to be universal. This view, of course, assumes that religion is indissolubly associated with belief in higher Powers, and while we must be on our guard against attaching exclusive importance to this element of belief, as though summing up the whole of religion, attempts to dissociate religious emotions from the factor of faith, pure and simple, are perforce abortive. Nor is it necessary to form a clear conception of the origin of man's faith in higher Powers in order to reach a satisfactory definition of religion. It is sufficient to recognise the fact that faith is an ingredient part of man's nature, whether existing in a semi-conscious condition among the untutored savages, or analysed and expressed in terms of philosophical thought (or doubt). Granting this, it matters little for our purposes in what way the Power or Powers are conceived. Whether we regard these Powers as personifications of natural phenomena, whether we accept the belief of an extra-mundane and super-mundane Being, or attach ourselves to a pantheistic conception of Deity, or simply recognise everywhere the workings of unchangeable law, the feeling of our dependence is one which we cannot get rid of, either by an act of volition or by a process of reasoning.

(3.) Starting with this feeling of dependence, there

naturally arises the desire to overcome it, and this aim is carried out in various ways, according to the grade and character of our religious thought. The savage will endeavour to flatter and cajole the Powers who control his existence; the religious man, impressed with the grandeur of a Divine Being, will send forth earnest appeals to Him and endeavour by conduct to gain His favour; the thinker will be prompted to regulate his life by ideals of conduct which to his way of thinking will best serve the aims of existence. Within these three broad groups there is an infinite variety of methods to which man has recourse in the attempt to establish proper relations between himself and the Powers outside of him.

(4.) We must recognise in the study of religion the tendency towards organisation. Religion as a mere emotion, as a simple feeling of dependence, or even as an abstract factor influencing to a greater or lesser degree human existence, has no real existence. It is only religion in some organised form that we encounter in the history of mankind. To be sure, this tendency towards organisation is part of the general disposition of mankind to unite for the purpose of carrying out aims felt to be common, but the reality of the tendency is for that reason all the more worthy of consideration. The manifold forms of worship are the outcome of this tendency, and here again, whether we turn to the lowest or to the highest forms of religion, we encounter a cult of some kind, forming part of the religious life. In tracing the development of the cult, other factors enter besides questions of belief, and it does not follow that the cult is always an adequate or a satisfactory expression of the state of belief, though this relation between the two ele-

ments ought to be maintained.   Indeed, we observe
a disposition in the cult to lag behind the doctrine
and frequently to assume such importance in the
eyes of the masses as to obscure the highest purpose
of religion, which is to regulate human conduct ; but
the undue emphasis placed in so many forms of
religion upon external observances is due in the
last instance to this same tendency to keep together those who are drawn to one another by
common aims, interests, and beliefs.   In view of the
force of this factor, it is inconceivable, judging from
the actual history of religion, that a religion will ever
exist unaccompanied by religious organisation and a
religious cult.   Such movements in our days as
Positivism and the Societies of Ethical Culture—the
former substituting a pure Ideal as its object of
worship, in place of a supposed Reality, the latter
relegating all questions of doctrine to the background
—may serve as illustrations of the force of this proposition ; for Positivism has a cult quite as elaborate
as that of the Catholic Church, and the distinguished
leader[1] of the Ethical Culture movement recognises
that if the movement is to be permanent, it will
develop forms of its own, which will adequately express the aspirations and beliefs of its votaries.

(5.) In regard to these four features of religion
there will be general agreement among thinkers, no
matter what their personal belief may be.   Not so,
however, with regard to a fifth and last point—the
natural origin of religion.   Reserving for a separate
chapter a discussion of this topic, which is manifestly
essential to a proper study of religion, it will be
sufficient to indicate here the hopelessness of effect-

---

[1] See an address by Felix Adler on "Worship" (New York, 1887).

ing a reconciliation between those who assume a special revelation as a necessary element in accounting for religion, and those who on the basis of historical studies find the explanation in natural conditions. However, so much at least may be conceded by the adherents of Revelation, that this question does not properly belong to the historical study of religion. Special Revelation can only begin where history leaves us in the lurch, unless indeed we assume the position that all history is a Revelation—which excludes the factor of any special dispensation. The representatives of both camps may therefore manifest equal zeal in tracing the actual course taken by religion. Accepting the historical attitude as outlined in the first chapter, we cannot escape the conclusion that religion forms as natural an ingredient of human nature as the possession of mental faculties and of physical features which distinguish man from the animal world.

With these five features clearly grasped, there is no difficulty in reaching a definition of religion, which, whatever its defects may be, and however much it may be improved upon, at least contains all essential elements, and covers the points of agreement to be noted in the various forms of religion, from the lowest to the highest.

Religion consists of three elements : (1) the natural recognition of a Power or Powers beyond our control; (2) the feeling of dependence upon this Power or Powers ; (3) entering into relations with this Power or Powers.

Uniting these elements into a single proposition, religion may be defined as the natural belief in a Power or Powers beyond our control, and upon whom we feel ourselves dependent ; which belief and feeling of dependence prompt (1) to organisation, (2) to specific acts, and (3) to the regulation of conduct, with a view to establishing favourable relations between ourselves and the Power or Powers in question.

CHAPTER IV.

THE ORIGIN OF RELIGION.

I.

WHILE such questions as the classification of religions and the definition of religion are of importance in beginning a historical study of religions, the problem involved in the origin of religion is one that can be postponed without serious inconvenience to the end of one's investigations. Indeed, it may be questioned whether the problem falls properly within the scope of a historical study at all. Like all other questions of "origins," the origin of religion is more a matter of speculation than of investigation; or if this seem too extreme, it will at all events be admitted that speculation is involved in a problem for which an entirely satisfactory solution cannot be found through historical investigation alone. We may trace a particular religion to its faint beginnings, we may even be able to determine the features which the most primitive form of religion presents, but we shall still be far from furnishing an answer to the question—How did religion arise? What is its source?

It is significant that the question did not seriously present itself to the minds of thinkers till the days of the English Deists. The Greek philosophers were indifferent to the question, while the Jewish, Christian, and Mohammedan theologians

assumed Divine Revelation as a necessary factor in
the rise of religion, either in the form of a primitive
Revelation vouchsafed to all mankind, or of a special
Revelation to certain peoples singled out for the
purpose; or combining the supposed primitive with
a special Revelation, the position was taken which
predicated a continuous Revelation of the Deity. A
sole exception is formed by sceptics like Lucretius,
who, regarding all faith as an illusion, ascribe the
origin of belief in gods to the sense of fear,[1] and who,
in consequence, view religious cult as a debased and
debasing superstition.

Setting aside Revelation, but at the same time
strongly maintaining the justification of faith, the
Deists sought the origin of religion in human
reason. Through the intellect, they claimed, such
fundamental doctrines as the belief in a god and
the immortality of the soul could be established with
a certainty that could not be shaken. They also
claimed that this religion of reason was natural to
man and therefore known to him from the beginning,
but through the machinations of priests, interested in
securing power over the masses, new elements had
been introduced and the religion directed into
deviating paths.

Hume,[2] reverting in a measure to the position of
Lucretius, rejects reason as a factor of any significance
in man's early state, and substitutes for it two others
—fear and hope. Man's fear of the forces of nature
led him to seek powerful gods behind them. By a
natural process he personified these beings, but his
fear of them was tempered by the hope of securing

---

[1] *De Rerum Natura.*
[2] *The Natural History of Religion* (1755).

their goodwill, and all his efforts were directed towards this end. Selfish interests led to placing one god or certain gods above others, and a continuation of this process finally had its outcome in the assumption of a single God in control of the universe. In the course of this process, however, an advance in religious thought was often followed by a reaction, superinduced by several causes, among which the priestly influence occupies a prominent place. The history of religion, therefore, is constantly "flowing backward and forward, between polytheism and monotheism."[1]

Despite the important points in which Hume differs from the Deists, he is at one with them in opposing the intervention of Revelation of any kind as a factor in accounting for the origin of religion ; and since his days the two camps—on the one side the advocates of Revelation in some form, and on the other side the opponents of Revelation—have been arrayed against one another in ceaseless conflict which at times waged fiercely, at times was carried on in milder fashion through attempts at a reconciliation. As typical of such attempts, Butler's famous work on *The Analogy of Religion, Natural and Revealed, to the Constitution and Course of Nature* (1736) may be cited for the eighteenth century, and Henry Drummond's *Natural Law in the Spiritual World* (1883) for the nineteenth.

Both authors stand on the basis of a Divine Revelation. The former maintains that there is a perfect correspondence between the tenets of revealed religion and the postulates of natural religion, and that therefore Revelation and Reason are but two

[1] Pfleiderer, *Philosophy of Religion*, vol. i., p. 131.

aspects of one and the same truth. Drummond, reversing Butler's argument, starts with the spiritual world and shows that it is guided by laws which find a complete analogy in material phenomena. Somewhat similar is the position of those students of religion whom we had occasion to discuss in the preceding chapter, and who claim that Revelation is merely a direct communication of what is ultimately ascertained to be true by the slower process of Reason. However, it must be admitted that all such attempts are unsatisfactory, inasmuch as they force the interpretation of Revelation to include either more or less than was originally intended by the term. If Revelation is to be so used as to cover the manifestation of Divine Power, which would make all the occurrences of nature, as well as the manifestations of the intellect, part of a general scheme of continuous Revelation, there is no place left for the *special* Revelation maintained by most of the advocates of the theory of Revelation. At all events, no criterion is forthcoming for distinguishing between a form of continuous and universal Revelation, and a special dispensation. The distinction, it is true, might still be theoretically maintained, but it would have no practical bearings upon the course of religion. The stretching of definite terms, which have acquired a specific meaning, is always an unsatisfactory proceeding, fraught with great danger. The result is that the term becomes vague and indefinite, and eventually loses all force. It is far better, and more honest, to maintain such a term as Revelation in its original sense, as covering a specific supra-natural phenomenon, and then to determine in how far, if at all, we may accept it.

II.

In his admirable *Prolegomena of the History of Religions*, Réville[1] shows how, from a historical point of view, the evidence is wanting which might warrant us in assuming a Primitive Revelation to mankind; and taking this term in the proper sense, it stands to reason that historical research cannot start with such an assumption. Even if Réville's argument be refuted, we should still have to face the problem how, if there were such a Primitive Revelation, we could prove it by a historical study of religions. Tracing religion back to its earliest manifestations, we find certain beliefs and certain rites. Granting that these beliefs and rites appear to transcend the intellectual limits which we assign to early man, the assumption of a Primitive Revelation to account for them means either that we give up the problem, or that we accept Primitive Revelation as a working hypothesis in default of a definite solution. The obvious conclusion is, that the theory of a Primitive Revelation lies beyond the scope of a historical study of religions; and the same applies to a supposed "Primitive tradition" which some scholars are disposed to substitute for Revelation.[2] We have reached the border line separating investigation from a form of faith, and so far from having any hesitation in acknowledging the existence of a limit to research, it is part of a proper method to clearly and cheerfully recognise such a limit.

So much then may be admitted by the adherents of both camps, that we may, by a process of historical research, trace back religious phenomena to a certain

---

[1] Pp. 35-48. [2] See Réville, *loc. cit.*, pp. 49-58.

point only.   At the same time, the advocates of the
natural origin of religion have a right to demand that
within this sphere no supernatural factors should be
introduced.   This concession applies to the entire
course taken by religion from its earliest manifestations to its latest, and hence, even when dealing with
religions in which we are personally interested, we must
be careful not to commingle with the historical method
such a factor as a special Revelation.   It will be found
that the advocates of the theory of Revelation make
the concession implied, so far as religions in general
are concerned, but when it comes to a special religion,
Christianity, Judaism, or Islam, as the case may
be, an exception is urged—either directly or
indirectly.   It would be unjust to assume that this
is done in all cases from a prejudicial opinion in
favour of a particular religion.   Men like Max
Müller, Tiele, and Réville—to mention only the most
prominent of modern students—are free from any
such prejudice when engaged in historical researches.
The exception is frequently urged from a scientific
conviction that the peculiar direction taken by
religion among certain peoples cannot be accounted
for by a process of purely historical development.
This position is indeed justified.   After due allowance is made for the natural causes that led to such
a remarkable religious movement as is represented
by the ethical monotheism of the prophets, or by the
appearance of Jesus, or by the rise of Islamism, there
remains an element which cannot be explained by
historical research.   So radical a critic as Wellhausen [1]
admits this for Prophetic Judaism.   Strauss's recourse
to the unhistorical " mythical" hypothesis in the case

[1] *Israelitische u. Jüdische Geschichte* (2nd ed., 1895), p. 35.

of Jesus amounts almost to an admission of failure to account for Jesus by natural causes, which is accentuated by the general rejection of this hypothesis, while whatever be our estimate of Mohammed, the secret of his mighty influence has not yet been grasped by the investigations of occidental scholars.

It matters little what name we apply to the hidden influences at work in shaping the religious fortunes of mankind; it is sufficient to recognise their presence. A question may of course arise as to the extent to which such influences are to be recognised, and here there will always be room for large differences among investigators. The personal equation in the shape of personal predilection, or mental disposition, enters into play, and it is perhaps hopeless to expect perfect agreement under such circumstances. It may, however, be granted that in all religious movements of a large character, there are influences at work which cannot be wholly accounted for by historical investigation. This is but equivalent to an admission that within this section of the historical study of religions there is a limit which cannot be transcended. The proper attitude of the student is to recognise this limitation, but at the same time not to permit it to interfere with the most perfect freedom of historical research. The existence of the limitation must not be used as an argument against applying the criteria of historical research to *any* phase of a religion under consideration; and so long as it is understood that historical research is to be carried freely to its utmost limits, the recognition that there are problems in the study of religion which such research cannot solve will act as a wholesome check to over-confidence in human endeavour.

Admitting then that the historical study of religion has to deal only with natural causes for the origin of religion, we are confronted by several theories that have been offered to account for the rise of religious phenomena.

III.

We may dispose briefly of the view—rendered popular by certain of the English Deists, and current among certain groups of thinkers in France during the latter part of the eighteenth century—which could see nothing in religion but the cunning devices of priests to keep the masses under their control.[1] The two fatal objections to this theory are: firstly, that it does not penetrate to the core of religion, but seizes upon certain external symptoms as embracing the entire scope of religious activity; and secondly, that it misinterprets the function of the priest, who is essentially a conservator. Religion is older than any form of priesthood. The priest avails himself of what is already in existence for his purposes (whatever they are), and he gains his influence from the hold which religion has upon man. He may strengthen this hold, but he does not produce it. There are other reasons which make the "priestcraft" theory a thoroughly unsatisfactory one. It suggests an unworthy cause for one of the most significant features in the history of mankind, and unless we are ready to take a cynical view of everything connected with human progress, and more particularly with the progress of human thought, the supposition that wilful deception has acted as a powerful factor in determining man's career, cannot be seriously entertained.

[1] See pp. 15 *et seq.*

It will also be found that those who advocate the
theory in question are filled with a decided prejudice
against religion, which disqualifies them from judging
religious phenomena calmly and dispassionately; and
there is no field of study in which calm and dis-
passionate judgment is so essential as in the study
of religion.   Our judgment once distorted, the facts
themselves become distorted and lend themselves to
an erroneous interpretation.   It will, accordingly, be
found that the advocates of the priestcraft theory,
ever on the look-out for priestly influence, scent it
where no such factor enters into play, and, besides
exaggerating the power of the priest, attribute motives
to him which are not borne out by closer investigation
of the facts.

IV.

A theory for the origin of religion which has found
much favour is the one brought into prominence by
the distinguished anthropologist, Edward B. Tylor,
and known as the animistic theory.   In his now
famous work on *Primitive Culture* he shows, by an
astonishing wealth of examples, that the view which
attributes life to the phenomena of nature—to trees,
stones, rivers, mountains, the sky, and the like—is
universal at a certain stage of culture, and starting
from this belief, Tylor thinks it possible to derive from
it, by a natural evolutionary process going hand in
hand with the advance of culture, all forms of worship, as well as the various religious doctrines.   There
are few modern writers whose researches have so
profoundly influenced the direction taken by the
study of religion as have Tylor's, and it is not surprising that the animistic theory, by virtue of its

simplicity and perspicuity, should have commended itself to the notice of modern scholars. That animism is a belief common to mankind at one time may indeed be regarded as a definitely established thesis, despite the opposition that it still occasionally encounters. The only question is whether Tylor is justified in regarding animism as the earliest form of belief. This has been doubted, and it would indeed appear upon closer investigation that animism, as a theory of belief, assumes a quality of reasoning which transcends the horizon of primitive man. The latter might indeed reach the conclusion that the flowing river is alive, and that there is life in the blossoming tree, but his experience is too limited to warrant him in connecting the life in the stone with the life in the tree, and to draw the conclusion that all nature is instinct with a single kind of life, manifesting itself in diverse ways. It may be maintained, therefore, that animism may be the earliest system of religious philosophy devised by man, but that he does not devise this system until well advanced on the road of culture. Religious manifestations, however, precede even the appearance of animism as an explanation of the universe, and hence, as a theory for the origin of religion, the latter would be defective.

Whether, however, we accept this position or not, there is another and a more potent reason why animism cannot be regarded as a satisfactory explanation for the origin of religion. Apart from the fact to which Van Ende[1] calls attention, that primitive man is only led to ascribe life to certain objects of nature—certain trees, certain stones, as the case may be—which in some way affect his movements, and not to all objects,

---

[1] *Histoire Naturelle de la Croyance*, p. 19.   Paris, 1887.

animism may prompt man to certain acts with a view of securing the favour of the personified object or power, or of warding off its attack, but the personification does not make so profound an impression upon him as to form the starting-point for a new line of development. In other words, if man was without religion before the animistic theory presented itself to his mind, animism by itself would not have led to the rise of religion. The emotions excited by a strange-looking tree or stone could not have been of such a character as to have kindled the divine spark in man; and however deep the impression made by such phenomena, as storms and lightning, may have been, the mere personification of these powers would not have led to bringing into play the religious feelings—hitherto dormant.

Granting that fear and hope play a large or even dominant part in the religious life of man, it yet does not follow that fear and hope are the source of religion; and what is more to the point, these two factors are not so closely involved in animism as to warrant us in making the latter a natural result of the activity of fear and hope in the relationship of man to nature. Animism does not enter closely enough into man's life at any stage of culture to be regarded as the source of so powerful an element of human life as religion. True, we have found that the bond between religion and conduct is loose during the early stages of religious development, but we must of necessity suppose that already on its first appearance religion must have stirred man sufficiently to make it henceforth of moment, in giving at least a new turn to his career. In seeking, therefore, for the origin of religion, we must look for something which

could stir his emotions deeply and permanently;
which could arouse thoughts that would henceforth
never desert him and would prompt him to certain expressions of his emotions and thoughts, so definite and
striking as to become part and parcel of family or
tribal tradition. Animism answers none of these conditions. Even the ceremonial to which it gives rise—
the propitiation of powerful spirits, or the exorcising
of evil ones—would have no chance of becoming
permanent institutions without a substratum of belief
that passes beyond the bounds of animism itself.

V.

Still less satisfactory is the theory chiefly associated
with Herbert Spencer,[1] which traces religion back to
the worship of ancestors under the guise of ghosts
as its sole factor. This theory rests on the supposition
that the deities worshipped by primitive man are, in
reality, the spirits of his ancestors. The awe inspired
by death, and the fear created by the dead who had
passed beyond the control of the living, constitute the
two factors which arouse a new sense in man. The
personification of the powers of nature likewise rests
upon ancestral worship, for the dead having powers
denied to the living, their spirits may choose a tree
or a stone as an abiding-place, and even the large
heavenly bodies are conceived as remote ancestors of
the living, under the influence of a primitive theory of
emanation. Totemism[2]—that is, the derivation of

---

[1] See especially his *Principles of Sociology*, chapters viii. to xvii.
Lippert, in Germany, is the most prominent adherent of this theory.

[2] See J. G. Frazer's admirable survey in his article "Totemism"
(*Ency. Brit.*, 9th ed.); Jevons, *Introduction to the History of Religion*,
chap. ix.

whole tribes or families from a plant or an animal—
is again a species of ghost-worship; and proceeding
in this way, Spencer claims to find everywhere confirmation of a thesis which commends itself, like that
of animism, for its simplicity.   This simplicity, however, is in reality its greatest weakness.   Religion is
too complex a phenomenon to be accounted for by
the growth and spread of a single custom.   Worship,
of however primitive a character, is not the expression
of a single thought or a single emotion, but the product of thoughts or emotions so complex, so powerful,
as to force an expression in the same way in which
a river, swollen by streams coming down the mountains
from various directions, overflows its banks.

Primitive man is not the highly sensitive being,
entirely at the mercy of emotions, that anthropologists
often picture him to be.   As a matter of fact, he is not
easily subject to impressions, and such impressions as
he receives readily wear off, as in the case of the child,
unless repeated with increasing emphasis.   A single
impression counts for little with him, and it is only
when impressions crowd upon his brain so as to overwhelm him that he will be led to seek some expression for them.   All this applies with special force to
Spencer's theory.   Mysterious as the aspect of death
may have been to primitive man, it is not more of a
mystery than the phenomena of nature.   Cain's sight
of Abel's death may indeed have produced a deep
impression, but since anthropological science does not
start with the "first pairs" of the human race, the
impression of the first sight of death cannot fairly be
taken into account, any more than the first sight of
the disappearing sun.   Starting as anthropology does,
with man existing as a species in considerable

numbers, Death is as regular, if not as frequent, a phenomenon as the changes in the moon's phases, and would leave no more lasting impression than the latter, even though the impression be of a different kind. Assuming that primitive speculation about the dead, their whereabouts, and about their power for good or evil, led to ancestor-worship, the same conditions should have simultaneously produced nature-worship.

Apart from the unsatisfactory character of any attempt to derive nature - worship from ancestor-worship, there is no reason why one should be dependent upon the other. It will certainly not be maintained that ancestor-worship is more primitive in character than nature-worship. On the contrary, the personification of the powers of nature suggested itself, if anything, more readily than the theory that an ancestral spirit has taken its abode in some object to which adoration must henceforth be paid. If animism as a system corresponds to a comparatively advanced stratum of culture, a religion based on ancestral-worship as a fundamental doctrine belongs, if anything, to a still higher category. Moreover, when we come to examine religion as it manifests itself among those occupying the lowest stage of culture, we do not by any means find the adoration of ghosts to be as prominent as Spencer would have us believe. A natural reverence for the dead, manifesting itself by a care for their resting-place, and periodical visits to the site of burial, must be distinguished from ancestor-worship. Even granting that the element of fear of the dead tempers this reverence, we are not justified in regarding all ceremonies observed in connection with the dead as due

to an actual worship of ghosts.   The tendency, which
is much in vogue at present, to seek for a religious
significance everywhere in the ceremonialism with
which primitive man surrounds himself, is apt to lead us
astray.   In the investigation of primitive customs we
must make larger allowance than is generally done
for the natural play of the emotions and of the fancy,
indulged in spontaneously without an ulterior motive,
or from any profound conviction.   Not all customs
that to us have a religious aspect are necessarily
connected with religion in the life of the savage.
The fact, therefore, that primitive man everywhere
cares for his dead, and carries out a more or less
elaborate ceremonial in connection with the burial,
does not warrant us in concluding that thoughts
about the dead form the starting-point of man's
religious development, or that the strictly religious
cult of the dead, when found, is necessarily the oldest
feature of primitive religion.

VI.

Neither the "animistic" nor the "ghost" theory of
the origin of religion goes to its core.   The source
of religion must lie deeper than in manifestations of
this character.   Animism and ancestor-worship are
symptoms of the actual religious experiences of man,
and as such their study is of great value, but from
the characterisation of religion which I endeavoured
to give in the preceding chapter, it will be evident
that religion must proceed from some strong emotion
aroused in the human soul through a thought at once
simple enough to be grasped at least vaguely by the
primitive mind, and at the same time strong enough

to make a positive and lasting impress. Starting from this point of view, we are confronted by a number of theories which cannot be reconciled with one another. A favourite one, which still finds many advocates, ascribes the origin of religion to a revelation of something divine in the universe made to man through nature, which, it is claimed, is so ordered as to lead even primitive man to the recognition of higher powers. This revelation, together with the attempt of man to put himself into proper relations with the powers recognised by him, leads to making man a religious being.

In discussing this theory, Tiele[1] has admirably pointed out its serious defect. The first part of the proposition—the revelation of nature to man —is correct, but the theory fails to account for the second half of the proposition—the endeavour of man to put himself into relationship with the powers recognised. This is the real religious element in man, and the question as to the origin of religion is satisfactorily answered only when we have determined how man came to have an element in his nature which made him receptive to religious influences. We are not led much further by the attempt, supposed to be natural to man, to derive religion from a process of pure reasoning as to the causes of things. It is true that primitive man manifests curiosity, just as the child does with regard to what is about, above, and beneath him; but granting that he succeeds in producing at an early period in his career some explanation of the universe satisfactory to him, it would yet not be apparent why his theory of the universe should lead him to

---

[1] *Elements of the Science of Religion*, vol. ii., p. 211.

put himself into relationship with superior powers, and this alone would convert his philosophy into a real religion. Thus there are to the problem two sides which need to be considered—the origin of belief in a higher power or powers, and the origin of man's endeavour to establish a relationship to this ᵣower or these powers.

To many thinkers it has seemed that man's consciousness of his own weakness, in the contemplation of the overwhelming strength of nature, furnishes the motive for seeking support in his endeavours, from certain powers of nature, and to accomplish this he must needs make them favourably disposed towards him. This theory, which has been made the starting-point for both a pessimistic and an optimistic view of man's position in the universe, has proved acceptable both to minds in sympathy with religious movements, and to such as regard all religion as an illusion. The reason for this is that the theory can be variously put. Man's recognition of his weakness is compatible with that sense of humility upon which many religions properly lay stress, and his endeavour to seek for aid from the powers of nature easily lends itself to the interpretation as a longing for communion with the divine. On the other hand, a thinker like Feuerbach explains the endeavour of man to supplement his own weakness by borrowing some of the strength of nature as "the desire of man to become God." God, from this point of view, is merely nature, and, moreover, nature as conceived by man. This God, thus created by man, is endowed with all kinds of powers, and man being limited in his powers and unlimited in his wishes and ambitions, seeks to supply what he lacks by association with God.

Hartmann[1] puts the theory from his standpoint even more succinctly when he says that "man desires to be happy, but is not happy." The recognition of this state, as it constitutes the source of human endeavour, furnishes for Hartmann the basis for his philosophical pessimism, and forms the basis of all religion. Siebeck[2] puts the theory in a rather novel manner in making man's dissatisfaction with the world, rather than his dissatisfaction with his inability to carry out his desires, the source of religion ; but whether we place man or the world first, the result is the same, since it is ultimately man's happiness or lack of happiness which is the chief factor involved. It must be recognised that this theory answers the conditions justly demanded of a hypothesis regarding the origin of religion ; it contains a fundamental religious thought, and explains the disposition towards worship, but the question may be asked, as in the case of the animistic theory, whether the recognition of his own weakness is sufficient by itself to make so profound an impression on him as to give a new direction to his life.

After all, by the side of his limitations, he would, naturally, be just as profoundly impressed by his achievements and by the possession of qualities which enable him, without the aid of the powers of nature, to accomplish his ends. He can destroy the tree much more easily than the tree can injure him. By cunning devices, he entraps animals much more powerful than himself, and gradually the animal world loses its terrors for him. It is true that he often finds himself at the mercy of the elements,

---

[1] *Das Religiöse Bewusstsein der Menschheit*, p. 27.
[2] *Lehrbuch der Religionsphilosophie*, chaps. i. and ii.

but limitations in the power of the personified objects of nature must have become apparent to him. His sense of pride would lead him to be on the look-out for these limitations and to dwell upon them with a certain feeling of satisfaction. The sun, moon, and stars do not appear to move about according to the dictates of their own desires. Certain positions and certain tracks are assigned to these bodies. The sun is obliged to hide himself from the moon, and the moon in turn seeks flight when the sun appears. The clouds are driven along by forces over which they have no control, and thus everywhere man sees limitations in the powers of nature as well as in his own career, and there is no reason why these limitations should not impress him as profoundly as the manifestations of power. If by a process of reasoning, primitive man comes to personify the powers of nature, that same process would be sufficient to deter him rather from allying himself to powers whose limitations are as pronounced as his own.

VII.

The mere personification of nature lacks a certain spiritual element which appears to be essential to the rise of a genuine religious feeling in man. Nature must be idealised, so to speak, before it can arouse the religious sense. Max Müller and Tiele, among modern scholars, have recognised the need of thus assuming some spiritual element in man's earliest view of the universe as essential to the rise of religion. Max Müller designates this element as "the perception of the Infinite." So strongly does Max Müller emphasise this "perception" that, as we

have seen,[1] he was at one time inclined to make it
the aim and substance of religion. From this position
he afterwards receded, but he continued to see in
"the perception of the Infinite" the yearning of the
soul after God, "the source of all religion in the
human heart."[2]   This perception is borne in upon
man through a general contemplation of the world
about him.   It is not dependent upon the personification of the powers of nature, though not inconsistent
with such personification.   However highly primitive
(or advanced) man may think of his own powers and
achievements, the sense of his insignificance in comparison, not with any particular element in nature,
but with the sum-total of what lies outside of his
being, cannot but overwhelm him.   Since with
ever-growing experience his mental horizon is extended, he comes to realise, albeit vaguely, that this
outside world is infinite when placed by the side of
his own finite existence.   The stability of stones and
trees, amid the changes which man himself experiences, the steady flow of the river, which already
in the days of his ancestors coursed by his hut, the
immortality of sun, moon, and stars, endowed with
never-ending life, whereas his own span of existence
is limited to a certain number of years—such phenomena would act as a further incentive to produce
within him a sense of the Infinite.

Be it understood that Max Müller does not accord
to primitive man anything more than the possibility
of the "perception" of the Infinite, or, as one might
also put it, an "apprehension."   It is, of course, out of

---

[1] See p. 163.
[2] *Theosophy, or Psychological Religion* (Gifford Lectures, 4th series),
p. 480.

the question to suppose that at the outset of his religious development, man should have had a clear view of a philosophical thought which has been a sore puzzle to advanced thinkers from the days of the Greek philosophers down to our own times ; nor is it necessary for establishing this hypothesis to assume that primitive man would be able to give a clear account to himself of this "perception of the Infinite." It is sufficient in order to leave a lasting impress, that the thought should once arise within him. Professor Tiele, indeed, recognising the difficulty involved in accounting for such a "perception" in the mind of primitive man, prefers to speak of "man's original, unconscious, innate sense of infinity"[1] as the source of religion. He is undoubtedly right in giving to this "sense" as vague and clouded a character as possible, for the character of the primitive intellect does not permit of clear and decided perceptions, but one may question the necessity of going so far as to make this sense of the Infinite "unconscious" and "innate." Inasmuch as man's actual experience helps him at any rate to the perception of the Infinite, it seems hardly accurate to designate it as "unconscious"; and again the term "innate" is of so unsatisfactory a character, and has been so much abused, that it seems best to avoid it if at all possible. The "sense of the infinite" may not be "inherent in man's soul," but Tiele[2] characterises it in a happy and succinct manner when he says that "it lies at the root of man's whole spiritual life," and that "it is revealed in his intellectual, his æsthetic, and his moral life."

[1] *Elements of the Science of Religion*, vol. ii., p. 233.
[2] *Loc. cit.*

13

This "sense of the Infinite" is naturally capable of various modifications. It has one meaning for the educated, and another for the ignorant. Definitions of it and interpretations of its scope will vary, but even the admission that such a concept as Infinity is a self-contradiction on the part of a finite intellect need not deter us from according to it a strong influence over primitive man, and all the stronger because of his failure to grasp it clearly. Moreover, it is a thought which, when once it has taken possession of man, never leaves him. He is conscious of it in almost every step that he takes in his career, and advancing culture will have the effect of leading him to realise it in its fuller significance. Philosophers will arise who will take hold of it and endeavour to define and to justify it, mystics will identify it with the soul's "yearning after God," and theologians will make it the basis for the doctrine of the divine spirit implanted in man from the beginning of his appearance on earth. No other thought is so well calculated to lead man to adoration of powers which will symbolise for him the Infinity of which he is dimly conscious; and by acts of worship, though primarily undertaken for his own protection, or as aids to carry out selfish aims, a realisation of his unique position in the universe will be borne in upon him, and prompt him to so regulate his conduct as to secure the favour of the powers symbolising the Infinite, and eventually of the Infinite itself. We have thus reached a solution of the problem on which we are engaged, that, whatever else may be said of it, answers the conditions required of a theory as to the origin of religion. To summarise the result, the perception or sense of the Infinite is furnished by an experience possible to primitive man in combination with a process of reasoning not transcending his powers. In connection with the personification of the powers of nature, also natural to primitive man, these powers will be viewed by him as symbols of the Infinite, and with such symbols, despite the limitations which he observes in any particular element of nature or natural phenomenon, he will seek to obtain from powers beyond his control, and upon some of which he is directly dependent, aid in supplementing what he lacks to carry out his ambitions. In this theory of the origin of religion there are involved three factors: (1) the desire to satisfy one's wishes, irrespective of the fact whether this desire is looked upon as the ambition to attain the goal of human life, or as a hopeless longing for unrealisable happiness; (2) the impulse to seek external help in overcoming obstacles or in avoiding dangers; (3) the spiritual influence of the perception of the Infinite, involving the idealisation of the powers of nature, and furnishing man with a thought capable of exercising a lasting influence upon him and of stirring the emotional side of his being.

The further question that suggests itself—how man comes to possess the *power* to attain to a perception of the Infinite, is one that transcends the limits of historical investigation, which is required only to answer the question of how the power is brought into action. The power itself, like the religious instinct, the emotional possibilities, the unsatisfied longings, and the intellectual phases of his nature, forms part of man's equipment, from which every science connected with man necessarily starts out. Just as anthropology assumes man to be existing and occupying the place proper to him in the universe, so historical science starts with man as a being endowed with reason, certain emotions and certain instincts, with the capacity of thought and the power to receive impressions on his mind.

Briefly put then, the origin of religion, so far as historical study can solve the problem, is to be sought in the bringing into play of man's power to obtain a perception of the Infinite through the impression which the multitudinous phenomena of the universe as a whole make upon him. The strength and the quality of this impression unite in suggesting to him at first, in a vague and dim way, that there is more in the universe than he can possibly take in with the help of his senses, that beyond what is visible and what is known to him, lies the vast field of the invisible and the unknown, that the power of which he can become conscious in the world outside of him represents only a portion of the power that really exists—in short, that the finite stretches out into the unbounded field of the infinite. The faint perception of this Infinite, so faint at first as to be merely a "sense" of the Infinite—a weak consciousness that there is such a thing—stirs his being profoundly. It strikes a responsive chord in what, for want of a better name, we may call man's religious instinct. He contemplates with a certain awe both himself and the world outside of himself, and the religious instinct thus stirred up leads him to realise his insignificance, his dependence upon higher powers beyond his control, which in divers ways he seeks to gain on his side in an unceasing activity which looms up now as an eternal chase for happiness, and again bears the appearance of a battling for some higher goal.

The religious instinct once aroused is never again lulled to rest. It accompanies man throughout his career, making its presence felt in every step that he takes on the "golden ladder of progress." His religious views at each round take on their colour from the grade of culture reached. The manner in which he strives to secure a proper relationship between himself and the Powers upon which he feels himself in the last instance dependent, will likewise be subject to frequent, if not constant change, as the conception of this relationship gradually takes on a more ideal shape. Instead of appealing to an indefinite variety of powers, he will concentrate his efforts upon a selection made from various motives, and from this position he will be led to placing one Power above all the others. Rising still higher in the intellectual scale, he will at last recognise that there is but one Power manifesting itself throughout the universe, and this Power he will, by an abstract process of thought, identify with Infinity itself. Instead of having recourse to magic rites, based upon a limited experience, the symbolical acts accompanying his religious worship will express his own aspirations in the endeavour to come into touch with the Infinite Power which seems so far off, and which for all that he feels to be watching over him. He may indeed, as his thought ascends higher spheres, be led to the position that all worship is vain, that silent contemplation of Infinite power alone remains for him, but for all that the "yearning after God" clings to him, giving direction to his efforts, helping to shape his destiny, presiding over all that pertains to his higher life. The religious instinct, aroused by the perception of the Infinite, abides amidst all changes in the kaleidoscope of mankind's history.   It is a permanent element in the chequered career of humanity—in a certain sense indeed, the only permanent element.

II.

SPECIAL ASPECTS.

CHAPTER V.

FACTORS INVOLVED IN THE STUDY OF RELIGION.

IT will have become evident from the discussions in the preceding chapters, that the study of religion is closely bound up with a number of other fields of investigation. In the first place, by its direct bearings on conduct, religion is closely linked to the study of ethics, and it is part of a proper method to determine the nature of the relation which exists between religion and ethics. Secondly, the doctrines of religion lap over into the field of philosophic thought. No system of philosophy is complete that does not take into consideration the problems which are fundamental to every form of religion. In consequence, it is of great moment to determine the point at which religion becomes philosophy, and, *vice versâ*, in how far philosophy is justified in trespassing upon the domain of religion. Thirdly, the formation of myths appears to be natural to religion at a certain stage. The process begins indeed at a very early stage, and in a certain sense it goes on even when religious thought has reached its most advanced form, but there are various grades in the process itself. It is necessary to trace these in order to reach a satisfactory conclusion as to the interrelations between religion and mythology, since not all myths are necessarily of a religious character. In the fourth place, religion being primarily a "psychical phenomenon," as Hartmann puts it,[1] it follows that psychology enters closely into the study of religion.

Each of these four factors is distinct in its bearings on religion. Their relationship to religion is far from being the same, and it is therefore essential to take up each in turn, and discuss as briefly as the importance of the theme will permit, the method to be followed in the general task of determining this relationship. At the same time, the general results reached by an application of this method will be indicated as a further guide to the student who takes up one of the numerous special phases within the broad field covered by the relationship of Religion to Ethics, Philosophy, Mythology, and Psychology.

Besides these four factors, however, there are others which call for mention. Religion entering so deeply into the life of a people, it is but natural that the history of religion should be closely bound up with the general history of mankind, and *vice versâ*. General history cannot be properly studied unless we understand the purely religious movements taking place in a community or a nation. Culture is a fifth factor closely bound up in the study of religion. All culture is to a large extent an offshoot of religion. The arts and sciences were, at their origin, closely linked to religious beliefs, but even after they acquired a position independent of religion, the relationship to the latter was far from being severed. From being merely phases of religious belief, the arts and sciences reached a stage which enabled them to influence the course of religious development. In our days, we have witnessed a notable illustration of

[1] *Religion des Geistes*, p. 3.

this influence in the profound change in religious thought brought about by significant discoveries in science, by the advent of new hypotheses, such as the Darwinian doctrine of evolution, and by historical methods applied to the study of the Old and of the New Testament. The so-called conflict between Science and Religion,[1] as will be pointed out further on, is merely a phase of this steady influence of culture on religion.

These two factors, history and culture, must therefore be included in our scope, but it will be sufficient to call attention merely to the salient features of their bearing on the study of religion. Their general relationship to this study is so evident as to require no elaborate elucidation.

[1] For the history of this conflict, we now have A. D. White's admirable work, *A History of the Warfare of Science with Theology in Christendom* (2 vols., 1897), supplementing Draper's *History of the Conflict between Religion and Science* (1875).

CHAPTER VI.

RELIGION AND ETHICS.

I.

IN all the more advanced religions, the bond between morality and religion is so close that the conclusion seems natural which predicates morality as the aim of religious organisation, or at least as one of the aims. For all that, the religious sentiment in man has an existence quite independent of morality, and one can even conceive of religions that do not foster morality.

Accepting the general definition which brings religion in some way—vague or definite—into relationship with the sentiment of man's dependence upon a Power or Powers beyond his control, it will be apparent that into such a definition morality does not directly enter. Whether we associate this sentiment of dependence with fear, or whether we account for it as due to the profound impression made upon man by the phenomena which affect his being, it is the superior strength of the powers which primitive man adores, and not their superior goodness that forces itself upon his notice.

The religious sentiment would thus, in its simplest form, lead man to place the highest value upon power. In so far as this sentiment would have any influence upon his acts, it would naturally prompt him to the utmost development of his own strength as the only means at his command for coping, not indeed with Powers with whom the struggle would be unequal, but with the more obvious obstacles besetting his path in his search for sustenance, and for such ease and pleasures as his tastes call for. The qualities thus engendered, while not necessarily antagonistic to the unfolding of ethical ideas, would hardly be of a kind that would raise religion to the rank of a moral force. With strength as an ideal, bravery and cunning would be carried to a higher degree of perfection, the intellect would be sharpened, but, on the other hand, unbridled prowess would have its natural outcome in a more pronounced accentuation of dormant or innate cruelty; and often the natural instincts of love would be sacrificed in order to gain some immediate end.

Passing from the mere religious sentiment to the primitive beliefs and customs, it will similarly be found that ethical questions are not at all involved. The view that whatever manifests life is controlled by some spirit partaking of a quality of vitality similar to that which man is conscious of himself possessing, is dependent upon a purely logical process of analogy, and Jevons[1] has shown most satisfactorily that the various rites practised by primitive society in order to ward off evils, or to secure the protection of dreaded Powers or spirits, are based primarily upon logical considerations. If a certain stone is regarded as sacred, it is probably because it is associated with some misfortune, or some unusual piece of good luck. Some one, after sitting on the stone, may have died; or, on sleeping upon it, may have seen a remarkable vision, which was followed by a

---

[1] *Introduction to the History of Religion*, chap. iii.

signal victory over a dangerous foe. The limited experience of primitive man leads him to deduce from a single event a fixed law, and hence the stone is made the responsible source for the good or evil incidents of life.

In all this, however, ethical considerations are conspicuous by their absence. Again, supposing that the unusual size, or unusual shape, or unusual position of a stone or tree has been the factor which has superinduced sacred associations with the object in question, we are still witnessing a logical process; for the impression made by an unusual phenomenon leads to unusualness in man's view of the phenomenon, and the degree of unusualness in this view is correlative to the logical impression made by the object. Taking again so common a belief among all peoples as the influence for good or evil exerted by the dead upon the living, and the numerous practices to which it gives rise—the recitation of incantations, the observances of various *taboos*, the provision for the supposed needs of the dead; all with a view of securing the good will of the dead, or of warding off their evil designs,—it will be difficult to discover in these beliefs and ceremonies the faintest suggestion of any ethical influence. It is not the good but the powerful spirits that are invoked; an appeal to them is not made by showing them examples of kindness, justice, or noble deeds, but by bribes, flatteries, and threats.

The question then arises, At what point in the development of religion does ethics enter? Upon the answer to this question depends the extent of the influence of ethics as a factor in the study of religion.

II.

It must not be supposed that, because morality is not involved in the religious sentiment, man does not possess a moral sense. So far is this from being the case that any definition of man which takes in more than a description of his anatomy and of his physical qualities and attributes, necessarily contains some reference to his ethical sense. The cruelty of primitive man has been much exaggerated by superficial observers; and the important fact has been overlooked, that this cruelty—the existence of which cannot, of course, be denied—is often only the reverse side of man's passionate love for those near to him.[1] To urge that this love differs in no essential point from the instinct of the animal for its young constitutes no valid objection, for, in the first place, there is no reason, *a priori*, for denying to animals an ethical sense; but, secondly, if we identify human and animal instincts, we are simply begging the question, since the assumption is that man, no matter in how primitive a state we suppose him to be, is distinguished from the brute creation by mental as well as by physical traits.[2] Love, in a human garb, being distinct from mere animal passion or animal instinct, may easily be shown to contain the elements necessary for arousing ethical feelings. The absolute authority of the father over his offspring, which characterises primitive society, is curbed by natural fondness, and introduces an element of mercy in his treatment of those dependent upon him. The check thus imparted to the abuse of authority will awaken also the sense of

[1] Wake, *Evolution of Morality*, vol. i., p. 63.
[2] Fiske, *Destiny of Man*, chap. iii.

justice; and this sense once aroused will have some influence, albeit at first a weak one, on his treatment of his fellows, to whom he is not bound by such close ties. Eventually, in the moment of triumph over a vanquished foe, chivalry will suggest milder forms of punishment than those meted out by his ancestors, and the thought will force its way into his mind and heart that even towards a hated foe justice must not be lost sight of.

There are other traits possessed by savage man that show him, even in the lowest stage of culture, not utterly devoid of ethical feelings. Writers agree that a high sense of personal honour distinguishes savages everywhere. It is evident, also, from the narratives of travellers that generosity is often met with among those whose form of social organisation belongs to the lowest possible order. But personal honour and generosity are traits which, in the natural course of development, become essential factors in creating an ethical view of human existence.

The fact is that the ethical sentiment forms as ingredient a part of man's disposition as the religious sentiment. As yet no people has been found in which the religious sentiment is totally absent, and with equal truth it may be said that ethical feelings are innate in man—form part of his being, without which he would not be human in the real sense of the word, any more than we should have the right to apply the word man to a being devoid of all mental power.

III

With Ethics, in some form, and Religion, in some form, characterising man in the earliest stages of culture, it is not difficult to see the point at which they tend to unite. In proportion as such natural, or, more correctly speaking, primitive feelings as love, honour, and generosity take hold upon man, his conception of the superior Powers will be modified by permitting similar qualities to enter into his view of beings who stand in close relation to his life. From the example which he himself furnishes to himself, as well as from the experiences derived from the conduct of his ancestors, man will learn to distinguish between appearance and reality. He will conclude that severity is not always the product of malice, but that its manifestation may be of a disciplinary character. If he can once be brought to connect love with his view of some powerful spirit, a simple logical process will force upon him the conviction that this Spirit cannot be animated solely by hostile motives towards him. A long time may elapse before he will gain the conviction that such a Spirit actually loves him; but even assuming that he continues for an indefinite period to be influenced in his conception of the Divine by personal experience alone, he will certainly conclude that there are times when this superior Power is stirred by emotions of love, mercy, and generosity.

Again, his own experience will come to his aid in drawing the further conclusion that there may be a justification for the evils that the Powers bring on. In other words, the sense of guilt will further modify his religious views in the direction of further emphasis upon the ethical qualities ascribed to the beings adored by him. As a consequence, in his endeavour to placate the angered spirits, or to secure their favour, man will have recourse to other

14

methods than mere bribes or flatteries. The relationship existing between himself and his own father will
find a counterpart in the position he assumes towards
his deities, and it will be his aim to please and placate
the latter by manifesting his obedience. Among the
numerous Powers whom he acknowledges, there will
surely be some who will show their appreciation of
some kind acts of man by granting him a fulfilment
of his wishes; and a single response to a request
made under such circumstances will be sufficient to
indicate to him proper conduct, as a necessary condition to further blessings.

From a modern ethical point of view, such motives
towards leading a proper life may not seem lofty, but
it cannot be denied that the motive is not merely
exceedingly human, and widespread in its illustration
even at the present time, but that it contains a distinctly ethical germ, capable of being unfolded to a
high degree of perfection. Indeed, it is difficult to
see how a pure system of ethics can be developed,
unless we take into account the influence exerted by
such factors as the desire for the fulfilment of one's
ideals—however low,—the ambition to be regarded
as good, and the wish to avoid misfortunes.

The natural growth of social life in the direction
of greater refinement will, in the various ways suggested, and in other ways that might be mentioned,
infuse an ethical spirit into religious conceptions
of the Powers, and when this process is once fairly
begun, the interaction between religion and ethics
follows as a necessary consequence. The link will be
forged uniting religion and ethics, and the further
progress along the path of civilisation will tend to
strengthen the link. Religion and ethics may thus

be likened to two streams that have an independent source, but which flow towards one another until they unite, and eventually become one.

IV

In the view here maintained, it will be seen that it is man's ethical sense that exerts an influence upon his beliefs, and not *vice versâ*. We cannot conceive man ascribing ethical qualities to his gods until he himself has proceeded far enough along the line of moral development to have established for his own guidance some ethical principles, however simple they may be. Religion, however, repays the debt it owes to ethics by stimulating the ethical sense of man. After the bond between religion and ethics has once been established, a divine sanction is found for the observance of moral precepts. Innate ethical sentiments are strengthened by being brought into direct connection with the will of the gods. To be merciful, just, and truthful, because in this way only one can secure the good will of the superior powers, must necessarily prove a more efficacious impulse in an early stage of culture than mere expediency, which is ever in danger of being set aside by more urgent considerations. Through the divine sanction for moral conduct, furthermore, the ordinary acts of life are apt to be raised to a higher plane. A definite code of ethics is evolved that will serve as a guide and a standard. The authority of religious leaders, who are certain of making their appearance the moment that religion becomes organised, will be correspondingly increased by the presence of such a code, even though for a long time it exists only by virtue of oral tradition.

The point may be raised that this influence of
religion upon ethics does not mark progress, but that,
on the contrary, the ethical motive was purer without
any ultimate appeal to the pleasure or dictates of
a superior power.   It may be questioned, however,
whether without the intervention of a religious
sanction the advance in morality would have been
so rapid and effective.   It is conceivable that a
system of ethics might have been evolved without
the aid of religion, but this system would have lacked
certain qualities which mankind could ill afford to
spare.   The element of self-sacrifice in such a system
would have been very feeble.   A heroic resolution to
pursue a noble ideal at all costs, and in the face of
the strongest temptations and most pressing dangers,
may be possible to-day after millenniums of discipline
under religious influence, but neither the ideal nor the
resolution would be in existence were it not for the
strength given to the ethical sentiment by bringing
the individual career into intimate contact with the
Divine.   The union of ethics with religion has
produced the feeling in the human race of the
sanctity of the individual.   The "categorical imperative" of Kant is the finest fruit of this union; and
the ability of the modern social reformer to appeal
to the sense of right, pure and simple, existing in
a community, is equally a direct outcome of the
education of the race through the divine sanction
established for the right and the good, for purity and
justice.

We have, hitherto, been considering the influence
exerted by the ethical factor upon religious beliefs.
This influence is less apparent in religious practices.
In the history of religion, strangely enough, it is

almost universally seen that religious customs lag behind religious doctrines. Long after conceptions of deities become current among a people in which ethical features are conspicuous, the manner of approaching these deities still proceeds after the fashion evolved when such features did not exist. The deities continue to be flattered, cajoled, threatened, and bribed through incantations that no longer form an adequate expression of the religious position occupied by the people. Rites continue to be practised in order to exorcise evil spirits, but to these rites, which are of a kind that would be applicable in the case of totally irresponsible spirits, there are added appeals which have a meaning only if addressed to beings endowed with ethical discrimination and judgment. So, to instance one example out of many that might be chosen, we find in the religious literature of the Babylonians [1] exquisite prayers put into the mouth of worshippers, expressive of their deep sense of moral quiet, and yet ending in a dribble of incantation formulas that have survived from a more primitive mode of thought.

To account for this more pronounced influence of ethics on religious beliefs than upon religious customs, it is but necessary to bear in mind that the advance in religious thought begins with those members of the community who are intellectually superior. It is they who first recognise the contradiction between standards of conduct evolved in a natural way, and views held about the gods, and who bring about an ethical transformation, more or less effective, in these beliefs. Only after this is accomplished, can the work of making religious

---

[1] See Jastrow, *Religion of Assyria and Babylonia,* chap. xviii.

customs accord with the new stage reached in beliefs
be taken up. The religious philosopher is followed
by the reformer, and even when the two qualities are
found combined in the same person, the chronological
sequence is still maintained in the individual's career.
Custom, accordingly, lags behind theory, and generally
to a considerable degree. Some writers, to be sure,
maintain that religious customs have a tendency to
become more deeply incrustated than religious beliefs,
and that for this reason there is a lack of correspondence between these two manifestations of
the religious sentiment, but in maintaining such a
position, we are not making any progress towards an
explanation of the phenomena.

People cling to beliefs as tenaciously as they do to
practices. The chief reason for this tenacity is the
same in both cases—mental inertia or ignorance; and
since it is manifestly easier to recognise the absurdity
of certain customs than to ascertain the insufficiency
or improper character of certain beliefs, one would
fairly expect to find practices more susceptible of
being attacked and modified.   If, however, we find
that the change invariably begins with the doctrine,
it is not because a senseless practice has a stronger
hold, but because neither the belief nor the practice
being clearly understood, or both being no longer
intelligible, the natural means for paving the way for
the reform of the practice is for leaders to convince
their followers of the imperfect character of their
religious conceptions.

In tracing, therefore, the relationship between
religion and ethics through the various religions of
the world, or through the special religion with whose
study we happen to be concerned, we must always

have before us these two factors—religious beliefs and religious practices.

V.

The special part played by ethics differs considerably in the various religions, so that it is manifestly impossible to do more than set up some general principles in a survey of the field. The suggestion has already been thrown out, that it is in solidly organised cults that we find the bond between ethics and religion closest. While even in the most primitive human society there is some attempt at a religious organisation, yet there is a wide scope for individual variation in the so-called primitive cults ; and we are safe in setting up this distinction between primitive and advanced religions, that the former are characterised by a very loose form of religious organisation, while in the latter there is a steady tendency towards rigid forms.[1]

Corresponding to this looser organisation, we must not expect more than that general tendency towards an ethical development of beliefs and customs in primitive religions, which we have already had occasion to refer to, while the counter-influence of religion on ethics at this stage is so faint as to be scarcely perceptible. The rise of an ethical standard in personal conduct leads, as we have seen, to the introduction of the ethical element into the views held of the higher Powers, but without an authoritative body of men to give to these changed conceptions a definite shape, the demands made upon the individual through the medium of religious influence will not be great. A conventional morality, without religious

[1] See above, pp. 78 *et seq.*

authority to remove its secular taint, will leave a large scope to individual preference ; and it is only an ethical system, deliberately produced and rigidly enforced, that will assume a thoroughly religious character. Religion, accordingly, among primitive nations, though influenced by popular ethics, will not be found to be a strong force making for morality. It will, by virtue of its union with ethics, curb to a certain extent the violence of savage instincts, but it will not give an ethical colour to either the religious or the secular acts of the individual. Ethical transformation of beliefs and customs has most definite limits in loosely organised religions. It is not long before these limits are reached, and the point where a decided ethical influence emanates from religion lies beyond the point reached by religions of a primitive form.

VI.

The appearance of the individual as a factor marks the point of demarcation, leading from primitive religions to the more advanced forms. It makes little difference whether the individual originally gains his authority by mental superiority, which naturally singles him out as a religious leader, or by virtue of the supposed possession of some strange power, or because differentiated from his fellows through no less mysterious bodily or mental defects—a rare or loathsome disease, leprosy, elephantiasis, epilepsy, idiocy, insanity,—his position in the community gives to his utterances an importance which has its natural outcome in the establishment of an orthodox system of religious conduct. His advice is sought, and what he says is regarded as embodying the divine pleasure.

To be sure, in some form religious leaders—whether as sorcerers, chanters of incantations, medicine men, guardians of sacred places, or what not—are found even in the most loosely organised forms of primitive religions, but they assume an authoritative position only when organisation of a definite kind takes place among them, and means are taken for the preservation of traditional methods in religious rites. In place of varying custom, the personal authority of a class of men in the community sets up fixed canons.

A loss of individualism is thus associated with progress in religious organisation, but in compensation for this loss, a more definite aspect is given to the ethical phases of the popular beliefs and customs. Even though the view arises that the gods and spirits are impressed by kindness and goodness, so long as the ethical qualities are subject to caprice, no great reliance can be placed upon their readiness to turn a favourable side to human endeavour towards kindness and goodness. Hence, just as the moral traits of people living under primitive conditions are marked by liability to constant vacillation, an act of kindness being rapidly followed by one of cruelty, a high sense of honour being yet unable to restrain outrages upon the rights of others,[1] so the ethical influence in religion does not proceed steadily. But when, through the direct or indirect influence of a body of men, certain standards of right are brought forward, and, through the authority of individuals, meet with acceptance, the established ethical principles will also have a permanent influence on the religion. There may still be occasional lapses

[1] For examples see Wake, *The Evolution of Morality*, vol. i., chap. v.

into primitive capriciousness, but they will be rarer and the reaction will only be partial. Mere speculations and fancies, derived from individual experience, will give way to theological doctrines formulated with more or less distinctness by those whose part it is to retain in their hands the spiritual guidance of the people.

However crude such doctrines may be at first, and however inadequate they may continue despite steady development, they will not be void of ethical content. It is the distinguishing trait of theological doctrines that, as they are unfolded, they embody the ethical ideas prevalent among the leaders of the people. As religious ethics advance from loose to more rigid forms of organisation, the bond between religion and ethics becomes closer, until, through the growing authority of the religious guides, the two factors in human society become inseparable. At this stage, likewise, the influence of religious beliefs and customs on ethical problems becomes marked. The ethical standards are determined by relationship to the doctrines maintained with reference to the gods. The divine sanction for proper conduct becomes complete. The inculcation of virtues proceeds with direct reference to their supposed source—the pleasure and will of the gods. Theory is put into harmonious accord with practice.

The religions of Babylonia and Egypt are the most suitable examples in antiquity of this relationship between religion and ethics, brought about through priestly authority. In the Euphrates valley and in the empire of the Nile,[1] authority in religious

---

[1] For illustrations see Jastrow, *Religion of Babylonia and Assyria*, chap. xxvi. ; Wiedemann, *Religion of Egypt*, pp. 9 *et seq.*

matters was vested in the priests. In the great religious centres—Sippar, Nippur, Babylon, Memphis, and Thebes—schools of theology arose which formulated religious doctrines, systematised the pantheon, transformed the popular traditions and myths in accord with later theological speculations, gave a literary form to cosmological and eschatological beliefs, and prepared rituals to be used for the occasions when the kings and the people sought the sanctuaries to ascertain the will of the gods, to seek healing from disease, help in distress, or to obtain advice through divine oracles. The priests, likewise, controlled secular education, and, as a consequence, the general character of the masses was shaped through their influence. Ethical precepts were closely interwoven with religious principles and religious observances. It was not enough to do the right thing. In order to please the gods, the observance of certain purely religious commands was equally essential. The displeasure and anger of the gods was enkindled by the failure to bring sacrifices or to offer tithes, as much as by wrongs inflicted upon one's neighbour or the omission of duties towards the state. Mistakes in ceremonial details were as certain of being punished as actual infringements of decrees involving the question of right and wrong.

The union between religion and ethics was equally close in such states as ancient Greece, where the family cult was a more potent factor than in Babylonia and Egypt. Religion being at the same time closely bound up with the state, the priestly authority was overshadowed by that of secular chiefs, but the function of the latter was, after all, only of an executive character in carrying out the decrees and statutes formulated under priestly influence. It is only with the growing strength of philosophical speculation in Greece, as will presently be shown, that the beginnings are made towards a separation of the two factors—religion and ethics.

In Judæa, where the theocratic idea of the state is carried to its highest theoretical perfection, the religion naturally gives colour to the ethics; and the high development reached by ethics among the ancient Hebrews is a notable instance of the capabilities of religion in this respect. Here the ethical transformation of the conception regarding the Deity produces the ethical ideals of the Hebrew prophets. The Old Testament and New Testament Ethics are not only distinctly religious, but are the outcome of religious thought developed under ethical influences. In this case religion returns with compound interest the debt it owed to ethics. Indeed, here the dividing line between religion and ethics is entirely wiped out, whereas in the case of the other ancient nations the two factors are merely united, neither of them completely losing its identity.

The reason for this phenomenon in the case of the Hebrews is to be sought in the place assumed by individual authority in the development of religion, as against a combined priestly authority in other states. For Babylonia, Egypt, Greece, it is the priest as an abstraction, the priest by virtue of his close position to the gods, that secures for him the *rôle* of religious guide. In Judæa we are confronted with personalities who, in consequence of their individual powers, impress their views upon the people. Moses, Samuel, Elijah, the first Isaiah, Ezekiel, and Ezra, constitute landmarks in the religious history of

Israel. The religion of the people is such as they have made it—whatever our theories may be as to the source whence these men derived their power. Similarly for Christianity, it is the personal influence of Jesus, of Paul, of Peter, that is impressed upon the religious movement inaugurated by them. Hence we meet in early Christianity with the confirmation of the phenomenon that characterises Judaism—the perfect coalition of ethics with religion. The further examples of Islam, of Buddhism, of Zoroastrianism, of the Protestant Reformation, warrant us in setting up the general principle, that religions which can point to an individual or individuals as potent influences, and religious movements inaugurated by the personal influence of certain individuals, result in the most perfect union of religion with ethics, and produce a system of ethics entirely derived from religious beliefs. Ethics become an offshoot of religion. It is in such religions that the relationship between religion and ethics finds its most perfect expression.

VII.

We must not, however, lose sight of the fact that, parallel with this coalition of religion and ethics, there runs also a tendency towards the dissolution of the bond. In Greece, where, as we have seen, the union of religion and ethics does not proceed to such an extent that each loses its independent existence, the partial separation of ethics from religion is brought about within the domain of philosophic thought. It was the Sophists who made the attempt to bring this about, by transferring the seat of authority for ethical conduct from divine sanction to the conscience and experience of the individual.

Socrates proposes a compromise by giving to this individualism a religious character,[1] but he is unable to resist the movement which finds its highest exponents in Plato and Aristotle, the former enthroning Reason as the ultimate source of ethics, the latter proposing instead to assign the first place to Will. Plato, who restricts the practical application of his philosophy to the intellectual aristocracy, maintains the bond between religion and ethics for the masses incapable of following the dictates of Reason, whereas Aristotle, more democratic in his thought, breaks totally with the theory of divine sanction for moral conduct by setting up instead the sole authority of the Will— which can be cultivated and exercised by all humanity. A factor which no doubt influenced Greek philosophy in the course that it pursued is the imperfect character of the ethics derived from the religion. The tales told of the gods and goddesses, whatever their original import may have been, did not make them worthy examples to be followed. Plato, who is strangely insensible to their poetic interpretation, takes these tales literally, and is shocked by them. He protests against ascribing to the superior powers acts prompted by jealousy and hate, thinks it dishonouring to hold the gods guilty of using such means as deceit, lying, and trickery to accomplish their ends. We may at least admit that part of Plato's criticism which implies that the continued popularity of these myths in an age that was far removed from the one that produced them, and that could no longer understand their original import, indicated an unfortunate limitation put upon ethical development

[1] See Pfleiderer's *Moral und Religion nach ihrem gegenseitigen Verhältniss* (Haarlem, 1871), p. 22.

by what must, after all, be included within the scope
of religious belief. The relationship between religion
and ethics thus ends for Greece in the separation of
the two, after a period of close union—though not,
be it borne in mind, of complete amalgamation.

We do not as yet know enough of the intellectual
history of Babylonia and Egypt to be able to determine the extent to which this tendency towards the
separation of religion and ethics developed, but turning to such a movement as Buddhism, we find the
tendency most marked. The pessimistic view of life,
favoured by the great religion of India, helps to remove
the religious sanction for ethics, although so strongly
maintained by some of the religious thinkers, and we
find systems of morality cropping up in which there
is no place at all for a central supreme supra-mundane
authority imposing His laws upon mankind. In
Judaism the tendency towards a dissolution of the
bond between religion and ethics, endangering the
basic principle of the derivation of all authority from
a Divine source, was checked by the weakness of the
philosophical spirit among the Jews. Through Greek
influence, it seemed at one time as though the sanction
for ethics was indeed to be removed from religion to
reason,[1] but the subsequent political misfortunes of
Palestine concentrated religious thought upon the
preservation of the ancient ceremonies of religion as
the only means of keeping the national life intact.

The intellectual movement in Islam received a
fatal blow at so early a stage through the complete
triumph of Mohammedan orthodoxy, that the tendency
towards a separation of religion from ethics was

[1] Such books as Job and Ecclesiastes betray the influence of Greek
thought.

effectually checked. The few sporadic attempts in this
direction remained without permanent consequence.
Coming to Christianity, the tendency crops up at
various periods with more or less force, but it is not
until the scepticism of the eighteenth century arises
that the bond between religion and ethics is loosened
in Europe. It is rather significant that in the case of
Christianity it is not philosophy, but a scepticism
as to the fundamental doctrines of Christianity,
which gives vitality to the movement to divorce ethics
from religion. Not until English and French sceptics
have done their work does German philosophy step
in, and, under the leadership of Kant, finds in the
"categorical imperative" the source of ethical authority.
Since Kant's time the religious movements, both
within and without the pale of the church, have been
in the direction of admitting in theory a line of
demarcation between religion and ethics. While
recognising that the two factors must be harmoni-
ously combined in order to further the highest aims
of mankind, the best thinkers are agreed that the
religious sentiment is independent of the ethical
sense, and that the cultivation of the former may
proceed independently of the latter.

It is rather curious that we should once more be
approaching a position rather similar to that which
existed in primitive society, when, as will be recalled,
religion was quite distinct from ethics, but the
resemblance is only superficial. While it is felt that
the sanction for ethical conduct is not dependent upon
the dictates of a higher Power, and would hold with
equal force if such a Power did not exist, yet the
thought that the ethical development of the individual is in accord with the destiny for which

man has been placed on earth, creates a new link between religion and ethics. The religious sentiment furnishes, according to this view, an aid to the ethical life.

Religion is no longer the source of ethics, but proves a stimulus to it. Matthew Arnold's definition of Religion as "Morality touched with Emotion," while defective as a definition, yet reflects this modern relationship between religion and ethics. The ultimate appeal for the confirmation of religious faith is the religious sentiment. The sense of harmony between faith and knowledge, for which all rational beings crave, produces a state of mind which has its influence upon our lives, even though the regulation of conduct proceeds independently of religious faith. But while religion thus furnishes the stimulus to morality, it must be confessed that in the most advanced, or, if you choose, the most diluted forms of faith, the influence of ethics on religion is reduced to a minimum. There may be ethical strains in these forms of faith, but if that is the case, it is due to the inevitable entrance of ethical considerations into any purely intellectual interpretation of the universe —and its mysteries.

VIII.

From this rapid survey it will be evident that in the study of religion the ethical evolution of the human race can at no point be left out of consideration, but that the relationship between religion and ethics is a constantly changing quantity, assuming a different character for each religion, and even within the same religion passing through various phases. There is a certain sense in which

15

the ethics of a people constitutes a gauge for the religious position reached, but we must beware of making this relationship the supreme test. There may be religions in which a high ethical influence will be found in combination with totally insufficient religious conceptions and antiquated forms of religious cult. Progress in ethics is dependent upon other factors than merely the religious state of a people.

On the other hand, philosophical interpretations of the universe may represent the finest products of human reason, and may also make due allowance for the play of the religious sentiment in man, and yet have but a minor connection with ethical ideals. The ultimate goal of the human mind is truth; and within the sphere of religion it is inevitable that this pursuit of truth will be carried on without regard to consequences—ethical or others. The purer our motives in the endeavour to attain truth, the clearer will be our grasp, the greater our courage in the willingness to follow our investigations, whithersoever they may lead, and the greater also our sense of assurance that in following this lead we are fulfilling the highest aims placed within the reach of the human intellect.

CHAPTER VII.

RELIGION AND PHILOSOPHY.

I.

IN previous chapters[1] I have already had occasion to touch upon the part played by the unfolding of philosophical thought in the modification of religious beliefs. It must be evident that from the moment an attempt is made to determine the laws governing the phenomena around us, and the phenomena presented by a contemplation of man himself, Religion is placed under the necessity of giving, as it were, an account of herself. The question suggests itself at the outset of an investigation as to the relationship between philosophy and religion, whether the rise of philosophy among a people is due to conditions presented by a prevailing religion or has its origin in an opposition to these conditions. A strictly historical survey forces upon us the conclusion that the spirit of philosophical inquiry is one of scepticism and not of faith. In a very broad sense, it might be possible to include the childish fancies of primitive nations as well as the systematisation of religious beliefs by priestly authority, under the term of philosophy, since such beliefs involve the interpretation of nature, the position of man in nature, and are attempts at formulating the best knowledge of the times.

[1] See Chapters III. and VI.

The late James Darmesteter has perhaps made clearer than any one else[1] the perfect accord existing between science and religion in the earliest periods of civilisation; and under the term science, as used by him, philosophy is included. There can be no doubt of the correctness of Darmesteter's position, that the earliest interpretations of natural phenomena made by religious guides reflect the actual knowledge of the day. Up to this point these religious systems merit to be called also philosophical, but there comes a time when scientific investigation cuts itself loose from religious authority, which at one time dominated all forms of human thought and intellectual activity. The observation of the movements of the planets and stars, undertaken at first for the purpose of ascertaining what these movements portended for the country, the ruler, and the individual, grows into the independent science of astronomy ; and even though practical purposes continue to be associated with the study, these purposes are independent of religious beliefs.

Medicine remains within the clutches of religious belief longer than one might be tempted to suppose, in view of the apparently materialistic basis upon which this science is grounded. To this day in the Orient, and among the lower classes in the very heart of Europe and America, magic is still resorted to as an adjunct to medicinal potions in the treatment of disease. It is, accordingly, natural to find that two sciences like theology and philosophy, which have so much in common, are not differentiated until a comparatively late stage in the course of civilisation. In Babylonia and ancient Judæa

[1] *Selected Essays* (1895), pp. 3 *et seq.*

philosophy continued to be an integral part of theological speculation. There was no philosophy outside of theology, that is to say, beyond the limits represented by the religious interpretation of the phenomena of the universe. There are indications that in ancient Egypt speculation was carried on in some centres independently of religious beliefs, but we know too little of the supposed esoteric systems of Egypt to speak with any degree of definiteness. India and Greece are the two notable examples in the ancient world of the rise of philosophical thought, either in direct opposition to prevailing beliefs or independent of such beliefs. For our purposes this distinction is immaterial, inasmuch as the source of philosophy in both countries was a doubt as to the capacity of the theories embodied in the popular religious systems to account for the phenomena of the universe.

The essence of philosophy consists in unfolding its theories on the basis of a study of the phenomena and laws of the universe, while the early speculations of peoples and the ancient systems of belief and of worship devised by theologians are based on conceptions and views, the truth of which are taken for granted. That these views at one time represented the science of the day may be admitted, but we must also bear in mind that this science antedates the period of systematic study of either man or nature. It was, no doubt, religion that gave the stimulus to such study, and in this sense religion merits to be called the mother of philosophy, but it would only lead to a confusion of terms to identify early religion with philosophy. It was because some men in the community, bolder than the rest, felt impelled to ask the question, independently of accepted tradition or systems, as to the meaning of life and of the universe around us, that philosophy in the true sense arose. But the rise of this spirit of inquiry, if not actually a symptom of the waning power of the established religion—whatever the form of this established religion might be—certainly indicates the existence among a minority of a disposition to strike out on independent lines.

This instinctive opposition between philosophy and religion may not have been clearly perceived by the first philosophers, but it could not long have remained concealed from those who were interested in preserving traditional views. Thales, for example, in declaring water to be the primæval element, took an important step towards the overthrow of Greek polytheism. There was no room for the gods in a theory of the gradual evolution of nature; and while the form in which Thales enunciated his doctrine may have been religious or theological, still the very fact that an adjustment was called for of popular or state theology to such a doctrine as that of Thales, points to a natural opposition between philosophy and what was after all, in its essence, a survival of a primitive form of belief.

II.

Such a theory as is here propounded seems required in order to account for the almost continuous conflict between philosophy and religion which characterises the process of the development of civilisation. The ill repute in which the Sophists stood in the eyes of the Greek populace is but a natural consequence of their maintenance of an independent position towards the current beliefs; and it is significant that Socrates' attempt at a compromise with the fundamental principles of the Greek religion, by giving to the individual conscience a divine character, was of no avail. Unless *everything* was ascribed to the direct influence of the gods, the popular religion was endangered. "C'est le premier pas qui coûte." The spirit of independent inquiry was the fatal step. Plato's direct hostility to the mythological tales,[1] and Aristotle's indifference to the entire system of the prevailing religion, are but further landmarks in the process which began when, for the first time, the question was raised, independently of religious authority, as to the origin of the universe.

It does not, however, follow that because philosophy takes its rise from a spirit of independent inquiry it also assumes an anti-religious character. Greek philosophy manifests this character because of the lack of proper spiritual guides, who, as leaders of the people, might have effected a readjustment of popular beliefs to scientific theories; and, on the other hand, the Greek philosophers, with some notable exceptions (*e.g.*, Socrates and Plato), were not distinguished by the possession of strong religious instincts. Religion in Greece was perhaps too much a matter of the state, and too strongly affiliated with family traditions, to be influenced by philosophical speculation. In India, on the other hand, we see philosophy, though starting out likewise in a sceptical spirit, assuming a religious aspect, and, indeed, leading eventually to the founding of a new religion.

[1] See above, p. 222.

Leaving aside the obscure problems connected with the religious literature of India, such a philosophical system as that embodied in the Upanishads,[1] while characterised by a spirit of hostility towards the spirit of the Vedas, is thoroughly religious; and Buddhism is but one of various forms which grew out of the opposition on the part of independent thinkers to the popular religion commonly known as Brahmanism. Significant as this religion was in many respects, its minute ceremonialism, its lack of definiteness in accounting for the phenomena of the universe, and, above all, the strong admixture of primitive notions that must have appeared childish to rational minds, aroused doubts as to its sufficiency among those who were bold enough to use their mental faculties, untrammelled by tradition or authority. Unlike the development of philosophic thought in Greece, the philosophy of India attempted a practical reformation of popular beliefs. The conflict between religion and philosophy in India has its legitimate outcome in the rise of various religious orders and sects, based on a thoroughly philosophical conception of the universe and of the problems presented by human life. Nevertheless, the old Brahmanism maintained its existence as well as its hold upon the masses, so that in one form or the other the conflict between religion and philosophy kept pace with the intellectual activity of India. The steady tendency towards a multiplicity of philosophical sects is an indication of the unbroken sequence of this conflict.

India thus furnishes an example of the relationship existing between religion and philosophy, which is

[1] See Hopkins, *Religions of India*, chap. x.

most instructive in determining in how far philosophy enters as a factor in the study of religion.   The tendency of every religion is to become rigid in its beliefs and practices.   This tendency is cffset by the spirit of independent inquiry.   The result is a conflict which leads either (1) to the adjustment of the existing religion to the science of the day, or (2) to an indifference to this science, so that a hopeless and impassable gulf is produced between religion and thought, or (3) to the rise of a religious movement embodying the results of philosophical speculation. The old Vedic religion, it is true, with its elaborate mythology and its intricate ritual, itself represents the result of an attempted reconciliation between religion and philosophy, for, together with survivals of primitive religious conceptions, Brahmanism contains elements that belong to advanced forms of religion, but the assimilation was not complete, and when further independent speculation ensued, the popular faith was in no position to accept further modifications.   The new sects that arise in India all pass through the same stage.   They originate as products of independent thought.   Whether representing a real intellectual advance or the practical surrender of philosophical problems by proclaiming the triumph of transcendentalism, the philosophical religions become fixed in doctrines and ritual until they, too, are totally incapable of any adjustment to some new phase of philosophical speculation.   So Buddhism and Jainism in turn give birth to other forms of religion, until it is almost impossible to thread one's way through the religious maze of India ; but these new forms are always produced as the result of a conflict between some established form of religion and further philosophical speculation conducted in a spirit of independent inquiry.

III.

The philosophical spirit would have been fatal to Islam had it not been checked by the triumph of Mohammedan orthodoxy, but in the case of Christianity we have another, and indeed the best, example for determining the part that philosophy takes in the development of religion, and just how far it must enter as a factor in the study of religion.

Professor Tiele[1] has recently shown the untenability of the popular view which makes Christianity solely a product of Semitic thought—the natural goal of Judaism. In addition to the Jewish elements, Christianity has taken up within itself certain religious conceptions which are sufficiently characteristic of the Aryan peoples to warrant us in regarding them as totally foreign to Judaism. According to Tiele, the contrast between Semitic and Aryan religious ideals can be summed up in the terms " theocratic " and " theanthropic."[2]

The Semitic ideal, best represented in Judaism, places God outside of the world, but in sole and direct control of all that occurs; the Aryan ideal, best represented by religious thought in India and Persia, emphasises the close relationship between God and man. The divine nature manifests itself in man, and the world is regarded as an emanation of the Divine Spirit rather than as an object called into existence by His fiat. Of the two conceptions it is

---

[1] *Elements of the Science of Religion,* vol. i., pp. 208 *et seq.*
[2] *Ib.,* p. 155.

evident that the theanthropic is the more philosophical, the other the more practical. Christianity
being the result of a combination of the theocratic
with the theanthropic ideal, gave rise to a theology
in which purely philosophical discussions had a much
greater share than in the theology of the Jewish
church. The latter concerned itself largely with
the specific relationship of God to his chosen
people, whereas the introduction of Aryan ideas into
Christianity gave an impulse to the development of
abstract theological doctrines regarding God's nature,
and the manner in which He manifests himself to man.
The close connection between early Christian theology
and the Hellenistic philosophy, the latter a mixture
of Semitic and Aryan thought, becomes intelligible
on the basis of Tiele's hypothesis, which views
Christianity as essentially a compound of two
different currents of religious thought.

As a consequence, the history of Christianity is
to a large extent a history of philosophic thought
applied to religious problems. The Christian dogmas
manifest at an early stage the tendency to become
philosophical formulas ; and so characteristic is this
connection between Christian beliefs and philosophical
thought, that the theology, from the time of its formulation in the Gospel of John, is as much a philosophical system as an attempt to establish a form of
belief and a religious organisation on a definite basis.

If we turn to one of the latest writers on the
subject, the eminent Professor Pfleiderer,[1] we see
that the early Christian theology is due largely to the
infusion of Greek philosophy into the religious ideas

[1] *Philosophy and Development of Religion*, vol. ii., Lectures v., vi.,
and vii.

of Judaism. Even in Paul, the influence of the
Alexandrian religious philosophy, though less direct,
is manifest. After breaking with the rabbinical
interpretation of the Old Testament, he plants
himself on the ground of Hellenistic speculation in
accepting, by the side of the earthly Jesus, an "ideal
heavenly man," and Pfleiderer[1] shows how this theory
rests on the Platonic idealism as developed in the
Jewish-Greek schools of philosophy. The Philonian
theory of the Logos, the divine word sent into the
world to assume a human form, underlies the gospel
of John, and what is even more important, the great
church fathers Clement and Origen carried yet
further the process of converting Greek philosophy
into Christian doctrine, while the final result of the
movement is to be seen in the system of Augustine,
which Pfleiderer aptly characterises as prompted by
the desire to work the Platonic doctrine of God
and the Pauline doctrine of salvation into a whole
through combining them with each other and with
the dogmas of the church.[2] The doctrine of the
"Trinity," as well as such doctrines as "Divine Grace,"
with its corollaries of "Election" and "Damnation,"
are apparently purely theological, while in reality
the conclusions drawn form an admirably constructed
system of philosophy, that is to say, an interpretation
of the phenomena of the world and of man's position
therein, undertaken in accord with the scientific
knowledge of the day and carried out with conscious
reference to this knowledge. During the Middle
Ages, the Platonic philosophy yielded to Aristotelianism, which acquired an exclusive hold upon

---

[1] *Philosophy and Development of Religion*, vol. ii., pp. 162 *et seq.*
[2] *Ib.*, p. 290.

intellectual minds. Whether under the influence of this change, or as part of it, Christian theology assumed an Aristotelian garb, but it was no less philosophical for that reason. On the contrary, the dividing line between philosophy and theology became still fainter. To the superficial observer it might have seemed that there was no philosophy outside of Christian doctrine. Hence the break with scholastic theology came with the downfall of the Aristotelian system. What is known as Modern Philosophy dates from the time of Descartes, when a fresh and independent attempt was made to solve the problems of existence. At this point Christianity follows the example characteristic of ancient religions. Unable or unwilling to adapt itself to the new order of thought, Christian theology enters upon a struggle with the new philosophy. Philosophy and Theology part company. Other factors which we need not stop to consider contributed to the disintegrating process which now sets in, and which leads to the deepening of the abyss, separating independent philosophic inquiry from a traditional and now antiquated system of belief. Had European Christendom still been united at the time that the Modern Philosophy arose, we might have witnessed the adaptation of Christian doctrine to the Cartesian basis, just as it had once before shifted from a Platonic to an Aristotelian basis, but with the spread of Protestantism threatening the authority of the Catholic Church, it was inevitable that at least this wing of Christianity should remain firmly rooted to the position once taken. Protestantism could better afford to change the scholastic garb for one of newer pattern, but when independent philosophic thought, under the lead of English sceptics, attacked some of the fundamental doctrines of religious faith, both branches of Christianity became involved in the struggle. Scientific discoveries that revolutionised the current views of the age of the world, and swept away traditional theories of man's place in nature, helped to accentuate this struggle between religion and philosophy, which under somewhat changed conditions is still going on. But while Christian theology and philosophy are no longer united, the fact must not be overlooked that there has been a persistent influence of philosophic thought upon the religion of Europe. As in India, speculation gave rise to new forms of faith, so in the occident, religious sects arose within and without the pale of the Church, aiming at restoring the harmony between the demands of faith and independent thought. The splitting up of Protestantism into various sects is one form which this process assumes, the rise of free religious bodies in the intellectual centres of Europe and America, and such movements as the Positivism of August Comte, Reform Judaism, and the founding of Ethical Culture societies represent other forms.

The relation of Religion to Philosophy may therefore be summed up as follows :—

Philosophical speculation takes its rise from a feeling of dissatisfaction with the current religious beliefs. Wherever it appeared in the ancient world it led either to the dissolution of the existing religions, as in the case of Greece and Rome. or to the combination of philosophy with religion, as in the case of the religions of India and of early Christianity. Within the range of Semitic culture, Philosophy

manifested but little vitality, and as a consequence
the highest forms of Semitic religion, Judaism
and Islam, are marked by their practical character
rather than by the theoretical development of a
doctrinal theology.   In India, speculative thought was
so completely absorbed in religious problems that
the continuation of this thought led constantly to
new manifestations in the sphere of religion.   In
Christian Europe, the combination of religion with
philosophy produced great systems of theology in
which the Semitic and Aryan elements of Christianity found expression.   Jewish doctrines are first
combined with Platonic philosophy in the modified
form of Hellenistic speculation, and afterwards with
Aristotelianism, until the rise of Modern Philosophy,
which, breaking loose from the Aristotelian form of
speculation, leads to a struggle between religion and
philosophy that bears a resemblance to the opposition
of Greek philosophy to Greek religion.   In the
course of this struggle, new sects arise within the
larger compass of Protestantism, and also independent
religious organisations are formed, all of which
represent attempts to harmonise religious faith with
the varying aspects of philosophic thought.

IV.

The question as to the legitimate limits to be
assigned to the influence of philosophy in the sphere
of religion is too large a one to be adequately discussed here.   Moreover, such discussion lies beyond
the compass of this work, but it must be evident
that in the modern conditions of life, no form of faith
can hope to maintain its hold which is in oppo-

sition to the progress of independent speculation. At the same time, the examples of India, and of Early and Mediæval Christianity, show that a combination of philosophy with religion so close as to make religion a pure philosophical system fails of its purpose, and at all events tends to a constant disturbance of the equilibrium of faith. We must distinguish here, as in the case of Religion and Ethics, between the legitimate demands of the religious sentiment and the inevitable consequences of continued intellectual activity. Philosophy can supply but to a limited extent the religious needs of man. As little as philosophy can hope to solve all the mysteries of the universe, and above all, the mysteries of human life, has it the right to encroach upon a territory in which human emotions necessarily play an important part, and a part quite independent of human thought. The sense of the mysterious is a factor in human life to which even philosophy must consent to pay a proper degree of respect; and the more keenly the philosopher recognises the limitations of human knowledge, the readier will he be to pay this tribute. Religion very properly protests against the assumption on the part of philosophy to enter a domain foreign to her, but religion commits a fatal error in opposing the advance of philosophical speculation, no matter in what direction it may lead. An influence of philosophy on forms of faith is inevitable, and, viewed in the proper light, this influence will be seen to be wholesome, but it is erroneous to suppose that a permanent religious system can ever be evolved from philosophic thought alone. Through philosophy, religion will be

enabled to clarify its doctrines, to cast off such elements as no longer are adequate to the advancing
human intellect, and to take up others which will
further the aims of religion.   It is not difficult to
foresee that the result of the conflict still going on
between philosophy and religion will help each to
recognise more clearly than before its proper sphere.
There are indications that the time is not far distant
when this truth will be admitted.   On the other hand,
philosophy can flourish only by remaining true to its
essence,—which is independent thought, untrammelled
by traditions, religious or scientific.   Every generation
of thinkers must grapple anew with the problems of
the universe.   The solutions reached must reflect the
best knowledge of the period, but at the same time
due allowance must be made for further modifications
that will assuredly be necessary with the advance of
research in the various branches of natural and
historical science.   There is no such thing as an
absolute system of philosophy ; and for this reason
alone it is erroneous to suppose that philosophy can
ever form an all-sufficient basis for religious faith.

V.

There is, however, another phase of the relationship
of philosophy to religion which remains to be discussed.   Philosophy, as we have seen, though origin-
ating from a spirit of independent inquiry, is yet
closely associated with religion; and the earliest
attempts at a system of philosophy are largely
theological.   The natural opposition between philosophy, as a science based on investigation, and
religion, as a compound of thoughts, aspirations, and

emotions, does not prevent religion from availing itself of the aid furnished by philosophy. Nay, the very existence of this opposition has acted as a stimulus to religious thinkers to justify, by an appeal to pure thought, the faith to which they were attached. Running parallel with the growth of philosophical speculation, we have the development of a philosophy of religion. This philosophy of religion must not be confounded with the mere formulation of religious doctrines, which is prompted by the natural desire to give to religious beliefs a definite form. Such formulation may lead to theology, but never to philosophy. In order that a philosophy of religion should arise, the doctrines themselves as formulated must be submitted to a further interpretation by being brought into connection with such phenomena of the universe as are involved in these doctrines. Thus, a fundamental doctrine, like that of the existence of a Deity, constitutes a large part of a philosophy of religion. It is this latter science which sets forth the manner in which this belief is reached, and endeavours to ascertain the reasons for the various ideas held regarding a Deity. More than this, a philosophy of religion touches the question of the origin of religion, not in the historical sense, but in so far as this origin demands an explanation from the peculiar nature of man. The factors involved in the development of religious thought constitute another department of the philosophy of religion, and no less essential is the investigation of the phenomena of religion as manifested in religious worship.

In this branch of the study of religion, it is evident that the history of religion and the history of philosophy must play a considerable part. It would be useless to attack any of the problems involved in a philosophy of religion without a knowledge of the actual manner in which the religious instinct or sentiment has manifested itself. Before we can advance to a philosophical explanation of the doctrine of God, we must observe and study the conceptions that men at various ages and in various climes formed of Deity, and, similarly, the problem as to the origin of religion cannot be attacked before we have made a thorough study of the facts of religion. Again, since the aim of the philosophy of religion is to discover not only the *raison d'être* of religion, but the justification for the basis on which religion rests, a constant reference to the postulates of philosophy is essential to an attainment of this end. It is especially modern philosophy that enters as a factor into this aspect of the philosophy of religion; for it is a characteristic feature of the various systems that arise after Descartes gave the impulse to a new order of thought, that they represent, each in turn, and in historical sequence, the conclusions reached by steadily advancing knowledge of the universe, its history, and the laws governing its phenomena.

In order to make this clear to ourselves, it is but necessary to recall to mind what has been briefly set forth above as to the relationship between religion and philosophy among ancient nations. One of the functions of philosophy at all times has been to systematise and summarise what may be called the exact knowledge of the day. The variations existing among the different philosophical systems produced among the Greeks are due to different interpretations put upon this knowledge, and it is evident that as long as systems arise which are based simply on different interpretations of nature and natural phenomena, without any advance in a knowledge of the universe, there may be attempts at an adaptation of religious beliefs to such systems as in India, though a growing hostility between religion and philosophy, as in Greece, is a more natural outcome; the shifting principles of philosophy, however, can in either case be of little value in accounting for the phenomena of religion. In order that this should be the case, philosophy itself must assume the aspect of a science with fixed canons, and its successive phases must represent the results of advancing speculation based on steadily increasing knowledge. This position was not reached in the Middle Ages, because all philosophical thought was chained to certain authorities—notably to Aristotle. It is, however, attained in what is generally known as Modern Philosophy, which, casting aside all claims of ancient authorities, enters upon an independent course. The various systems that arose after Descartes stand in a logical as well as in a historical connection with one another. One cannot understand Spinoza without Descartes, nor Leibnitz without either, while Kant but carries the thought of his predecessors—notably the tendency of English thought—to its logical outcome. While much in these systems has merely an ephemeral value, yet we see a distinct advance as we pass from one generation to the other. Definite propositions are put forward and established as principles once for all. New problems naturally arise as rapidly as old ones are settled, but the existence of these new problems is itself a symptom of the increasing horizon of human knowledge.

It is not necessary for our purposes to indicate here the various factors that have contributed to give to modern philosophy so totally different a character from that which philosophy showed in ancient times and in the Middle Ages. We may content ourselves with merely recalling the growth of knowledge through travels and explorations, through discoveries in chemistry and physics, the progress in such sciences as astronomy, biology and philology, and the rise of new disciplines like psychology and the science of religion. Modern philosophy being thus the expression of modern science in the broadest meaning of the term, religious inquiry can avail itself of its principles without committing itself to any special system. Not only *can* religious inquiry do this—it is bound to do so, because the foundations upon which religious belief rests are involved in the problems with which modern philosophy deals. We may take as an example such a problem as the credibility of the evidence furnished by our senses and our reason. Before we can hope to find a hearing for the reasonableness of a belief in the existence of an ultimate First Cause, we must make sure that we are not deceived in our judgments of things as they exist. Now one of the most certain acquisitions of modern philosophy is the recognition of the limitations of our knowledge through two factors so entirely beyond our control as Time and Space. The bearings of this limitation upon the doctrine of a creator of the universe are obvious; and unless religious inquiry takes these bearings into consideration, it will necessarily go astray. Similarly at various points, indeed at almost every turn, when we come to investigate the bases of religious belief, we are confronted with the postulates and principles of Modern Philosophy.

There is a sense, then, in which the philosophy of

religion takes its rise only with the advent of Modern
Philosophy.   At all events, the study of this aspect
of religion is indissolubly associated with the philosophical systems that have arisen in Europe during
the past three centuries.   Even those who, like Rauwenhoff,[1] are of the opinion that the history of
philosophy, and more particularly of modern philosophy, forms the second part, and not the first, of
the philosophy of religion, admit this close connection.[2]   Indeed we may go so far as to say that no
philosophy of religion worthy of the name is possible
without a constant reference to the course of Modern
Philosophy, and it is a fundamental error of so well
written a book as Sabatier's recent *Esquisse d'une
Philosophie de Religion*, that it leaves this reference too
frequently out of view, or puts it in the background.
Sabatier's fine periods impress one with the high religious fervour of its author, but carry no conviction.
In contrast to Sabatier, Rauwenhoff, Pfleiderer, and
Siebeck[3] may be quoted as illustrations of the valuable results reached by philosophy of religion through
the application of the proper method to the study.
The difficulties involved in this part of the study of religion are obviously enormous.   It is advisable therefore for the student not to approach it until he has
advanced considerably in his investigation of the
phenomena of religion, nor can it be carried on with
profit unless one has also made himself familiar with
at least the outlines of the chief systems of ancient
and more especially of modern philosophy.

[1] *Religionsphilosophie* (Germ. transl. by J. R. Hanne), Braunschweig,
1889, p. 20.

[2] *Ib.*, pp. 3 *et seq.*   [3] See the Bibliography, sec. ii.

CHAPTER VIII.

RELIGION AND MYTHOLOGY.

I.

THAT myth plays a large part in all primitive religions as well as in the advanced religions of antiquity is beyond dispute, and it may also be admitted that the religions of the present contain many survivals falling within the domain of mythology. It is, indeed, no exaggeration to say that no religion ever obtained a hold upon the masses that did not contain mythical elements or did not eventually give rise to myths. A myth-making faculty is the common possession of humanity. The power that this faculty manifests among those peoples who represent the lowest stratum of civilisation and culture is not only significant, but furnishes the key to the problem as to the precise relationship existing between religion and mythology. It is but necessary to take up any of the numerous accounts of travellers among savages, wild tribes, or groups that have proceeded only a short distance along the path of civilisation, to arrive at the conviction that myth forms the natural medium for primitive man in giving expression to thoughts lying beyond the daily range. Scholars are not agreed as to the strength of the instinct of curiosity among savages. Some, like Herbert Spencer,[1] go so far as to deny this instinct or faculty altogether in those who live in a

---

[1] *Sociology*, p. 98.

state of rudeness and ignorance, but an extreme position like this is untenable. Even though the ordinary phenomena which man witnesses, such as the rising and setting of the sun, and the change of seasons, rains and storms, may make little impression upon him, or at all events not enough to arouse in him the desire to account in some way for these phenomena, yet unusual occurrences are bound to affect him. Eclipses of the sun or moon are perhaps too rare—relatively speaking, of course—to be taken into consideration in discussing this topic, though, for that very reason, the impression will be all the more striking when eclipses do occur; but the terror aroused by the roar of thunder, or the fear produced by the flashes of lightning—a fear completely justified by the mischief frequently wrought by the lightning— must prompt him to seek an explanation for phenomena affecting him so profoundly. In these explanations, whatever they may be, he comes into contact with the more ordinary phenomena. The sun, obscured when a storm arises during the day-time, naturally suggested the thought of a conflict between the sun and some hostile power; and when out of a dark sky he sees a flash of light suddenly appear, he will almost inevitably be led to bring this manifestation into some connection in his thought with the two great bodies of light—the sun and the moon—so familiar to him. The moment that this connection is brought about, the path is cleared for the rise of explanations regarding the more ordinary phenomena. All that is needed is that man's attention should be directed towards the latter; and it is inconceivable that, even though his sense of curiosity be weak or almost entirely lacking, some accident should not arise in the course of his career which will suggest such questions as, What does this constant change of night and day mean, what happens to the sun when it sinks below the horizon, why does the moon now appear in a round shape and again only as a thin stripe? The answer that man gives to these questions leads to the formation of nature-myths; and it is only necessary to remind the reader how large a proportion of religious myths deal with natural phenomena to illustrate the import of the theory just advanced.

One feature of these answers, which of itself is sufficient to produce nature-myths, is the personification of the powers whose manifestations man witnesses. The storm will be personified as a huge bird; the sun will be regarded as a human being, sun and moon being viewed as husband and wife, or brother and sister, or two rival rulers; the lightning will be a dragon.[1] This personification is not to be interpreted as a poetic metaphor, though to a later age it may appear so. To ascribe life to all things is an axiom of primitive man's science, and since the only life of which he knows anything is that of which he is a witness in himself, in his fellows, and in the animals about him, the powers of nature are likewise conceived as animate beings—either in human or animal shape. Naturally, the greatest possible diversity exists among peoples in the particular kind of personification selected. Climatic conditions, habits of life, and, to a certain extent, mere chance will control the personifications. Still less agreement have we a right to expect in the myths

[1] For examples see various chapters in Lang's *Myth, Ritual, and Religion* (London, 1887; 2nd ed., 1899).

themselves, in what is related of the personified powers of nature to account for their appearance, for what happens to them, and for what they bring about; but in all there is a large predominance of what to us appears to be an irrational element. Animals are introduced as gifted with powers of speech, human beings are given the power of changing their form, taking on in turn the guise of certain animals or of certain plants, or they are turned into stone.

Here again we must beware of mistaking for metaphor what to primitive man is a stern reality. It is the merit of Andrew Lang to have shown conclusively that belief in such metamorphoses is natural with men at a certain stage of intellectual development— nay, that he comes to such a belief almost inevitably. It is forced upon him by evidence that he is unable to interpret otherwise. Similarly, in ascribing powers to beasts, which appears to us to be a purely fanciful procedure, man was guided by a process of reasoning peculiar to him at a certain juncture in his course along the path of civilisation, for nothing is more characteristic of different periods of culture than the variations in logical processes that they present. Progress in thought is to a large extent merely an advance in reasoning powers. Viewed in this light, the irrational elements in the myths of ancient nations are the most natural factors, and such as will inevitably make their appearance. Thirdly, we note the tendency of the primitive myths to become exceedingly complicated. Contrary to popular prejudice, the mind of the savage is not a simple but a very complex apparatus. In accounting for phenomena, he does not hit upon obvious explanations, but, on the contrary, is more apt to form an elaborate theory in

which simplicity is conspicuous by its absence.
Modern hypotheses of natural science may be called
simple, but not the attempts of savages to explain the
mysteries of creation.   Hence, as we examine the
myths current among primitive nations which account
for the creation of the world, we are struck by their
exceedingly elaborate and complicated character.
A factor which serves to maintain this complicated
character of myths even among comparatively advanced peoples is the combination that is attempted
among related myths.   Stories told in one place pass
to another, but instead of being adopted in their
original form, they are combined with such as are
already current, and have with the imported tales
some features or traits in common.   So long, therefore, as myths continue to retain their hold upon
people, they also maintain the trait peculiar to them
in being not simple but cumbersome explanations of
natural phenomena.

Without entering upon the perplexing question
as to how the belief in deities arose among mankind, it is important for our purposes that the
myth-making faculty is strengthened by this belief.
In the same way that stories will arise in connection with purely natural phenomena, they will
also be produced regarding the relationship of gods
and goddesses to one another.   In many cases these
tales will again resolve themselves into nature-myths
—that is, stories originally invented to account for
the phenomena of the universe,—while in others faint
historical traditions will be interwoven in these tales.
Greek mythology furnishes notable illustrations of
such a combination of historical tradition with pure
myth, but among other nations also examples will

be found. The last stage in the process of myth-
formation is reached when literature avails itself of
the material furnished by the popular tales of natural
phenomena and of the gods. When myths receive
a literary form, a certain amount of trimming and
systematisation is inevitable. It matters little whether
the myths are embodied in epics or introduced into
hymns, modifications of the original material will be
the result. In the study of myths we must therefore
distinguish between old and original elements, and
such as have been added at a subsequent period, and
with clear intent. Yet such is the persistency of
tales once obtaining a hold upon the people, that
even an advanced age cannot free itself from their
subtle influence, and although the original import of
the myth is forgotten, it continues to survive even in
literature with all those features which to a later age
must necessarily appear irrational or revolting. This
brief exposition of the nature of myths and the
course pursued by them will prepare us for approaching the question as to the place to be assigned to
mythology in the study of religion.

II.

Scholars are still far from having reached an agreement as to the method to be employed in the interpretation of myths. With that tendency towards
complication, amalgamation, and assimilation which
we have seen to be characteristic of the development
of myths, it is perhaps impossible to solve all the
problems involved. This much at least is certain, that
there is no single key that will unlock all mythology.
The ancients already occupied themselves with the

interpretation of myths.   Among Greek philosophers
we have attempts at a symbolical, an historical,
and an ethical interpretation.[1]   The early Christian
scholars were inclined to look upon the stories told
of the Greek deities as literally believed, and therefore found in them an admirable weapon for dis-
crediting the ethical standards of Paganism.   The
discovery of myths in Sanskrit literature bearing
a resemblance to the Greek stories broadened the
horizon of scholars, and when it was further found
through accounts of travellers and through students
of folk-lore, that the tendency to myth-making was
practically universal, and that among the masses, even
in occidental Europe, primitive myths survived in
the form of fairy tales and legends, it was clear
that in accounting for the origin of myths we must
have recourse to mental traits common to mankind
at a certain stage.   From this point of view, the
elaborate Greek myths, as embodied in Homer and
other literary productions, are for the greater part
"survivals" of primitive ideas and primitive methods
of interpreting the phenomena of the universe.

The same view is to be taken of the rich mythology
in Sanskrit literature, and the abundance of myth-lore
found in Egyptian, Babylonian, and Hebrew literature.
Among modern attempts at interpretation of myths,
it is sufficient for our purposes to note the theories of
Max Müller and of Andrew Lang. According to Max
Müller, the irrational element in the myths, such as
the change of human beings into animals, the supposed descent of groups of people from animals or
plants, the immoral and fanciful tales recounted of

---

[1] For a full exposition, see Gruppe, *Die Griechischen Culte*, pp.
14 *et seq*.

the gods and goddesses, are due to a confusion of
terms. Mythology resolves itself into a species of
calembours, or, as Professor Müller was fond of putting
it, represents a "disease of language"—the original
import of certain terms being no longer known, an
accidental resemblance of these words to others gives
rise to the myths. The manifest objection that has
been urged against this theory is that it does not account for *all* the facts, but only for a small proportion.
Indeed, Professor Müller's key can be applied only to
the elaborated myths of Greece and India, and in
part to those of Egypt and Babylonia, but not to
those found among primitive nations. Andrew Lang,
approaching the subject from the standpoint of the
anthropologist, is more successful in showing the
mental state which produces myths, but at the same
time, it must be confessed that Lang's theory cannot
be applied throughout. There are late elements in
myths which have a totally different origin from the
earlier ones. The process of myth-formation, in fine,
is so complicated as to make one despair of reaching
any general series of principles to account for it,
but in so far as mythology has a bearing on religion,
it is sufficient to make clear to ourselves the universality of the myth-making faculty, its great antiquity,
and the mental conditions reflected in the myths
themselves.

It does not follow of course that all myths are of
religious import. Indeed there are many which have
no connection with religious beliefs, primitive or
otherwise, but, on the other hand, it is not difficult
to see how the religious element naturally makes its
entrance into a myth. The personification of the
powers of nature constitutes perhaps the most notable

entering wedge.   When with such personification, the worship of the power personified is combined or involved, as must frequently happen, it is inevitable that conceptions of the deity or spirit in question, and of man's relationship to the same, are introduced into the myth.   In both storm and dawn myths, which form a large proportion of nature-myths everywhere, religious views regarding such deities as the sun, moon, and certain planets are thus embodied, while on the other hand, the personification of thunder, rain, and lightning leads to the creation of special storm gods if such are not already in existence. Again, in the large series of myths which aim at accounting for the existence of the world, its products and animals, its order and apparent laws, religious beliefs form a necessary feature.   Not that the creation of the world is always ascribed to the gods; for it is rather a characteristic of very primitive myths that they bring the world into existence without the fiat of the superior powers, but at some juncture in the cosmology the gods are certain to be introduced, and it is to them that such features as the regulation of the seasons and vegetation are ascribed. When we come to a third class of myths which deal with the fate of mankind after death, the conception of some gathering place for the departed is of course of a religious character, and as a general thing special gods are hypothecated under whose dominion the dead are placed.

Through the mythology of a people we are accordingly introduced to certain phases of the religious beliefs entertained from time to time, and what is of special significance, it is the popular side of the beliefs that is brought to our notice in this way.

Whatever theory we adopt to account for the rise
of myths, it will not interfere with this important
conclusion—that it is the popular mind which reveals
itself in the myths. Distinguishing, as a proper
method must, between form and contents of a myth,
it will not be difficult to determine exactly what
parts of a myth are essentially popular in character,
for though it may be said that any formulation of a
myth is due to some individual or individuals, still
the people as a whole have a part even in this
formulation, for only that form which finds a response
in the minds of the masses will obtain a hold upon
people and maintain its sway. It is this popular
aspect of mythology that constitutes its importance
in the study of religion—an importance that is fortunately independent of the interpretation that we
may be inclined to place upon any myth or series
of myths.

III.

The question suggests itself at this point as to
the precise influence exerted by mythology upon the
religion of a people? From what has been said, it
will be obvious that this influence is strongest in the
earlier stages of religious development. Through the
popularity of a myth produced at a time when what
seems fanciful to a later age was perfectly natural,
beliefs will be maintained which no longer adequately
represent the mental state reached by a people. In
this way it happens that the tales of the gods continued to be current among the Greeks long after the
people had outgrown the conditions which produced
them. It is impossible to conceive that any
intelligent Greek living in the age of Sophocles

should have accepted literally the stories told of Zeus, or Aphrodite, or Apollo, and yet but for these stories, belief in the reality of the gods would have been undermined long before the advent of Christianity The hoary antiquity of the tales lent to them an almost sacred character. The Greeks knew nothing of a time when these stories did not exist, and hence an extreme scepticism could not go further than to attempt an explanation of the tales that might remove those features in them which appeared objectionable to a more sensitive age, features which appeared to place the gods on a lower moral level than that reached by human beings. The stories, it was held, had originally a different import; and various schools of interpretation arose, but not even Plato ventured to go so far as to deny all real basis for the myths. In some sense or the other they were not only true, but they responded to some kind of reality. The mixture of historical tradition with pure myths was a factor which helped to maintain this belief in reality, and, in a still stronger degree, the literary form given to the ancient stories deepened their impression upon the intellectual portion of the population. The beauty and charm of Homer were too powerful to be resisted, and people could not bring themselves to believe that what had inspired a mortal to such wonderful flights should turn out to be merely a mass of idle tales, the product of human fancy. Elsewhere we may note the same influence of mythology in maintaining primitive religious conceptions. The hymns of the Rig-Veda were even more precious to the people of India than Homer's poems were to the Greeks. As part of the religious ritual, the truth of the stories embodied in these hymns could

17

not be questioned without endangering the entire fabric of the religion.   The inconsistency existing between the beliefs expressed in some of these hymns and the advanced notions found in compositions almost entirely free from allusions to the ancient stock of mythical tradition was calmly ignored. That which had acquired sanctity by virtue of its age was not to be tampered with.   As a consequence, the breach between ancient popular conceptions and later doctrines grew ever larger, until finally new forms of faith were evolved which corresponded to higher religious conditions.   Yet, even in these forms, much of the old mythology survived, and when, as a reaction against the attempts to convert religion into a form of philosophy, Brahmanism reasserted itself with vigour, there was also a recrudescence of mythological elements in the religion.

The religion of the Hebrews forms no exception to the rule.   The notion at one time prevalent that the Semites had no mythology, or were at best poor in producing myths, has long since been exploded. Not only is the Babylonian literature rich in examples of myths, but we now know that the early chapters of Genesis have an equal right to be included in the domain of mythology with the stories of the gods embodied in Homer.   The creation story is based on a nature-myth portraying the winter storms and rains as a contest between a monster and the finally triumphant sun-god.   A combination of the same myth with perhaps some faint historical traditions can be recognised in the Biblical deluge tale, ending with the division of mankind into three great groups. As we proceed to later periods the historical element becomes stronger and the mythical admixture weaker,

without however disappearing altogether.   The story
of Sodom furnishes an illustration of such weaker
admixture.   In Abraham's career myth begins to give
way to legend, though there are scholars who detect
in most of the adventures that befell Abraham
genuine myths transferred to the life of an individual.[1]
Myth as well as legend prevails in the story of Jacob.
His contest with an unknown power during the night
is the old story found among so many nations, which
represents the change from night to day as a fight
between two powers; and even at so late a period as
that of the "Judges," we find mythical elements
entering for example in the account of the adventures of the famous Samson.[2]   In the story of
Jonah an ancient myth is introduced, but made
to serve the purpose of an allegory.   There can be
no doubt that the incorporation of these myths
in literary productions which acquired a sacred significance not only served to maintain the belief in
the numerous myths that were once current among
the Hebrews—many of which they shared with other
Semites—but also proved a powerful factor in maintaining among the Hebrews standards of belief that
correspond to the myth-making period.   That the
ancient myths were given a totally different turn in
the sacred writings did not materially affect the real
influence wielded by the tales.   For the masses, the
importance of the stories lay in their contents, shorn

---

[1] *E.g.* Winckler, *Geschichte Israels.*

[2] See H. Steinthal, "Die Sage von Simson," *Zeits. f. Völkerpsy-
chologie,* ii., pp. 129 and 178; and Moore, *Commentary on Judges* (New
York, 1895), p. 395.   Even though we are not justified in going to
the length of declaring Samson to be a *pure* solar myth, there is no
doubt but that many of his adventures are nature-myths, transferred
to an individual and combined with historical traditions.

of all moral and purpose. They were adapted by the religious leaders to advanced ideas, because it was through the ancient tales that they could best reach the people, and indeed the stories had such a strong hold upon the people that no efforts of the leaders could have driven them out. By the side of the myths embodied in the sacred books, numerous others were current, some of which found a place in the later Rabbinical literature; but it is curious to note that the purpose of the Biblical writers to raise the religious level of the people was offset in a measure by this very incorporation of myths in their literature.

Among the Egyptians and Babylonians the same observation may be made; it is the popularity of the myths which acts as a powerful factor in preserving traditional beliefs; and while it is true that these beliefs are constantly undergoing some transformation, ancient Egypt is an admirable example of a country where this transformation is reduced almost to a minimum. It cannot be accidental, therefore, that it is precisely in Egypt where we find certain myths—particularly that of Set and Osiris—honeycombing, as it were, the entire religious system, controlling to a large extent the religious ritual, entering into the eschatology and regulating the funeral rites and the elaborate ceremonials of homage to the dead.

IV.

The mythology of a people may be designated as a conservative force in religion, and indeed we may go further and declare that the popularity of myths, and the respect they inspire by nature of their antiquity, serve to keep alive religious conceptions that belong to the myth-making period of a people. It follows that mythology, from being originally a natural expression of man's theories and fancies of the universe, becomes a hindrance to his passing beyond totally inadequate religious conceptions, acts as a check to progress in religious thought, so far at least as the masses are concerned. The mythology of a people does not only find a permanent place in its sacred literature, but, as already intimated, enters the ritual and religious customs. Festivals of a permanent character are among most nations closely connected with some myth or the other. Significant in this respect are the solar festivals. Throughout the Semitic world, the Tammuz or Adonis myth was current. The story was told of a spirited youth who was loved by the goddess of love and fertility, but who meets with a tragic death. In some places—notably Babylonia—the goddess is held responsible for the death of the youth, but after his death she bitterly bewails her loss. The myth belongs to the class which symbolises the change of seasons. Tammuz is the youthful god of spring. The union with the goddess represents the fertility in vegetation and among animals that takes place upon the re-awakening of nature in the spring, but the heat of summer comes and kills the god of spring, who is thus portrayed as being snatched away from the world and compelled to pass a long imprisonment in the nether-world, where the dead are congregated, until once more released through the influence of the goddess who loves him. This myth underlies a fast of mourning for the lost Tammuz which was widely observed among the Semites.

There was also a festival of Tammuz celebrating the
return of the god, and in later times the fast and
festival were combined, the days of mourning for
Tammuz being immediately followed by merry-
making in honour of his return. From the Semites,
the Tammuz myth and the festival made its way to
the Greeks, and it is significant of the hold that the
tale had even upon people of advanced religious
thought, that as late as the days of Ezekiel [1] the
inhabitants of Jerusalem still clung to the worship of
Tammuz.

In Greece, Rome, and Egypt some of the most
important festivals were similarly in close association with certain myths. The question whether
in such cases the festival has given rise to the myth
or the myth to the festival, has been the subject of
much discussion among scholars. No doubt the
influence has been mutual. The festival has not
only served to keep alive the memory of the myth
and popular belief in the same, but there is
plenty of evidence to show that the form of the
myth has been modified in order to bring about
a more perfect accord between myth and festival—
to bring the myth, so to speak, "down to date." On
the one hand, the fact that a myth symbolised so
striking a phenomenon as the change of seasons
seems to preclude the possibility of its having been
suggested by a spring or summer festival. The
startling contrast between winter, when nature is
stripped of its glories, and the spring, when a new
life seems to be infused into the earth, is just of a
kind that would arouse the attention of primitive
man, because it directly affects his comfort. The

[1] Chap. xiv.; see W. R. Smith, *Religion of the Semites*, pp. 390 *et seq.*

character of such a myth likewise bears all the marks of having been evolved at a period when man's thought was at the lowest level. The personification of spring as a youth, the union between the spring and fertility represented as a goddess, the personified death of spring, are all primitive features that are perfectly intelligible, even though no fast or festival existed, whereas the dependence of the fast and festival of Tammuz upon the myth is so evident as to require no further demonstration. Logically at least, the myth precedes the festival, and the logical precedence in this case appears to correspond to a chronological order. While, therefore, it is quite within the range of possibility that myths should also have been produced on the basis of a religious custom, still the myth-making period is earlier than the production of a ritual, and hence it is the myth that in the first instance gives rise to a religious rite and not the reverse. But however this may be, the influence of the myth, when once it has been imbedded in the ritual, is materially increased. Myth and ritual in this combination present a solid front against attacks on current religious conceptions. The abandonment of religious custom is at best a very slow process, and when a custom is reinforced by connection with popular tales, it is almost impossible to kill the rite. Even though driven out of the official religion, the rite will find a place elsewhere, or it will survive as a popular custom none the less virile for being denounced as a "superstition." Through literature and through the ritual, mythology continues to exert a strong influence upon the religion of a people; and in both cases the influence is of the same character, tending towards the maintenance of a low order of religious conceptions, and successfully blocking the attempts of religious thinkers to raise the popular religion to a higher level. The result of the conflict that ensues when the mythology of a people is no longer adequate to the religious level reached—even though this level be reached by a minority alone—is a compromise. The old tales are carried over into the higher forms of the religion, and the attempt is made to interpret them in terms corresponding to the new order of religious thought. The myth, from being a theory of primitive science, becomes a poetic symbol to convey ethical ideas.

Philosophy also takes hold of the myth and reads into it philosophical truths. In this way, the material elements and objectionable features so prominent in the myth are accounted for to the satisfaction of those who can no longer accept them in naïve fashion. Finally, when even in this diluted form mythology is no longer capable of being introduced into some higher form of religion, some of the most tenacious myths are by a popular process transferred to favoured individuals who have absolutely no connection with the myths, but who lend themselves to this species of adaptation, and now instead of myths we have religious legends. There is scarcely a great religious leader in Judaism, Christianity, and Islam, into whose life some ancient myths have not found an entrance in the guise of legend. The mythical elements introduced into the life of Abraham, Jacob, Moses, Joshua, Samson, Elijah, are obvious to scholars. There is scarcely room for doubt that in the story and ritual of the Resurrection, mythical elements illustrative of the change of seasons have been embodied, just as in fixing the celebration of Jesus' birthday at the end of the year, tradition was influenced by an old winter festival celebrated among the Aryans.[1]   In Mohammed's career, likewise, myths have been recognised.

Not to speak of the vast quantity of folk-lore which preserves many an ancient myth, the actual survival of mythology in even the most advanced religions is sufficient to indicate the important part that the study of mythology must play in the investigation of religious phenomena.   Without having recourse to mythology, it is hopeless to attempt to analyse religious beliefs, and carry them back to their source.   It may safely be said that the earliest forms of all the fundamental doctrines in the great living religions are to be found in the mythology of one or other of ancient nations.   The continuity of religious beliefs through the long course of development and evolution through which they pass, finds illustration in the survival of ancient myths both within the pale of present religious thought and beyond it in those boundless regions which we call "popular superstitions."

For the study of religious literature, as well as for the investigation of religious rites and customs, we must have recourse to popular mythology.   Mythology, in short, is the scarlet thread that has been woven into the pattern of religion in such a way as to be apparent everywhere.   We cannot escape

---

[1] The 25th day of December corresponds to the 25th day of the Hebrew month Kislev.   On this day there is now celebrated a festival among Jews commemorative of their liberation under the lead of the Maccabeans from Greek rule (165 B.C.), but the festival is much older than the historical event which has been connected with it.

mythology the moment we enter upon a thorough study of any religion. There are few religious doctrines which, when scratched, do not reveal a lower surface of myth.

To some this connection between religion and mythology may appear as an unholy alliance, or at all events as an unworthy one. If religion is to so large an extent involved in mythology, in what is, after all, either crude thought or pure fiction, what becomes of the supposed reality of our religious beliefs? If mythology survives in modern religions, is there not here a mixture of absolute falseness with supposed pure truth? Natural as the question is, it nevertheless starts from a wrong assumption as to the nature and essence of religion. If religion were simply a question of truth and reality, and if its doctrines were of a kind that could be tested by the methods of the intellect solely, the feeling of repugnance for the association of mythical fancies with sublime aspirations would be justified; but religion, as need hardly be emphasised again, corresponds to other needs besides those of scientific curiosity as to the meaning of life, the government of the world, and the fate of man after death. The moment that emotions come into play, as is the case in every religion, the intellect is no longer the sole ruler of the situation. The head must be willing to divide authority with the heart. The emotional needs must be satisfied by religion, if religion is to exert any influence over human lives. A religion that dispels the sense of mystery which the phenomena witnessed by man arouses, commits suicide.

Myth takes its rise, as we have seen, from this sense of mystery. Man is impressed with the strangeness of certain occurrences in nature. At first it is an unusual phenomenon, one that seems to interfere with the regular course of things—as an eclipse or a destructive storm—that arouses his attention; and from trying to solve the mystery attendant upon these unusual occurrences, he comes to ponder also upon the ordinary phenomena, such as the change from day to night, the movement of the seasons, the varying phases of the moon. Upon such reflection as he is capable of, he finds these ordinary phenomena to be no less miraculous than the exceptional ones. He proceeds further and encounters the problem as to the origin of all the things that he sees, of the waters, of the earth with its vegetation, of the animals, of himself. With every advance in thought the mystery becomes more impressive. The struggle that he undergoes in his endeavour to pierce all this mystery, has its outcome first in the worship of powers of whose existence he cannot be in doubt, since he sees their manifestations, and secondly, in theories to account for the various phenomena. In these theories his emotional nature has an equal share with his mental composition; and the natural result of such workings of the savage mind is the production of a myth. At this stage in man's mental development, there is no sharp distinction between metaphor and reality. Abstract ideas have no meaning for him. He is bound to personify all powers of whose manifestations he is convinced through the evidence of his senses. All forms of life being, according to his notions, of one and the same kind, a change from one form of life to the other is perfectly rational. Men can be produced from animals and plants. Gods as well as men can be changed so as to take on the shape of animals. Since even in dealing with the ordinary phenomena of nature, he is necessarily concerned with things lying entirely beyond his control, his play of fancy is unchecked. Strange as the explanations which he offers for the phenomena of the universe may seem to a more advanced generation, they will, after all, not be any stranger than the phenomena themselves. The mystery inspired by the latter is maintained in the myths, and for this very reason, the myth retains its hold. It continues to satisfy man's sense of the mysterious, even when he reaches a point where the myth is no longer adequate to serve as a scientific interpretation of nature. Moreover, the irrational elements in the myth are the very ones that lend themselves to a symbolical explanation. The fancies of one age, produced through the overwhelming impression of nature's mysteries, become poetic metaphors to another, which, despite all advance, still requires as much as the earlier one to have the sense of the mysterious satisfied. To see things of the world darkly, as through a glass, is a condition imposed upon man in all states by the limitations of his powers.

Myth accordingly meets the requirements of religion, even in an age which no longer produces them. The religious thinker gifted with spiritual insight may find in the myths a support for his endeavour to reach out to an understanding of things that belong to a higher realm. For the philosopher the myth may also have a meaning. He feels that his system of thought is not in contradiction with the traditions of the past, since he can pierce the real import of these traditions; and there are but few philosophers

so bold and so confident of their own powers as to
willingly forego, by an appeal to the past, a confirma·
tion of their views. To seek the new in the old has
always been the aim of religious innovators and
reformers, and the sharper the break between the new
and the already existing conditions, the greater the
anxiety to find a connecting link between the innovation and the remote past. It is manifestly
unjust, therefore, to apply such terms as "false" to
the realm of mythology. The myth always corresponds to a reality. One age may view this reality
in a different light from another, but this change
of view does not affect the truth comprised in the
myth. To argue that this truth is not complete is
but to assert that it is a human attempt to seize
what lies for ever beyond the grasp of finite mind
and limited intellectual powers, whereas to claim
that this truth should be freed from mystery is to
make a demand of man in an early state of development which the best intellects of the most advanced
age are unable to satisfy.

V.

Reference has already been made to the severe
denunciation, in which various Greek philosophers
indulged, of the immoral elements in the myths, but
their claim that the trickery and knavery attributed
to the gods, and the downright crimes of which they
are guilty, must have had a demoralising influence
upon the masses, cannot be admitted. The people
through their very reverence for the gods easily
reached the position which admitted a different code
of morals for the higher powers from the one which

held good for mortals. We may feel certain that no
Greek ever urged that it was right to steal because
Prometheus indulged in this privilege, any more than
he would approve of infanticide because Kronos
swallowed his children. We may feel quite sure
that it was the immoral elements in the Greek myths
which appealed to the people, as did the irrational
elements, because both helped to satisfy the sense of
the mysterious. Even without having recourse to
symbolical, allegorical, or philosophical modes of
interpretation, the people perceived, albeit vaguely,
what these immoral and irrational elements portended.
They served their purpose if they deepened in the
masses the conviction that the phenomena of nature
were controlled by powers that had but little in
common with the restrictions under which man
suffered. Despite the sunny skies of Greece, the
people must have felt keenly the tragedy of human
life, that was always obliged to pay a severe penalty
for transgressing the apparently arbitrary decrees of
the gods, or this tragedy would not have found such
a sublime expression in the dramas of Sophocles and
Euripides.

In studying the mythology of primitive and
advanced nations, we come closer to the religious
needs and aspirations of humanity, than through the
study of Ethics and Philosophy so far as they bear
on religion. There is only one other factor which
touches religion so closely as the mythology of a
people, and that is the ritual. Through the ritual
likewise, the distinctly popular aspects of a people's
faith are revealed, not indeed the ritual as definitely
shaped by the systematic efforts of long successions
of theologians, but the religious customs as evolved

through the popular genius with the help of priests whose functions, it is well to bear in mind, are quite different from those of the theologians. This analogy between the mythology of a people and the oldest parts of its ritual may be carried a step farther. In the perfected cult of an advanced faith, not all of the ancient ritual is preserved, but what is not officially recognised survives as popular superstition, often outliving the legitimate ritual which is subject to more frequent modifications. Similarly, a part only of the mythology is carried over into more advanced forms of belief and makes its way into religious doctrines that are appropriate to a higher condition of religious thought ; the rest, or at least a great part of the rest, survives as folk-lore in the shape of fairy tales, or becomes mingled with popular legends. For a complete study of mythology we must not rest content with an examination of the mythology of civilised nations, nor is our task completed when we have gathered from the accounts of travellers the myths current among savages and those living in a backward state of culture ; we must push our investigations into the domain of folk-lore. Right about us and on all sides we have survivals of popular myths in the tales of elfs and wizards current among the ignorant classes of European and American towns,[1] in the stories that nurses relate to children,[2] in the well-known tales of "Uncle Remus," just as in many a popular game now played by children, we have the last traces of some religious rite that belongs to the myth-making period of a people.

[1] See, *e.g.*, Jacobs' collection of *English Fairy Tales*.
[2] For examples, see Fiske, *Myths and Mythmakers*.

Naturally, we must not press the mythical elements in folk-lore too hard. Just at present, when folk-lore studies appear to run riot, a warning of this kind is in place. It is manifestly absurd to identify folk-lore with mythology, or to make the one domain co-extensive with the other. Folk-lore will not help us materially in solving the problem as to either the origin or the nature of religion, but it is of value in enabling us to trace the course taken by a myth, to supply missing elements in the same, and to establish the connection that binds the present to the remote past. For such purposes, only a small amount of the material collected with such patience by the folk-lorists is of value. One cannot help harbouring a suspicion that much of this material is indeed worthless for any scientific purpose whatsoever; at all events, granting that it may be useful in other fields of research, it has nothing to do with mythology or religion.

CHAPTER IX.

RELIGION AND PSYCHOLOGY.

I.

THE factors involved in the study of religion, which we have hitherto been considering,—Ethics, Philosophy, and Mythology,—are all such as enter into direct relationship to religion. Ethics is an integral part of religion, the field of Philosophy overlaps that of religion, and Mythology is closely bound up with religious belief. In the case of religion and Psychology, to which we now turn, the relationship is indirect. One can study any particular religion in all its phases without entering the province of psychology. In order to trace its history, to lay bare its doctrines, to examine its ethical principles, and to investigate its myths, a consistent application of historical methods is all that is required, but when we proceed further and endeavour to determine the causes of its growth, to penetrate to the secret of its influence and to account for its decline, historical research needs to be supplemented by a study of human nature. The religious instinct, though first aroused, as we have seen, by the aid of an intellectual process, is essentially of an emotional quality.

It follows that, since this instinct is present in all the phases of religious development through which mankind passes, the emotions are invariably brought

18

into play in religious manifestations. To such an extent is this the case, that, as will be recalled, some thinkers—notably Schleiermacher—have been inclined to seek in the emotions the real strength and main support of religion. One-sided as such an attitude towards religion is, the frequent predominance of the appeal to the feelings made by many religions over the appeal to the intellect cannot be denied, and even where such predominance does not exist, an appreciation of the actual influence exerted by any religion, and by religion in general, is impossible unless we enter sympathetically into the peculiar workings of the human heart. The imagination, the will, the passions are brought into requisition, all the senses are frequently appealed to in religious cults, and the reaction of the senses upon the mind must therefore be appreciated if we would understand the power of religion itself.

II.

In view of this it seems rather strange that until the last century the psychological study of religion should have been almost entirely neglected. Neither Spinoza nor Leibnitz, neither the French Deists nor the French Materialists, endeavour to establish the relations which exist between the play of the emotions and the nature of religious belief.

Even the English Idealists and Kant do not appear to appreciate the full force of the problem, and what Hegel and his followers understand by the "psychology of religion" is merely speculation as to the subjective side of certain religious doctrines. Schleiermacher is among the first, by the emphasis which he lays upon "feeling" in religion, to direct investigations into this channel, the immediate result of which was to lead thinkers like Feuerbach, in a natural reaction from the exaggerated sentimentality of Schleiermacher's view of religion, to the conclusion that all religion was but a psychological illusion. Starting with an emotion and feeding upon emotions, it was held that there was no external reality corresponding to the sensations aroused by religious belief. Hartmann in part gives his adherence to this view, though only in part,[1] for he appreciates the difficulties involved in supposing religion to be altogether illusionary; but it is to the "New Psychology," which arose too late to influence Hartmann materially, that we owe the demarcation between emotion and thought in religion. The modern school of Psychologists, under the leadership of Wilhelm Wundt, has set itself the problem of determining, from a study of the physiology of man, the character of what are commonly regarded as psychic phenomena.

Until a short time ago the investigations of this school were confined largely to the study of mental impressions, dreams, illusions, hallucinations, the rapidity of thought, sensations of pain and pleasure, and language concepts, but quite recently there are indications of the extension of the scope to religious phenomena.

The first larger attempt to apply the new physiological-psychological method to the sphere of religion has been made by E. D. Starbuck,[2] who takes up so

---

[1] See *Die Religion des Geistes*, particularly pp. 16-18.

[2] *The Psychology of Religion* (Contemporary Science Series), London, 1899.

significant a phenomenon as "religious conversion," and endeavours to determine, by means of an elaborate series of statistics, the conditions of age, of temperament, and of surroundings favourable to its taking place.

Professor Starbuck has done well to choose as his theme a phenomenon that does not belong to the class of the "abnormal," but is consequent upon the educational and religious influences to which most persons in occidental countries are subjected. It is from similar investigations, applied to other phases of religion, that we may expect to reach clarified views as to the peculiar workings of the religious spirit in man. Much, too, may be expected from statistical studies of religious hallucinations, and from such "pathological" phenomena as religious mysticism.

At the same time it is well to recognise the necessary limits of such psychological studies. The tone of assurance assumed by some of the modern psychologists, as though the new science would finally solve all the mysteries of life, is not justified. While it is true, as Leuba has recently pointed out,[1] that a large part of the necessary groundwork of a philosophy of religion is furnished by psychology and psychological analysis, yet his severe arraignment of the historians and philosophers of religion is unwarranted and merely illustrates that same one-sidedness with which he charges others. If his utterances may be taken as an indication of the present trend of psychological investigation, the fundamental error of the new method consists in assigning too large a place to the merely subjective phenomena of religion. Religious

[1] "Introduction to a Psychological Study of Religion," *Open Court*, 1901, pp. 195-225.

emotions do not by any means constitute the whole of religion. They form the starting-point of speculations which sooner or later pass over into the domain of pure reason, and when this transition has taken place, the play of the intellect reacts upon the emotions, and eventually secures control over them. Leuba complains that the investigators of religion, however much they may differ among themselves, have represented the situation as though the existence of a god (or a superior power of some kind) were the real problem involved, whereas this question is suggested by purely practical considerations, hinging ultimately upon the relation, or supposed relation, of man to this power. In offering this criticism he appears, however, to overlook the fact with which the historian of religion is confronted at the outset of his investigations—that it is precisely some practical consideration which brings the religious emotions into play. The mere impression—to a large extent involuntary—made upon man by the circumstances in his own life, and by the life of nature around him, would spend its force without leading to any issue were it not that these impressions are brought by him into connection with real necessities involved in existence. Granting that the earliest manifestations of religious life are purely instinctive, still they are also called forth by a recognition, however faint, of the possibility of establishing proper relations between man and the universe about him. There is, therefore, involved in the religious life of man from the very start a problem capable of taking on a philosophical aspect, and the persistence of this problem, as much as the persistence of religious emotions, constitutes the connecting link between the most primitive and the most advanced religious phenomena. The explanation for the emotions themselves belongs properly to psychology, and in this domain much is to be expected from the new school, of which Starbuck and Leuba are worthy representatives; and in view of the part played by the emotions, even in the highest forms of intellectual activity, psychology is an indispensable factor in the study of all phases of religion and of all periods in its history.

At the same time, the very principle upon which the new psychology rests, the interdependence between the play of the emotions and the physiological accompaniments of such play, suggests another necessary limit to investigations of this order. Although we may have determined what physiological phenomena accompany certain emotions, we have not yet answered the question as to the cause of these emotions. The workings of the human mind remain no less mysterious after we have laid bare the conditions under which pleasure and pain are experienced, and have determined what nerve-centres are set in motion when the sense of fear or of awe or of joy is aroused. Physiological psychology leads us further into the domain of soul-life than speculative Philosophy, but it, too, must confess its inability to explore the innermost recesses of this mysterious domain. There will, it is safe to say, remain many a query to which psychology will be unable to give an answer, and above all, the primary question—what is it that makes us conscious of possessing something which, for want of a better term, we have been accustomed to speak of as soul-life? The true value of the new psychology consists in enabling us, by a keener and more scientific appreciation of the emotional side of human nature and of the manner in which the human brain performs its functions, to strike a proper balance between the play of the emotions and the control of the intellect. The physiological study of the brain having determined what psychic manifestations are due to diseased states or to abnormal conditions, a safe standard is secured by means of which to distinguish between healthy and sound manifestations of the religious spirit and such as are due to influences, affecting either individuals or entire communities, which lead of necessity to eccentricities, and to more or less harmful aberrations in religion.

Despite the fact that the "new psychology" has scarcely outgrown its swaddling clothes, and that there is a vast amount of work, particularly in the investigation of religious phenomena, still to be done, the results of the elaborate study of brain functions[1] and of hypnotism and insanity are of considerable import, and have a direct bearing on the psychological study of religion.

III.

The large scope of the psychological study of religion is thus apparent. In a sense it covers the whole horizon of religious experience, but it is concerned more particularly with the emotional aspects of religion.

The observation has long since been made, that the main difference between an educated and an ignorant

---

[1] See especially the works of Wundt himself; the *Philosophische Studien*, edited by Wundt, and containing the investigations of his pupils; the monographs of Hall, Ladd, Joseph Jastrow, Cattell, Baldwin, Witmer, Scripture; and the *Amer. Journal of Psychology*, edited by G. Stanley Hall.

person is the extent to which the emotions are
controlled by the intellect. The child and the man
of primitive culture stand in this respect on about the
same level. Both are largely at the mercy of the
impressions they receive. It follows that in the
earliest forms of religion the emotional phases are
predominant. Fear and hope are easily excited;
and while, as we have seen, the origin of religion is in
part dependent upon a process of reasoning, the very
simplicity of this process is due to the large part that
the emotions have in it.

The whole process of the religious development of
man may indeed be viewed as a constant struggle
between the emotions and the intellect, in which
the latter gradually obtains the mastery. It is
the intellect which makes the first attempt to classify
and systematise the impressions that through man's
contact with nature crowd in upon him. By
slow degrees he comes to control his fears, and
through the influence of the intellect, the spiritual
element which we have seen present in man's
earliest perception of the Infinite is linked to his
moral impulses, and the bond is thus brought
about between religion and ethics which we have
discussed in a previous chapter. The most significant
result of the gradual mastery of the intellect over the
emotions is the crystallisation of confused impressions
into religious doctrines. As the perception of the
Infinite from being faint and indefinite becomes more
sharply outlined, the doctrine of supernatural powers
takes shape. The idea of the Divine that first " wells
up in consciousness" (to borrow Spencer's famous
phraseology) is taken up by the intellect and becomes
a theory of God's government of the universe. The

belief in the immortality of the soul similarly starts
up in man as an intuition—suggested by his hopes
and fears—and only afterwards is it unfolded as a
genuine doctrine. The suggestion that certain
persons are divinely inspired, and that to their
utterances, therefore, extraordinary value is to be
attached, does not arise from a process of reasoning,
but from the awe inspired by individuals whose
appearance strikes the observer as abnormal, or whose
actions deviate from conventional lines ; and when
we come to a " mystery " like the Trinity, it is even
more evident that the doctrine is later than the belief,
and represents the crystallisation of emotions, impressions, and sensations which were at first vague and
undefined.

The control of the intellect over the emotions never
becomes absolute, and there is a point at which the
strongest intellect succumbs to the force of unre-
strainable feelings. As a consequence, even the
development of doctrines into a hard and fast
bound system of theology does not altogether drive
out the play of the emotions in religion, which are
given free scope in the cult of even the most advanced religions. A purely intellectual cult is almost
a contradiction in terms, for unless in religious
worship an appeal to the emotions is also included,
it degenerates into a cold scholastic exercise, devoid
of all real influence on the individual. This feature
is recognised by even rationalistic thinkers, and the
only question is how far the intrusion of the emotions on the intellectual life is to be permitted.
It is evident that if the emotions are allowed untrammelled scope in the cult, the result is a species
of hysterical performances, such as the ecstatic

dance of the dervishes, bacchanalian orgies, and camp meeting exercises, which cannot be regarded as promoting the healthier religious instincts. On the other hand, the suppression of the emotions is scarcely less harmful, and in our days, when all conditions favour such suppression, emphasis should be laid upon the value of allowing our emotions freer play. There is a decided tendency, as intellectual growth leads to refinement of feeling, to become afraid, as it were, of our own emotions, as though they necessarily lead us astray, whereas, as a matter of fact, emotions, as long as they are kept within bounds by the control of the intellect, may safely be followed as a guide in determining conduct. Applying this principle to the religious cult, it is eminently proper for our emotions to be aroused by soul-stirring chants, by the resonant peals of an organ, and even by symbolical acts—such as are prescribed by the Catholic Church—which affect the sense of smell. The proper limits of the process are not hard to draw. Where the appeal to the emotions reaches a point which is so extreme as to destroy self-control, the borderland has been crossed, and we have entered the dangerous region of religious hysteria.

The emotions being the basis, as has been pointed out, for the development of religious doctrines, the vital question suggests itself, as to how far those doctrines may be regarded as corresponding to reality. If religious belief is a structure built upon a subjective psychical foundation, is there any escape from the conclusion of Feuerbach that all religion is an illusion? The "new psychology," in demonstrating that processes of thought are as distinctly physiological in

character as the play of the emotions, suggests a way
out of the dilemma.   There is no reason why impressions made upon our feelings should be less trustworthy than those made upon our thoughts.   The
workings of our intellect being as distinctly psychological as the play of our emotions, the evidence based
on the latter is as worthy of serious consideration as
the data of the former; and since the intellect, as little
as the emotions, is able to take us outside of ourselves,
all that can fairly be demanded is a correspondence
between the data furnished by the two.   To be sure,
if it is claimed that religious belief to be acceptable
must have the stamp of absolute certainty attached to
it, the attitude of those who regard religion as an
illusion would be justified, but Hartmann well points
out [1] that all that need be expected of religious belief
is that it should possess a measure of probability.
Religious belief is to be regarded as a working hypothesis—like so many hypotheses assumed by science
—to be accepted because best answering the required
conditions.   Absolute certainty (unless based on the
theory of a special Revelation) being out of the
question, whether we rely upon the evidences of our
reason or on our imagination, it follows that reasonable certainty may be supplied at least in part by
our emotions, and not exclusively by our intellect.
Confidence in the doctrines set up by religions need
not be shaken because these doctrines rest ultimately
on emotions or on pure intuition.   The test of
these doctrines is their correspondence with results
reached by an intellectual process.   It might be
supposed that we could still go further, and in case
of a contradiction between the emotions and the

[1] *Die Religion des Geistes*, p. 16.

intellect, give preference to the former instead of to the latter. Thinking and feeling being both purely subjective processes, this position would be justified but for one circumstance, namely, that we are so constructed that the *normal* being revolts against such a concession to the emotions. If the concession, however, is made, the result is Mysticism, Spiritualism, Christian Science, and similar religious phenomena, which, whatever else may be said of them, represent the willing or unwilling surrender of the emotions to the intellect.

We are thus led by the psychological study of religion to set up a standard by means of which we may test, not indeed the absolute truth of religious belief, but the normal and sound character of belief as against "abnormal" and pathological manifestations of the religious instinct. This test is to be applied not merely to individuals but to movements affecting an entire community, or a portion of it. The mystic from this point of view is an "abnormal" phenomenon. Through contemplation and introspection he reaches a certain conception of God and the universe, but the very strength of his conviction is due to the reliance he places upon his intuition, and while mental processes undoubtedly enter into every "mystic" system, the correspondence between thought and reality is intentionally neglected. The pathological phenomena of religion are naturally of great interest to the student, often much more so than the normal manifestations. There are periods in the religious life of every people when in consequence of some extraordinary occurrence—an earthquake, a plague, an invasion—the emotions of the masses are stirred up to such an extent as to lead to strange

religious outbreaks.   Such were, in the Middle Ages,
the dancing manias[1] which seized hold of entire
districts, such the processions of the Flagellists.[2]
Again, in days marked by excess of intellectualism,
accompanied by extravagant tastes in modes of living,
there is apt to be a turning of the current of religions
into the muddy streams of mysticism of one kind
or another.   Such a period sets in in Greece and
Rome when faith in the ancient gods begins to
decline, and instead of a purification of this faith, we
find primitive religious ideas imported from the
Orient and with a mystic interpretation, taking the
place of the ancient faith, until young and vigorous
Christianity sweeps like a fresh breeze across the
ancient world, and brushes away the cobwebs of
mysticism and superstition.   Later on, Christianity
itself, in some of its phases, falls a victim to exaggerated emotional tendencies, with the result of
encouraging morbid views of life, as emphasised in
the ascetic orders.   Judaism and Islam likewise
have their "emotional" periods, leading in the
case of the former to a complete sway of cabal-
istic lore which, beginning in the eleventh century,
still maintains its hold upon large bodies of Jewish
communities in eastern Europe.   In Islam we
encounter in the Sufites one of the most significant
of mystic sects, besides many others marked by
strange teachings and by hysterical cults.[3]   As for
Buddhism, it still retains the impress of indifference

[1] See J. T. Hecker, *Dancing Mania of the Middle Ages* (translated
by B. J. Babbington).

[2] Wm. W. Cooper, *Flagellation and the Flagellants*, London, 1896.

[3] See J. P. Brown, *The Dervishes, or The Oriental Spiritualism*,
London, 1868; Guyard, *Fragments relatifs à la Doctrine des
Ismaelis*, Paris, 1874.

to reality given to it by its founder, and evinces an inexhaustible vitality in producing a succession of mystic sects.[1]

From this very brief survey it will be seen that pathological phenomena form no inconsiderable feature in the religious life of mankind. There is no religion which is entirely without its pathological side and its abnormal manifestations. There are religious communities and religious sects which, whatever else their merits be, the psychologist cannot view in any other light but as diseased manifestations of the religious spirit, produced by overexcitation of the emotions, and it may indeed be questioned whether there are many individuals who at some period of their career have not been subject to "unhealthy" religious influences and affected by them in some way.

The study of these pathological phenomena of religion with the aid of psychology thus becomes a matter of practical importance as well as of theoretical interest; and at the present time, when there are indications of a reaction against over-intellectualism, which accounts for the hold which such movements as Spiritualism, Theosophy (in the current acceptation), and Christian Science have taken upon the intelligent elements of the public, this study is of special moment.[2]   Only in this way can we expect to keep a watch on our religious development and distinguish between healthy and diseased tendencies in the religious life of our times.

---

[1] Hopkins, *Religions of India*, chap. xvii.

[2] See a chapter on "The Modern Occult" in Joseph Jastrow's *Fact and Fable in Psychology*, Boston, 1900.

IV.

The aspects of the "new psychology" must not make us indifferent to another phase of the psychological study of religion which deals with the purely subjective features of religious belief and religious practice. Until the "new psychology" arose it was the determination of these features, their character, sub-divisions, and scope that constituted all of what was known as the "Psychology of Religion."

One might perhaps relegate these aspects of religion to the "philosophy of religion," where philosophers like Hegel and Schelling treated them, but there is a good deal to be said in favour of dealing with them under the head of psychology. The sphere of the philosophy of religion is properly the tracing of the chief ideas running through the various historical religions. But since these ideas stand in close connection with the history and culture of a country, they are not as specifically and exclusively psychological in character as is the substructure of religious belief, which belongs to all forms of religion, and which is directly due to the bent of the human mind. But whether we place the subjective phases of belief under philosophy or psychology, one is justified in protesting against any attempt to relegate these phases to the background, as of no importance for the historical study of religions.

Important as the results of the "new psychology" are, and however significant future experimental researches may be, the "old psychology," which concerns itself with the speculative study of human nature, will still retain its place. Experiment and speculation are not deadly antagonists, and there is no reason why they should not supplement each other.

Perhaps the most satisfactory outline of the subjective phase of religion in recent times is the one embodied by Hartmann in his profound and suggestive *Philosophy of Religion*,[1] though it requires supplementing in an essential particular. Starting with a twofold division of what he calls the "religious function" into the individual human phase and into the mutual human and divine phase, he distinguishes between the religious function as a concept, as feeling, and as will.

The religious function of necessity requires an object upon which to direct its attention. This object is, according to Hartmann, in every case, God. It will be seen that his use of the latter term is peculiarly wide. He does not connect with it any special conception, and it includes the most primitive notion of a personified power of nature, as well as the most advanced conception of a single Power controlling the universe. An essential quality of the object of the religious function is that it must be regarded as superior to the subject, which is man. In agreement with the conclusion we reached in a previous chapter, Hartmann defines the religious function as the establishment of the relation between the subject and the object, between man and God. The representation of an object of some kind is thus not only the first requisite to religion, but man is unintentionally led to conceive of an object superior to him, transcendental in character, and with which he can enter into some kind of relationship.

The religious function, in the second place, manifests itself as feeling. In view of what has already

[1] Part II. " Die Religion des Geistes," A., *Religionspsychologie*, pp. 1 *et seq.*

been said, it is needless to enlarge upon this phase, which imparts life to the concept. It is the emotions, as Hartmann well says,[1] which reveal to us the deepest abysses and the highest peaks of the religious life.

The religious function as will, is merely the natural impulse towards giving expression to one's concepts and feelings. Hartmann defines religious will as the Alpha and Omega of religion.[2] The determination of man to establish by his conduct and by his symbolical acts, a communion between himself and God leads to ethics, which, even in its highest form, cannot sever itself from the religious function without becoming a stiff and rigorous morality, devoid of any spiritual glow.

It is not necessary to follow Hartmann in his interpretation of these three phases of the religious function in order to recognise them as convenient sub-divisions of one of the provinces of the psychological study of religion. It is the part of psychology to determine the mental conditions under which religious concepts are formed, and, by a study of the feelings and will, to determine the scope of these phases.

But concept, feelings, and will, embracing as they do the entire psychological activity of man, constitute the religious disposition of man, and may thus be viewed under a single aspect. By virtue of its relationship to God, this disposition has its natural outcome in "belief." Every religious act is at the same time an expression of religious belief. Since, however, as we have seen, this belief is not merely the result of an intellectual process, but in its earliest form, as the perception of the Infinite, is furnished

[1] *Ib.*, page 29. [2] *Ib.*, page 55.

in conjunction with the emotions, religious belief manifests two sides,—(*a*) what to the religious mind is "revelation" as against (*b*) intellectual belief. An ultimate agreement between the two is essential to the healthy growth of religion. In the earliest form of religion this correspondence is always to be found, and it is only when the intellect progresses rapidly that a conflict between revelation and intellectual belief arises which must eventually lead to an adaptation of the former to the latter.

By the side of pure belief, man also experiences the longing to be happy, or, negatively expressed, to be relieved from evil. An analysis of the evil to which man is subject shows that it consists of two kinds—misfortune and sin. From Hartmann's pessimistic point of view, both are due to the necessary constitution of things, and man's dependence upon the universe is thus the ultimate cause of all the ills that human flesh is heir to.

The desire for the release from pain is the practical phase of the religious function as feeling, and Hartmann is undoubtedly correct in regarding this desire as inherent in all forms of religion, though more prominently dwelt upon in some—notably Buddhism and Christianity—than in others.

The practical exercise of the religious function as will in the relationship between man and God, leads to the accommodation of the human to the divine will, or what is regarded as such. Moral freedom and moral energy thus represent the highest goal of religion. Hartmann fails to include in his outline of the psychological phases of religion the psychological basis of the religious cult. His discussion has reference almost solely to the subjective phases of belief, but the forms of worship are no less an expression of mental states than religious concepts, and the longing for release from evil.

De la Grasserie, in his *Psychologie des Religions* (Paris, 1898), endeavours to make good this defect, and devotes an equal share of attention to religious doctrines and to religious cults, but his investigation, valuable as it is in some respects, lacks system, and he fails to bring out the salient psychological features in the cult. We may distinguish two such features— sacrifice and adoration. The former, which plays so large a part in all religions, has its source in the natural disposition of man to pay homage to the object of "the religious function." It matters little that this homage is, originally, at least, suggested by selfish motives for the purpose of securing the protection and aid of God, who, to retain Hartmann's phraseology, is this object, and that no sacrifice is made without some ulterior motive, for behind this motive there is still the instinct of reverence for something regarded as superior, and the instinct of gratitude for a performed service. Without these instincts it is inconceivable that the religious spirit should manifest itself in a form which certainly involves reverence and gratitude as factors. Similarly, adoration, though again suggested by selfish motives, and including the direct appeal for some divine favour, is nevertheless due ultimately to a feeling of awe and devotion, inspired by the thought of a superior and transcendental power.

V.

There are thus two aspects to the psychological study of religion, one proceeding largely by experi-

mental research with a view of determining the mental
conditions under which the religious instinct is aroused,
and the underlying psychological causes for both the
normal and abnormal phenomena of religion, for the
hold which certain doctrines have on mankind, and for
the strange freaks appearing in religious history; the
other largely speculative, concerned with the substratum of belief, and seeking to determine the various
ways in which the religious instinct manifests itself,
both in religious doctrines and in the cult.

Through the former we will be able to account for
the various phenomena coming under the head of
animism, the rise and spread of such movements
as mysticism, spiritualism, theosophy, and Christian
Science, affecting entire communities, while the study
of the individual mind will throw light on the secret
of the power acquired by leaders of religious thought,
and will also make clear the reasons which lead the
thought of one man towards pantheistic conceptions
of the universe, of another towards mysticism, and
of a third towards genuine or apparent atheism.
Speculative psychology, on the other hand, will
enable us to realise the elements essential to every
form of religion, and why certain features are
embodied in all religious cults.   It is only through
the combination of these two aspects of the
psychological study of religion, that we can be led to
determine the exact relation existing between
religion and psychology.   This relation, as pointed out
at the beginning of this chapter, is indirect.

Psychology has important bearings, not on the
truth or falsity of the contents of any particular
religion, but on the general nature of religious belief,
and on the character of the manifestations of the

religious instinct. Its most important practical
function, as clearly indicated, lies in the fact that it
furnishes us with a standard by means of which to
distinguish healthy religious phenomena from such
as are either due to diseased mental conditions,
affecting for a time or permanently individuals or
entire communities, or are " abnormal " in consequence
of a surrender of the intellect to the emotions.

No less significant, however, is the bearing of
psychology on two vital questions, the one as to the
permanency of religion and the other as to ultimate
justification of religious belief.

The study of the human mind by experimental
and speculative research confirms the conclusion that,
however profound may be the modifications which
religion will undergo, religion, as such, can never
disappear. The " religious instinct," or the " religious
function," or by whatever other name we choose to
call it, is an integral part of human nature. Man is
forced to attach himself to some object regarded as
higher than himself, and conceived of as transcendental. His speculations about this object cannot
suppress his longing for it, and even though he proves
to his satisfaction that the object has no existence
outside of his brain, the " yearning after the Infinite "
still haunts his restless spirit.

But are we justified in supposing that because the
basis of all belief is psychological, that this belief does
not conform to any reality? Psychology can as little
give a definite answer to this query as can philosophy. Bounded as we are by the limitations of a
finite intellect, the old Kantian problem is ever and
anon stirred up,—we cannot know things as they really
are. We can only see with *our* eyes, and think with

our minds ; but once admitting that in some way
—whatever the solution of the problem we adopt—
there is a reliable correspondence between the image
on the retina as conveyed to the mind, and the
object itself, the psychological study of religion must
strengthen our confidence in the correspondence
between the natural impulse to predicate an object
on which to exercise an inherent instinct or function,
and the reality.

In addition to this, the " new psychology " justifies
the position that the play of the emotions is not to be
set aside as an unreliable guide, but, on the contrary,
furnishes us with a view of reality which, if not
reliable to the same degree as are the postulates of
reason, is of direct value in clarifying our relationship to the universe. If, in addition to this, it be borne
in mind that all we are called upon to look for in
testing the value of religious belief is probability of
truth, psychology, by establishing the proper balance
between the emotions and the intellect, is of direct
help in determining what classes of beliefs are probable. By a purely intellectual process we can
scarcely expect to reach satisfactory conclusions on
this point. As at the beginning of man's religious
development, the emotional element in his nature
enters into play, so even the most advanced thought
needs an emotional spark in order to kindle it into
a glowing flame. As long as intuitions, yearnings,
and faint perceptions do not conflict with the results
or even the trend of thought, there is no reason
why they should not be put to service in man's
endeavour to obtain the highest possible degree
of probability for his religious beliefs. Such an
attitude does no violence to the authority of reason,

nor does it involve a surrender of our reason to human authority, which Balfour[1] regards as essential to the establishment of belief. A surrender of this kind cannot seriously be considered without opening the door again to the abuse of human authority, of which the history of religion furnishes so many examples, but by linking reason to the feelings, by the combined effort of the healthy intellect and the sane emotions, that measure of probability in religious belief will be reached which must satisfy us. Is it so hard to resign ourselves to this recognition of the limitations of human power?

Surely the achievements of man, despite his limitations, form not only a consolation, but also an assurance that just as by means of working hypotheses in science and art, great results are obtained, so also in the domain of religion, beliefs which have proved a help and a stimulus to mankind, which have helped to establish high standards of conduct and have promoted lofty ideals, which have stirred men to deeds of valour and to acts of goodness, which have consoled millions, and illumined at some time the path of every individual who has walked on this world of ours—such beliefs may surely be accepted as a working hypothesis which, by virtue of the actual tests to which it has been put in the long and chequered career of humanity, corresponds to that absolute reality which will always remain "the mystery of mysteries."

[1] Balfour, *The Foundations of Belief*, Part I., Chap. III , and Part III., Chap. II.

CHAPTER X.

RELIGION AND HISTORY.

THE most notable element in the relationship of religion to history is the gradual separation of religion from the political organisation of a people. In the earliest stages of religion, to be sure, religion appears to be something apart from both the political and social life of a community. Whatever cult there was, appeared to concern individuals rather than the community at large; but the moment that an organisation of this cult assumes a fixed shape, partly by the force of tradition, partly through the influence of individuals within the community, the cult, and with the cult also the doctrines, become linked to the fortunes of the people as a whole. As the community develops into a state, religion becomes an affair of the state.

This is the general condition in the ancient Orient and Occident; and it is perhaps best exemplified in the case of the Greek states, where citizenship was so closely bound up with religion, that no one could become a Greek citizen without adopting the worship of the Greek gods.[1] In centres such as Babylonia, Palestine, and Egypt, where admission of foreigners to citizenship was not regarded as a

[1] Fustel de Coulanges, *The Ancient City*, chap. i.

possibility, it was considered even more as a matter
of course that religion was as much a part of the state
as were military affairs and the execution of justice.
Closely bound up with this intimate association was
the view, current at even the most advanced stage of
ancient civilisation, which limited the jurisdiction of
the gods to certain districts. The gods, originally personifications of nature, became local deities, as religion became a part of political life; and only by the
enlargement of a town into a district is the god of the
town supposed to extend his sway. The ultimate
limit of this process is reached when the city
becomes the centre of an empire—as in the case
of Babylonia, where the chief god of the city of
Babylon, Marduk, became the head of a Pantheon,
extending his jurisdiction over a territory equal to
Babylonian control. This extension, however, does
not interfere with the local cults, nor does it affect
the position of gods supposed to preside over the
destiny of other nations. In so far as these gods
are associated with a certain territory, they retain
their authority. Hence when the Assyrians, after
conquering the kingdom of Israel, sent people from
other conquered districts to take the place of Israelites
deported from their homes, the new-comers are not
urged to adopt the Assyrian cult, but quite naturally
seek out the god of the place, who happened to be
Jahweh,[1] and endeavour to secure safety from besetting dangers by proper devotion to him. Despite,
therefore, the comparatively high state reached by
religious thought in Babylonia and Egypt, as exemplified more particularly in their religious literature,
despite even an apparently close theoretical approach

[1] 2 Kings xvii. 25-29.

to Monotheism,[1] the barrier represented by the union
of the national existence and the religious cult was
overthrown in each of these two empires as little as
it was in the case of Greece and Rome. The first
decisive step in the direction of a divorce between
the two factors was taken by the Hebrews, among
whom, under the leadership of the exilic and post-
exilic Prophets, the doctrine arises that Jahweh's
jurisdiction is not territorially limited. None of the
earlier prophets, indeed, went so far as to declare that
Jahweh was not essentially the national deity of the
Hebrews, but they suggested the possibility of a
divorce between religion and the state. Isaiah and
Jeremiah shock the prejudices of the age by declaring
that Jahweh might not only survive the destruction
of his central seat in Jerusalem, but would contribute
to the downfall of his people because of his displeasure with them. The continuance of the Jahweh
cult among the Judæans deported to Babylonia was
the triumph of a new conception of religion.

An example was furnished for the first time in
human history of the worship of a deity "without a
country," by a people dwelling in a foreign land.
To be sure, the experiment was on a small scale, for
probably not many of the Hebrews actually took
part in Jahweh worship conducted in Babylonian
cities, but this in no way affects the importance of
the step. The return of the Hebrews to Jerusalem
under the edict of Cyrus, and the restoration of
Jahweh worship at Jerusalem, checked to a certain
extent the further growth of the doctrine that religious worship could be separated from a visible
centre for a natural deity, but it could not altogether

---

[1] Jastrow, *Religion of Babylonia and Assyria*, p. 696.

stamp out this view   The restoration of the Jews
to their country was never carried out completely.
Indeed the numbers of those who lived outside of
their native land, notably in Babylonia and Egypt,
and later on in Rome and the Roman provinces,
continued to increase until they far exceeded the
Jewish population in Palestine.   The teachings of
the prophets bore fruit in bringing about the
attachment of these scattered Jewish colonies to the
cult at Jerusalem, which, from being the seat of
Jahweh as a tribal god, became a spiritual centre for
the worship of a god practically deprived of political
power, and depending upon the fidelity of subjects
bound to him by spiritual rather than by moral ties.
The lack of political independence was a powerful
factor in leading to the establishment of the doctrine
that Jahweh's seat was "a house of worship for all
nations."[1]   The ethical monotheism of the pre-exilic
prophets became, in theory at least, universal monotheism in post-exilic days; as this idea progressed,
a struggle naturally ensued between national and
religious ideals.   The majority of Jews still clung
to the old idea that religious life could not be
divorced from political organisation, but when the
final conquest of Jerusalem by the Romans dashed
the hopes of the Jewish patriots, the new idea gained
a notable triumph.

It was reserved for the young and vigorous offshoot of Judaism, Christianity, to carry the prophetical
doctrine of universal monotheism into the remotest
corners of the ancient world.   Those who clung to
the old faith were likewise impelled, through the
destruction of the visible centre of the old national

[1] Isa. lvi. 7.

cult, to give to their worship of the universal god a purely spiritual character; but, not fully weaned from the union between national organisation and religious cult, they sought to maintain their natural identity amidst such adverse circumstances by punctilious observance of elaborate regulations controlling all phases of private life, and by looking forward ever to a restoration of the national cult.

But Christianity, too, was unable practically to carry out the theory which forms one of its foundation-stones. As it made its way into the western world, the doctrine of the union of political and religious life once more came to the front, though in a modified form. When Christianity became the official religion of the Roman Empire, the doctrines of the church derived their authority from the political organisation of the empire. The universal monotheism of the prophets accorded with the theory of a single universal empire upon which the Roman Empire was founded. One state and one church in inseparable union became the political and religious creed of the times. We no longer find national deities or tribal gods exercising jurisdiction over limited districts and conditioning the title of citizenship in a community, but under the modified form of church and state the old union between political and religious life is not only continued, but emphasised during the Middle Ages with a vigour and consistency which is unparalleled in ancient days.

The Protestant Reformation marks the first indication of the weakening of this union. The schism in the church resulted in imparting to the claim of one church and one state, a theoretical rather than a

practical character, and as independent states increase in number, the possibilities of a practical
realisation of the hope become still further diminished. Within the separate states or kingdoms,
likewise, the union between the political and religious organisation, though maintained, manifested
a steady tendency towards disruption. The growth
of the ideas of religious liberty and of civil freedom
contribute to the weakening of the union until, with
the advent of the French Revolution, the important
step is taken, first in France, and then in other
countries, which divorces citizenship from adherence
to the official creed.

Bound, however, by the force of tradition, the
European kingdoms still clung to the association of
religion with political organisation, and it was reserved
for the republic established at the close of the last
century in America to set the example in its constitution of a complete divorce of church and state.
The republics of South America and of Switzerland
followed in the footsteps of the United States,
whereas, in the Republic of France, a curious compromise was effected, granting to the various large
church organisations—the Catholic, the Protestant,
and the Jewish—state recognition and state support.
Such an arrangement amounts practically to an
establishment of the principle of divorce of church
and state. Historic events, as well as the trend of
thought, point to the continuance of the movement
which, unless an unforeseen reaction ensues, will
eventually lead everywhere to the theoretical recognition of what has practically been secured—the
complete divorce of the religious life from the political
organisation and from the control of the state.

This evolution of a certain phase of religion is of special interest, because it affords the best illustration of the interrelation between history and religion. There are other phases of religion, the development of which is likewise bound up with historical evolution, and if we turn to the religious history of India and to the history of Islam, we shall detect the same conditions. What applies to the larger aspects of religious evolution also holds good for the development of religious thought, which is not merely dependent upon intellectual conditions prevailing in a country, but upon historical occurrences. There is in the religious life of every people a constant flow and ebb conditioned upon the circumstances by which a people finds itself surrounded. There are periods of religious activity followed by ages of apparent inertia ; religious faith manifests at times great vitality only to sink back into seeming lethargy. The observation has been made that a great national excitement, such as war, leads to the increase of religious faith, whereas long periods of peace promote religious scepticism. Commercial prosperity, again, dulls the religious sensibilities of a people, and they receive new strength when national calamities — such as a famine or a commercial panic—ensue.

It may be confidently asserted, therefore, that every movement in religious history assuming the proportion of national importance stands in some connection with the trend of historic events. This aspect of the history of religion lends to the subject much of the interest which it arouses; it also imparts to this interest a vitality which it would not otherwise possess. The bond between history and religion illustrates better than any long argument could dis-

close, the way in which religion enters as an important
factor—in many respects the most important factor—
in the course taken by human history. Every step
forward in that course is not only accompanied by
changed religious conditions, but religion itself largely
brings about this step; and it must be sadly confessed that the reverse likewise is true, that religion
is often found to be a force aiding, if not impelling, a
movement that marks a decline from the highest
ideals of mankind. The very power which religion
possesses, its close connection with human history,
makes it a factor for evil as well as for good; and the
so-called crimes of religion, upon which those who
are hostile to it are wont to dwell, are illustrations of
the manner in which religion may blot the pages of
history. An impartial judgment, however, must
admit that religion, on the whole, has been a force
linked to progress, to justice, and even to political
advance. If some of its devotees have appeared to
put spokes in the wheel, it must not be forgotten that
more have put their shoulder to it and helped to
push the cart forward towards the goal. If church
organisation is often found to be in league with forces
that stand for political oppression, it must not be
overlooked that those who are arrayed on the other
side are no less the offspring of the church — the
children of some religious faith—than their opponents. And after all, the acts of individuals, and
even the attitude of large organisations, do not count
for as much as we are inclined to suppose in the
history of religion. Until studied closely, such acts
are apt to assume a much larger place than they in
reality deserve. To judge them in their proper proportion, we must consider the place taken by religion

in the history of mankind as revealed by a bird's-eye view from an eminence of impartial thought. Such a view reveals to us religion as a river winding its way across meadows and valleys, ravines and crevasses, now rushing with impetuous force, now sluggish, but always imparting to the landscape its general tone, lending life to it and feeding the soil.

CHAPTER XI.

RELIGION AND CULTURE.

I.

THE suggestion has already been thrown out that culture is, to a large extent, an offshoot of religion. The various arts and sciences are linked in their origin to religious beliefs, and to the mental stimulus that emanates from them. Medicine, though the most materialistic of the sciences, is at its origin the profession of the priest *par excellence*. To the priest people come for relief from ills, and he grants it by virtue of his closer touch with the gods and his control over the evil spirits which are supposed to cause the ills and worries of human flesh. The priest prescribed the magic formulas which would drive the evil spirits out of the body of the sufferer. He accompanied the utterances with medicaments or salutary advice, the efficacy of which was dependent again upon the proper performance of incantation rites.

The oldest tribunal is the sanctuary. To it parties went for a decision when a dispute arose, and it was the priest who sought by means of an oracle to discover what the pleasure of the local deity was. He indirectly stimulated the sense of right and wrong by encouraging the worshippers to carry out the will of the gods. To secure the favour of the latter may

20

appear to be far removed from an ethical standard of life, but the motive underlying the desire to stand well with the gods had at least an ethical colouring. As religion came to be more closely in touch with conduct, the execution of justice became the sole prerogative of the priest, who thus assumed directly the *rôle* of the promoter of right and the punisher of evil. Legislation in this way arose in connection with belief in the sanctity attached to the priest as the representative or controller of the deity

Astronomy is a science even more intimately associated with religion than Medicine and Law. The planets and the conspicuous stars being associated by the theories of the theologians[1] with certain deities, it was of importance to watch their movements and determine from coincident events what positions foreboded good and what presaged misfortune. The study of the heavens was followed with a minuteness in ancient Babylonia that testifies to the acuteness of the observations made by the priests, and it is not astonishing to find the latter becoming the teachers in astronomy to all of western Europe. The first steps in decorative art and in architecture were taken in connection with the desire to do homage to a god by beautifying his dwelling-place ; and long before the thought arose of making one's own dwelling more than a shelter against inclemencies of nature, a religious architecture had developed into respectable proportions.

Passing into the domain of pure thought, philosophy is originally identical with theology, and the literary talents of ancient nations were at first employed wholly in the service of religion, producing prayers,

[1] See Jastrow, *Religion of Babylonia and Assyria,* chap. xxii.

hymns, and rituals, while even the epics partook largely of a religious character   But while in the early stages of civilisation it was religion which produced culture and continued to give colour to it, the situation was reversed when, by the natural process of differentiation which accompanies progress in civilisation, the sciences and arts one by one cut themselves loose from the leading-strings of religion, and assumed an independent position.

The process was a slow one, though it was more rapid in the case of certain sciences and arts than in others. Medicine continues to this day in the orient to be associated with magic practices, and as long as the intimate union between Church and State prevailed, Law was not fully differentiated from religion even in Christian Europe. When astronomy cuts itself loose from religion there remains behind astrology clinging to the skirts of religion, until the latter itself throws astrology off.

II.

A feature of the process is the natural struggle which religion makes to retain her hold on her offspring. She instinctively feels that these children may turn against the parent, and her fears are well grounded. No sooner is astronomy well established as an independent science, than theories arise which contradict traditional views regarding the movements of the heavenly bodies. The observation of the workings of nature leads men to recognise the presence of immutable laws, which seem to make the intervention of the gods both superfluous and impossible. Medicine, once freed from association with religious practices, views with contempt the methods formerly in vogue for expelling disease; and on the other side, the votaries of religion looked upon the bold attempts of medicine in fighting disease as a trespass upon the Divine purpose.

Art and Music alone appear to have remained at all times on good terms with religion. For a longer time than Medicine, Law, and Astronomy, they continued to draw their inspiration from religious belief. Religious architecture, down to the Middle Ages, far exceeds in its grandeur and beauty secular architecture. The Greek sculptors to the latest period chose their subjects chiefly from the gods and from current myths; and the best specimens of the art of the Renaissance are the religious pictures of the Italian masters. But even painting and architecture finally became independent of religion, and likewise music—so long a valuable adjunct of the cult—became secularised.

The bitterest enemy, however, which religion encountered among her offspring was philosophy. From being the handmaid of theology, which appeared to be her function upon her first appearance as an independent discipline, she soon developed into a rival which threatened to displace theology entirely. All efforts to restrain the intellect of man from bursting the fetters with which religion attempted to chain it proved unavailing; and soon it appeared that men had to choose which mistress they were willing to serve—philosophy or theology The result of the struggle between medicine and magic was a divorce. Each went her own way, and magic continued to sway men's minds even after the independence of medicine was recognised by religion.

Similarly, Astronomy and Astrology entered upon a compromise, and the contempt of the astronomer for the astrologist in no way interfered with the popularity of the latter, who found a recompense in the converts he often made among the best intellects of the day. The hostility, however, between the philosopher and the theologian admitted of no *modus vivendi.* Philosophy, including as it did until recently both the natural sciences (under the designation natural philosophy) and speculative thought, covered the same field which religion regarded as her province. The so-called conflict between science and religion is largely the history of this struggle between philosophy and theology. In studying this conflict we must not commit the error of supposing those who stand on the side of theology to be necessarily the representatives of intellectual reaction. The philosophers had their vagaries as well as the theologians, and it was wholesome to have in theology a check upon the spreading of views and conclusions wholly unwarranted by the reasoning which the philosophers employed. The course taken by the history of philosophy is strewn with the wrecks of discarded systems, and the disagreement of the philosophers among themselves lent more than a semblance of justification to the warnings of the theologians against man's dependence upon his intellect. Indeed this conflict, as the conflict in general between religion and culture, must be viewed as a process essential towards bringing about true progress, on the one hand preventing errors from spreading too rapidly, and on the other, restraining superstitious beliefs from wholly engulfing man's intellect. The relation between religion and culture thus turns out in one of its phases to be an exceedingly peculiar one. Religion at first is the stimulus which produces the earliest definite manifestations of culture. It gives birth to the arts and sciences, and not only encourages all manner of intellectual pursuits, but presides over them. It is but natural to find religion at this stage also putting the various arts and sciences in her service. In the course of time one mental discipline after the other becomes independent of religious guidance, and a struggle arises as religion attempts to check this independence. The failure of the attempt changes the aspect of the relationship of religion to culture. Instead of religion being the inspiration of culture, it is culture which now endeavours to exercise an influence over religion, and with ever-growing success. This process appears in what is generally termed the conflict between science and religion, which is largely the struggle between philosophy and theology for intellectual supremacy.

III.

Various stages are to be distinguished in this process which is admirably set forth in the two standard works of Draper [1] and White,[2] but in every case the struggle ends by the accommodation of religious belief to the new conditions produced by important discoveries in the laws of nature, or by historical researches contradictory of traditional views and opinions. At the same time, the opposition manifested by religion, which in the

[1] *History of the Conflict between Religion and Science*, New York, 1875.

[2] *A History of the Warfare of Science with Theology in Christendom* (2 vols.), New York, 1896.

conflict with the new represents the conservative force, serves as a wholesome check in preventing the acceptance of the new in an immature state. It is erroneous, therefore, to view the later relation of religion and culture as a hostile one. Such is far from being the case, although it is true that religion, when once the arts and sciences have become independent of her guidance and authority, ceases to become an innovator, and assumes the *rôle* of the conservator. The function of the former may appear more attractive, but the importance of the latter is not diminished by this circumstance. Whether the task of the innovator is the more thankless, or that of the conservator the more gratuitous, is an idle question. He who serves the cause of civilisation in the hope of personal reward has mistaken his calling. The innovator often falls a martyr to his cause, and the conservator is just as frequently misunderstood and denounced as an enemy of progress.

Here, too, that same care must be exercised as in studying the relation of religion to history, not to exaggerate the importance of the individual or of organisations. In the case of the large movements in the history of mankind with which we are concerned, individuals and organisations are merely the instruments for carrying out certain ends, the value and meaning of which we are only able to discover after the process, of which the particular movement is a symptom, has come to an end, and the next step is about to be taken.

Before dismissing this subject, however, the question remains to be answered,—which is the ideal relation that should exist between religion and culture? The hands on the clock of time cannot be turned backward, and it is idle therefore to look forward to a period when religion shall again become the mainspring of intellectual and material progress. Nor is such a condition to be desired. The true sphere of religion lies elsewhere. • Its province is not the investigation of scientific problems nor the creation of new arts, but the directing of human life into proper channels, and the serving as a beacon light in illumining the path of mankind towards its goal, whatever we conceive that goal to be. On the other hand, it is most unfortunate when religion steps forward as an opponent of the free play of the intellect, or of scientific theories, or of movements looking to the improvement of the lot of humanity. In doing so, religion is unfaithful to herself, and always pays dearly for her error.

Recognising, as a historical study forces us to do, that religion is a permanent factor in human history, there must surely be a place for her consistent with the best interests of mankind. A feature in the earliest forms of religion which must strike the observer forcibly is the perfect accord existing between religious belief and actual knowledge of the universe. James Darmesteter, in a notable essay on "The Future of Religion," [1] dwells on this feature and sets it forth in an admirable way. While it is true that this accord is due to the circumstance that the religious guides at this early stage are also the depositories of knowledge, yet whatever science the priests, even in the form of oracle-seekers and soothsayers, possessed was the highest in existence, and indeed the only science known. Under the changed conditions,

---

[1] *Selected Essays of James Darmesteter*, p. 3 (Boston, 1895).

brought about by the process of civilisation, it is impossible for the representatives of religion to be such depositories. The task is one beyond the power of any individual, but the accord between belief and actual knowledge may still be set up as the proper ideal, regulating the relationship of religion to culture, and it is the true function of religious guides and religious thinkers to bring about this accord. It is also within their power to do so. With a sympathetic attitude towards new discoveries, and towards the result of researches, they can impart this attitude to their followers. Under such conditions, the conflict between science and religion ceases to be a quarrel urged by two opposing hosts, the one aiming at the destruction of the other, but the fruitful combination of the two factors essential to genuine progress—the factor of innovation and the factor of conservatism. The conflict itself may then go on, and indeed will necessarily go on, but each phase of it, instead of ending in a temporary truce or an unsatisfactory compromise, leading only to the renewal of the struggle, or in a forced submission on the part of religion or science, will produce results beneficial to art, science, and religion—religious belief becoming the representative of the most matured thought, and science held in wholesome check, lest in its vaulting ambition it overleap itself. Darmesteter, in the essay referred to, offers the alternative of science taking up the work of religion, or religion putting herself once more in accord with science. The former alternative is impossible, and Darmesteter himself points out, with dramatic force, how incapable science is of satisfying the spiritual hunger of mankind. She has no answer for the questionings of the human heart, she cannot still the yearnings of the soul; but while we cannot accept the conclusion that if religion is to maintain her place in modern life, she must again assume the guidance of thought, it is certainly not visionary to look forward to a time—not too far distant—when religion and science will once more be in that perfect accord which characterised religion in its earliest stages. Through the very fact that the tendency of religious development is to bring religion into closer touch with life,[1] it is essential for such an accord to be established in order to attain the best results from both.

IV.

In conclusion, it must again be emphasised that the conflict between science and religion represents but one phase of the relationship between culture and religion. There are other phases of culture which precipitate no conflict whatsoever. In this category belong inventions like the steam-engine, the telegraph, and the telephone, which have changed so materially the aspects of modern life; discoveries like gunpowder and dynamite, which have altered methods of warfare. Again, there are many discoveries in science—in physics, astronomy, biology, and geology—which in no way conflict with religious doctrines or the corollaries of these doctrines, and which yet profoundly influence the culture of mankind.

In regard to all these phases, however, it will be found that they have some bearings on religious thought, so that here too, as where a conflict between religious tradition and new thought arises, it is religion

[1] See Chap. VI., " Religion and Ethics."

which falls under the influence of culture, while religion no longer gives the colour to culture. Religion is a single factor, culture is many-sided, and it is natural therefore to find the relationship the reverse of that at the earlier stage, when culture was merely an aspect of religion. In view of this, it is manifestly misleading to attach to modern culture a religious tag. Modern civilisation, while of course largely influenced by Christian beliefs and the Christian view of things, cannot properly be spoken of as Christian civilisation, for Christianity is but one of the factors that go to make up modern culture. In the Middle Ages there was still some justification for the phrase, for then Christianity still controlled many of the sciences; but even at that time there was a powerful non-Christian element — Arabic civilisation — which largely determined the thought and general nature of the centuries preceding the Renaissance. With the revival of interest in classical learning, the old Greek and Roman culture was brought to the front, and henceforth entered as an important factor in moulding the culture of the Christian states of Europe. In fact, European culture is an exceedingly complicated product, drawing its first inspiration from a period that antedates Judaism, Christianity, and Islam, appearing gigantic merely because it rests upon the various cultures of antiquity—Babylonian, Egyptian, Grecian, and Roman—and contains elements that may be traced back to one or the other of these four.

It is chiefly, however, because of the obvious fact that with the independent position of the arts and sciences cultivated by man, they exercise an influence on religion, and not the reverse, that

modern culture may not be specifically connected
with any particular form of religion. The Arabic
culture of the four centuries following upon the death
of Mohammed comprises more than Islam; and
similarly European culture embraces more than
Christianity. The recognition of this relationship
between religion and culture, and of the dividing
line between the two, is in no way derogatory to the
former. The function of religion is not restricted
by the consideration that she is not the controlling
factor in modern culture, since this is a condition
brought about by the law of differentiation of functions, the operation of which is indispensable to
progress. On the contrary, the concentration of
religious function to a restricted field should intensify
its energy; and this increased intensity, leading to a
profounder influence on conduct and on human
ideals,—on the soul-life which after all contains the
noblest elements of our being,—should be more than
a compensation for the loss experienced by religion in losing her authority over the various
branches of human culture.

III.

PRACTICAL ASPECTS.

CHAPTER XII.

THE GENERAL ATTITUDE IN THE STUDY OF RELIGIONS.

I.

THE traits of the historical method in the study of religion having been set forth in the first chapter, it is hardly necessary to dwell at any length upon the importance of a strict adherence to this method. To successfully accomplish this, not only is a proper training in the method essential, but equally so, a conscious effort to maintain an impartial attitude. Even the best-equipped scholar must keep watch, lest on a subject touching personal predilections and personal convictions so closely, he find himself influenced in his investigations by his preferences or dislikes. The best safeguard against this besetting danger is to cultivate a sympathetic attitude towards the manifestations of the religious spirit, viewed as the continuous effort of the human mind to attain religious truth, and as the endeavour to carry out the dictates of the religious conscience. Unless indeed we enter sympathetically into the multitude of beliefs which we shall encounter in our researches, it is hopeless to look forward to an understanding of them. Even in what appears to us to represent the lowest form of superstition, there may, and there frequently does, lurk the inkling of some higher truth, but we shall never be able to find out what it is, if we persist in measuring the distance separating us from these " superstitions," or ever keeping before us the superiority of our own beliefs.

A sympathetic attitude does not as a matter of course imply that we are to approve of the beliefs and rites which happen to form the subject of our investigation.   Apart from the fact that such a contingency is absolutely impossible, it is quite as undesirable as it is impossible; but for the time being, at least, we must be able to put ourselves in the position of those to whom these beliefs and rites appeal.   If, for example, we are dealing with a phase of the taboo superstition, according to which it is ordained that a certain kind of food must not be eaten, the sympathetic attitude involves the effort on our part, not merely to study the circumstances under which this peculiar belief arose, but to appreciate the mental state which would be impressed by the belief in question.   Let us suppose that the prohibition is against eating the meat of a certain animal, and that we have ascertained that this animal is regarded as sacred by the tribes who feel bound by the prohibition.   It may upon further investigation transpire, that at a remote period a prominent member of the tribe, of unusual endowments, had the power to assume the guise of this animal, and on one occasion did so for the purpose of frightening off some enemy.   The problem for us in such a case consists in putting ourselves in the position of those to whom such a tale would appeal. Under what circumstances can people believe that a human being can voluntarily change his appearance? Now, among many tribes in a primitive state of culture, the belief exists that they are actually descended from some animal. It is not difficult to account for such a belief. The strange appearance of individuals, with features that suggest an ape or a dog, would be one factor, while the knowledge of instances of actual copulation between men and animals would be another. The belief once established would easily lead to the notion that under extraordinary circumstances a human being could appear under the guise of an animal. A connecting link at least between the human and animal form would be determined in this way, and to people of limited experience, whose imagination is therefore given free play, a possibility readily becomes a probability. The supposed greater credulity of children and savages is due largely to an unbridled imagination, and a goodly part therefore of the sympathetic attitude consists in our ability to conceive of the extent to which the human imagination, uncontrolled by reasoning powers which are developed by the increase of experiences, may dominate us. Once having obtained a firm grasp of the mental state which would be inclined to regard as quite natural what to us appears impossible, we shall, instead of feeling tempted to indulge in a contemptuous smile at primitive beliefs, be led rather to recognise in them an element which shows the capacity of people in a low condition of culture to idealise their surroundings. The belief that an animal is sacred illustrates the force which the idea of sanctity has already acquired.

The example chosen in elucidation of the sympathetic attitude belongs to the lowest stratum of religious belief; and this choice was purposely made, for, if even the grossest superstitions can be shown to have phases which commend themselves to us, it follows that when we come to beliefs which are the outcome of higher conditions reached by man, we must recognise a more or less close approach to the mental impressions by which we ourselves are swayed. The mythology of the Greeks may serve as a simple example, and one familiar to all. The question that we must ask ourselves is: How could the Greeks—cultivated and refined—bring themselves to believe in stories about gods whose acts are so much like those of man, holding court, feasting, quarrelling, travelling, intriguing—in short, doing everything except dying? To answer this question, we must not have recourse to the symbolical interpretation, for it was only the choice spirits among the Greeks to whom these stories appealed purely as illustrations of certain truths, or as a means of inculcating certain moral principles. No doubt in the days of the decline of the Greek religion, the myths were no longer accepted even by the masses as literally true, but it is precisely at the time when the Greek intellect produces its choicest fruits that the attachment to religion as handed down from former days is strongest, despite the scepticism that already manifests itself in the works of some of the dramatists.

It is to a study of the Greek character that we must in the first instance turn for a solution. Responding keenly to impressions, as an artistic people invariably does, the Greeks were attracted by the poetic spirit so liberally diffused through the stories. The majestic figure of Zeus, sitting in solemn state, surrounded by his court of gods and goddesses, at whose glance mountains quake, who controls by his word the fate of gods and men, stirred the imaginations of the people to such an extent as to repress the spirit of inquiry with regard to the reality of the conception. The splendid character of the public rites with their processions, their solemn chants and their sacrifices, served to deepen the impression and to heighten the appeal to the æsthetic sense and to the poetic imagination of the Greeks. Add to this the force of tradition and the influence of parental teachings imparted to children at the most impressionable age, and we shall at least have approached the solution of the problem in hand. In any case, proceeding in this way, we shall be able to put ourselves in the position of those to whom the myths appealed, and shall understand the religious attitude of a people who cling to these myths, as embodying religious truths of the highest order.

It is comparatively easy to acquire this sympathetic attitude towards primitive religions, or towards religions that belong to a dead past; but more serious difficulties are encountered when we approach the study of religions that belong to the present, and more particularly to such forms of religious belief as are in direct opposition to the views to which we are more or less strongly attached.

It is only within comparatively recent times that fair judgments regarding Islam and Buddhism are to be met with in the works of European writers, and as yet the percentage of those whose attitude of mind enables them to view these religions in an impartial manner is quite limited, while the number of those who consider it worth while to carefully study these two great religions is even smaller. This being the case, there is no longer any reason for surprise to find, when we enter the circle of the history of Christianity, the judgments of writers with but rare exceptions warped by their individual preferences or prejudices. Indeed, it may be questioned whether *absolute* impartiality is possible in studying aspects of religious history in which we are directly interested, and it is also an open question whether such absolute impartiality is desirable. The personal equation cannot be set aside altogether. If we hold any convictions on religious questions—and who does not?—our view of beliefs opposed to those to which we are attached is necessarily coloured to some extent by virtue of this opposition; and if the sympathetic attitude demanded the abandonment of our own convictions as a condition of our comprehending those held by our opponents, it would be a most mischievous and dangerous factor in the study of religion.

Fortunately, no such sacrifice is involved. So far indeed is this from being the case, that the student who has not passed through actual religious experiences misses an important preparation for the study of religion, and the stronger our grasp on our own convictions, the better shall we be equipped for appreciating the manifold workings of the religious spirit and the exercise of the religious function. It is therefore a pre-requisite towards acquiring the sympathetic attitude, to have decided convictions of one's own, and to have experienced in ourselves the power of the religious sentiment. There is a sense in which only the religious man, that is one in whom the religious sentiment is active, is qualified to study the history of religion, just as only one gifted with appreciation of music, who has deeply felt the charm of the art, can deal effectively with an investigation of its province and its subtleties. All that the sympathetic attitude demands of us is, so to attune our souls as to respond to the vibrations produced by the souls of others; and there is no *inherent* reason why our own religious preferences should prevent us from maintaining this high standard. While acknowledging freely, then, the difficulties involved in extending the sympathetic attitude towards the study of religious phenomena diametrically opposed to our own ideals, yet, since this end can be accomplished without any injury to our own beliefs, the cultivation of this attitude may properly be urged. No further argument is required to show that this attitude is even more important in studying religious phenomena of present interest than in the study of such as belong to the domain of history. The bitterness which so frequently crops out in the discussion of religious questions, leading to estrangement among those naturally attached to one another, may in most instances be traced back to a lack of ability on the part of the contestants to enter into the mental state of those from whom they differ. If for no other purpose than to aid in the disappearance of this bitterness—which is surely not a healthy manifestation—it should be the aim of every student of religion to watch himself at all times, lest his personal views so obtrude themselves as to prevent his understanding of religious convictions different from his own. In so far as living religious interests are concerned, the sympathetic attitude merely demands of us to understand opposing views, and to appreciate the mental state of those who differ from us.

It has been necessary to dwell at some length upon
the character and scope of the sympathetic attitude
in the study of religions, chiefly because of the
exceedingly delicate problems with which the study
deals.   The feeling of instinctive opposition to the
scientific investigation of religious phenomena, which
still largely prevails even in intelligent circles, is due
to a great extent to the fear that such an
investigation will not treat with the proper consideration things which are dear and sacred to
thousands and tens of thousands; and the proposition
has at various times been put forward to exclude
problems of present and living interest from the scope
of the study.   Such a limitation, however, is entirely
out of the question. We may indeed, as has been
set forth in a previous chapter, draw limitations as to
the *possibilities* of the historical study of religion, but
one cannot in the case of any science draw an
imaginary line, and say, beyond this point you *must*
not investigate.   A study is hopelessly defective, and
the conclusions drawn from it utterly untrustworthy,
that leaves out of consideration any phase of the
subject under investigation ; and in the case of a
theme like religion, the careful study of modern
religious movements furnishes a most valuable adjunct for grasping the nature of the religious
instinct.

II.

All sciences touch the present at some point; why
then should the study of religion form the exception?
The various sciences may be compared to so many
roads leading from diverse directions towards one
point — living humanity.   The most theoretical of

sciences—even astronomy and mathematics—have their practical side, and while they may not be consciously cultivated for this purpose, the factor which unconsciously serves as the stimulus to the pursuit of any science is its ultimate connection with man and his interests. In so far, then, as the study of religion has bearings on problems of living and practical importance, it does not occupy an exceptional position, but shares this feature with other sciences, while the fact that the practical bearings of the study involve matters requiring delicate handling, cannot be urged as a reason for avoiding these bearings entirely. It is therefore both indispensable and inevitable that the historical study of religion should include in its scope living religions, and even the particular religion or sub-division to which we happen to be attached ; and in doing so we cannot avoid considering aspects of religious problems which have a present importance. It must not, however, be supposed that the connection of the study of religion with living issues implies an obligation, or even an encouragement, to enter the field of religious controversy. If that were the case, the study might properly be denounced as mischievous.

The line of demarcation, fortunately, between study and controversy is very distinct, and there is not the slightest possibility of an unconscious overstepping of the boundary line. Indeed nothing is to be gained by doing so, and, as a matter of fact, it will be found that students of religion are only too anxious to avoid trespassing upon the thorny field, so much so that the charge is sometimes brought against them of being indifferent to practical religious

interests, or too cowardly to express definite
convictions. This charge of cowardice, when made,
should be pocketed by the student with pride and
satisfaction, for it furnishes a guarantee to him that
he has kept within the prescribed limits of scientific
impartiality. Without, then, in any way limiting the
scope of the study of religion, it may properly be
demanded of the student, when dealing with the
history of modern religions, and more particularly
with those aspects of it which have a direct bearing
on present movements in the religious world, that he
treat with due consideration the feelings of others,
and that he exercise care not to shock popular
sensibilities in treating of matters which are regarded
as sacred possessions. This being premised, there is
no subject which cannot be dealt with in such a way
as to carry out the aims of the study—the elucidation
and interpretation of religious phenomena. On the
other hand, the demand may be made of the religious
public to divest itself of the prejudice and fear that
in some way the study of religion is subversive
of religious faith. The previous chapters will have
surely demonstrated one point—the permanency of
such a factor as a part of human nature and as an
indispensable element in human culture. The study
of religion, pursued with an application of the
historical method, can but emphasise this truth and
strengthen the position of religion itself. Whatever
changes in our own beliefs may be brought about
by the study of religion, it is inconceivable how
any earnest student can be led, through the study, to
a rejection of religion, or to a position of opposition
to it. The enlargement of one's sympathies, which is
almost a necessary result of the study, will certainly

be sufficient to prevent either contingency, not to speak of other influences, all tending in the same direction, to which the student will be subjected. It is a short-sighted policy, therefore, which seeks to check the growing interest in the historical study of religion. Religion has nothing to fear from a searching investigation, pursued in a spirit of sympathy towards the manifestations of the religious instinct, and it is incumbent upon those who have the practical interests of religion at heart to encourage this study, and not to injure their own cause by raising a suspicion that it cannot endure the test of scrutiny.

But the question may still be asked—Granting that the cause of religion in general is not weakened by the study of religion, but, on the contrary, strengthened, may not investigation prove disastrous to certain tenets to which the masses or large bodies of people are attached? It would be idle to disguise the possibility of such a contingency arising, but, on the other hand, it must be born in mind that modification in religious beliefs, or the setting aside of certain tenets altogether, is, as a general thing, brought about, not by the deeper study of these beliefs or tenets, but through the influence which discoveries and advances made quite outside of the circle of belief exert upon the religious temper. Historical investigation of any tenet by itself furnishes no argument either in favour of the belief or against it, and it is not therefore from the study of religion that the real danger comes. Biology, Philosophy, Astronomy, Geology, Philology—these are some of the factors which profoundly influence religious thought and religious belief. So far as the study of religion is concerned, its chief effect must necessarily be, as already pointed out, to enlarge our sympathies. In so far as this enlargement involves a change in particular beliefs, the study must also be taken into account as a factor, but as a minor one compared with the bearings of new aspects of various natural sciences and of speculative thought.

III.

There is, however, a danger of another kind lurking in the sympathetic attitude, against which we should be on our guard. It is possible, from an over-zealous desire to be impartial in our judgments, to allow our sympathies with all forms of religion to go to the extent of making us indecisive and wavering. The career of Renan furnishes an illustration of this danger. In his desire to be entirely just, he developed, as years went on, a tendency to advocate with equal force the two sides of disputed questions, and according to his changing moods would now appear to be an adherent of one side and again of the other. So pronounced was this tendency, and so great the influence of his example over his contemporaries, that the term Renanism arose, to describe an attitude towards religious belief, half cynical and half sentimental, which made impartiality almost synonymous with indifference. It was undoubtedly Renan's excessive sympathy with all efforts of the human mind in the struggle for truth that developed in him what proved to be a serious defect, endangering the effectiveness of his important and brilliant services to the science of religion. The attitude of the justice of the peace, who, after listening to two contending parties, declared each to be right, and upon receiving a remonstrance from a third party that both could not be right, declared "You are right also," is bound to lead to intellectual confusion.

The way out of the difficulty seems simple enough. While maintaining a disposition that may be described as "open to further conviction," we should at all times make sure of where we actually stand on important matters of belief, or failing in that, assume some position as a *provisional* standpoint, and as best answering the conditions involved, in so far as they are known to us. Recalling that religious truth, as pointed out in a previous chapter, can be expected to respond only to *reasonable* probability, there should be no difficulty in formulating our beliefs, whatever they are, with sufficient definiteness to enable us to occupy some positive platform and at the same time to hold ourselves in readiness to shift that platform, should the necessity arise. It is a delicate matter, to be sure, to adjust the mental balance in such a way that belief and knowledge should equal each other, but the task is within reach of all who have trained themselves in clear and logical modes of thinking.

But while this danger lurking in the sympathetic attitude should be recognised, it is well to bear in mind that the number of those prone to it is small, as compared with those whose real difficulty will consist in cultivating this attitude to the necessary extent. Most of us, by virtue of surroundings and early influences, are apt to cling too tenaciously rather than too loosely to accepted beliefs—so tenaciously as to prevent us without a strong effort from entering sympathetically into the beliefs of others. For the present, therefore, it is the cultivation of the sympathetic attitude that needs to be urged as an essential aid to the study of religion.   There are as yet but few persons who can boast of being free from religious or—what is more—anti-religious prejudices.   To see things as others see them is still for most of us a task that is sufficiently difficult to call all our energies into play; and yet, unless we divest ourselves of all prejudiced opinions as to the value or worthlessness of any particular form of belief, unless we throw aside all species of intolerance, purge our souls of all hatred, except the hatred of injustice, free our minds of bitter thoughts, remove every taint of cynicism and of the assumption of superiority, it is hopeless to carry on the historical study of religion with any success.   We may gather facts by patient toil, we may fill our minds with much valuable information, we may make a most thorough study of the sources of religion—and yet we shall fail in the interpretation of the facts, we shall obtain a distorted view of any religion and of all religions, and we shall be unable to understand the sources without a sympathetic appreciation of what the facts, the information acquired, and the sources studied, meant for others.   We must feel the beating of the human heart beneath the surface.

CHAPTER XIII.

THE STUDY OF THE SOURCES.

WHAT distinguishes the genuine student from the dilettante is, mainly, that the former goes directly to the sources of his subject, whereas the latter acquires his knowledge from second-hand, and usually third-rate mediums. By the latter method one may acquire quite as much if not more actual knowledge than by the former, but it is only the exceptionally gifted who will also be able in this way to enter into the true spirit of the subject investigated. There are some subjects in which this is impossible to even a man of genius, and religion is one of them. It may be set down as an axiom that no religion can be understood except by a direct study of the sources of that particular religion. These sources will naturally vary in character with different religions. In the case of primitive religions which possess no fixed or written literature, the direct study of the people among whom a religion of this character is found constitutes the main source. A traveller like the late Frank Hamilton Cushing,[1] who lived with the Zuni Indians, acquired their language, took part in their daily occupations, shared their festivals and ceremonies, furnishes an illustration of the method

---

[1] Died in Washington, April 10, 1900. Cushing's early death is a great loss to ethnological science in America. His chief works related to the Zuni Indians.

of studying primitive religions (though not unmixed with elements pointing to the influence of a more advanced culture) from the sources. In the case of religions that have produced literatures, it is of course the study of the latter in the original form that constitutes the primary source.

I.

Returning for a moment to religions without fixed literatures,[1] it is manifestly given only to a few to study a religion in the direct manner followed by a Cushing in America, or in Arabia by Charles Doughty,[2] one of the most remarkable travellers of all times, who exposed his life for two years to constant danger by his intercourse with Bedawee of a fierce type. To read and carefully study the works of such travellers is naturally the best compromise that can be effected; but in doing so, we must also be ready to resign our claims to acquiring authoritative opinions on the subject of primitive religious beliefs. We may of course accept the opinions of others, and by dint of well-directed comparative studies fortify these conclusions, but all such efforts will not compensate us for the benefits to be derived by direct contact with people still clinging to what are designated as primitive beliefs.

It is only necessary to take up two or three modern ethnological compilations to convince oneself how difficult it is to grasp the true character of the

---

[1] The term "fixed" is used to exclude the prayers, incantations, and exorcising formulas of primitive peoples, which are also in a certain sense literary products.

[2] *Travels in Arabia Deserta* (2 vols.), Oxford, 1888.

savage or of groups living in a state of primitive culture. Even keen travellers are often deceived in their judgments through misleading statements made to them by one of the natives, or through a misunderstanding of what they see. So far from being simple-minded, the mind of primitive man is a more complex piece of machinery in its workings than that of civilised individuals, whose thought by virtue of being clearer is also simpler. The savage, like the child, is apparently a tangle of contradictions, generous to a fault and cruel to the extreme, with a high sense of honour in some matters and treacherous in others, full of superstitious fears and yet endowed with genuine courage. His moods change rapidly, and from our point of view without sufficient cause; he appears to be at the mercy of his emotions, and yet shows at times indomitable will-power. How is it possible, then, to enter thoroughly into the workings of so complex an organism, except by means of direct and prolonged observation? Limited opportunities are afforded nowadays for such observation, without proceeding to the native haunts of primitive man, by means of such exhibitions as were arranged for the first time on a large scale at Chicago in 1893. The objection urged against the primitive peoples brought to that place, that they had all encountered the influence of Christian missionaries and occidental civilisation, holds good for the savage and primitive peoples visited by travellers, since there is no district, unless it be the remote interior of Africa, where one can now encounter primitive culture in its pristine state.

Again, since the value of direct observation consists largely in our being able to approach closer towards the working of the primitive mind, the study of the lower and ignorant classes in a community furnishes some compensation in default of extensive travels to the outskirts of civilisation. In the United States, students are fortunately placed in having, in the case of a large portion of the negro population, persons only two or three generations removed from the stage of primitive culture, and the large mass of negro folk-lore still extant in the south shows the abiding character of former influences.

In the third place, the study of child-nature is a valuable adjunct towards understanding the mind of primitive man, and in so far constitutes another compensation to make good the loss of direct observation. The child, as has frequently been observed, passes in the course of its development through the various stages of culture, beginning at the lowest, and if one may judge from the startling resemblance between the fancies of children and the conceptions found among primitive people,[1] we may go further, and regard child psychology as a direct source for the study of primitive religions. We might, therefore, arrange the means at our disposal for the study of religions in their earlier forms in a descending scale as follows :—

(1.) Direct observation and contact with primitive peoples, though it should be recognised that primitive culture untainted by modern culture is practically extinct.

(2.) Study of child nature.

(3.) Observations of the ignorant and lower classes in a community.

---

[1] See an interesting series of answers given by children to questions of a religious nature, in the *Topical Syllabi* for 1894-95 (No. XV.), edited by G. Stanley Hall.

The first constitutes the chief and primary source ; the other two are secondary sources, of which again the former possesses more direct value than the latter.

II.

Naturally it is not possible for any single individual, supposing him to be so favoured that he can avail himself of the primary source, to come into contact with all divisions of primitive peoples. This, however, is not necessary. The advantage of direct observation lying in the facility afforded for understanding the workings of the untutored mind, the general similarity of human nature at the same mental stage—an axiom requiring no further demonstration—dispenses us from extending our observation beyond perfectly feasible limits. The ideally equipped student of religion in its primitive form would be one who has had the opportunity of observing at close range religious rites of a primitive character, and to have studied carefully from various points of view the different character, thoughts, beliefs, aims, and mental methods of the people practising these rites. Such a student may lay claim to speak with authority regarding primitive religious beliefs, assuming of course that his previous training has been such as to enable him to observe in a truly scientific spirit. This proviso must be added, for, as a matter of fact, the travellers who fulfil this condition are exceedingly few. Many of these travellers are missionaries, and valuable as the ethnological work of some missionaries has been, the great bulk of it is worthless, because of the lack of training—and in part also the lack of sympathy—on the part of the observers. To see

22

correctly is not a natural but an acquired gift. It is to the poor judgment and lack of training displayed by missionaries that many of the erroneous notions still current concerning primitive religions are due, as it is to them also that we owe the existence of the belief, which finds expression in such a work as Sir John Lubbock's *Origin of Civilisation*,[1] that there are savages devoid of any religion.

Contact with a single people living in a state of primitive culture, if prolonged, is sufficient to give us that insight into the workings of the religious instinct which must form the basis of our studies; but having secured this basis, it is essential that the range of our observation should be extended by abundant reading, so as to determine wherein the particular people forming the object of our study differs from others occupying about the same culture level. The greater the amount of comparative material gathered by us, the better equipped shall we be for forming ripe judgments in our special field. The specialist in the science of religion is the only one who can make contributions of value to the science, but the usefulness of the specialist depends to a great extent upon the amount of knowledge he possesses not strictly belonging to his speciality. If he remains within his sphere he may learn to observe well and accurately, but it will be left for others to interpret and make scientifically available what he has seen.

III.

This becomes even more apparent when we turn to religions that must be studied through the literatures

[1] Chap. v., pp. 208-213 (London ed., 1882).

which they have produced. Direct contact in the
case of primitive religions is here replaced by the
study of the religious productions in their original
form. The study of a people's language is of itself
an important adjunct for an understanding of their
religion, since it is in its language that the peculiar
genius of a people manifests itself. The existence of
certain terms reveals their spiritual grade, the turn
given to a certain word or phrase may afford a key
to the solution of an important problem in the
religious history of a people. For this reason the
study of its religious literature in the original tongue
is an absolutely indispensable condition towards
attaining an authoritative knowledge of their religion.
To take an example from the domain of the Old
Testament, in what a new light the term " redeemer,"
which plays such a *rôle* in Christian theology, appears
when by turning to the Hebrew we observe that the
word used—*goël*—belongs to a period in the life of the
people antedating the organisation of courts of justice.
The *goël* was the " blood-avenger," upon whom, by
virtue of his relationship to some one who had met
with a violent death, the obligation rested to
"redeem" the loss incurred by the family or tribe
through suitable vengeance or compensation. A
latent sense of justice evidently underlies this formal
recognition of primitive lynch-law, but how far removed is this original application of the term from
the designation of the single Power of the Universe
as the one who will " redeem" the wrongs of the
sorely-tried Job, who feels that he has suffered un-
justly. Yet it is not so much the distance separating
the later from the earlier meaning of the term which
arouses interest, as the intermediate stages, by means

of which we are enabled to follow the religious and
social development of the people itself.[1] With the
introduction of legal modes of procedure, the function
of the *goël* as avenger ceases, but he becomes the
kinsman whose duty it is to protect and aid those
rendered helpless by being deprived of their natural
support.   It is part of the duty of the *goël* as
kinsman to "redeem" the property of a relative
who has been impoverished, and hence when the
Hebrews lost their land through defeat at the hands
of the Babylonians, it is to their god that they look
for "redemption" from the misfortune.   The national
god, Jahweh, becomes the *goël* of his people, and,
as this conception of a deity of restricted power and
interests is extended until thé higher conception of
a universal ruler, imposing duties upon mankind, is
evolved, the term *goël*, as applied to this deity, is
spiritualised and made to do service as expressing
supreme confidence in the justice and loving kindness of the great Judge of the Universe.

But *goël* is merely one of many terms in the
Hebrew language which throw a light upon the
religious history and the religious aspirations of
the people; and illustrations in abundance could
be adduced also from other sources.   All the great
religions are marked by a rich religious phraseology, the close study of which yields as valuable
results as the study of the religious texts.   But,
naturally, these results can only be utilised in
connection with the study of the religious literature; and, where single words are of such import-

See a paper by the writer, "Blood-Avenger, Kinsman and
Redeemer in the Old Testament" (*The Independent*, Aug. 27th,
1896).

ance, it is quite superfluous to emphasise the necessity of studying this literature likewise in the original. Indeed, in no other way can we be said to reach the sources of a religion that possesses a literature. A translation, however meritorious, can never replace the original, and while through the medium of a translation we can gather the facts of a religion,—a view of its doctrines, a conspectus of its rites, its ethical phases, and the like,—a translation can never bring us close to the spirit of the religion in question. We must resign ourselves to probing near the surface if we have recourse to translations. It is only through a study of religious texts in their original form that we can penetrate to the core of the religion. Through acquiring a knowledge of the language in which these texts are written, we fill ourselves, as it were, with the spirit of the people among whom the texts were produced, we enter into their way of thinking, and fit ourselves for appreciating in a sympathetic manner their religious ideas, their practices, and their hopes. The language of a people supplies that direct contact which, in the case of nations of the past, it is no longer possible to secure in any other way.

IV.

The proof of the correctness of this proposition is furnished by the history itself of the study of religion. No sooner did men turn their attention towards studying in a direct manner the sources of other religions than their own, than the views with regard to these religions began to change. As long as even scholars derived their knowledge of Islam from translations of the Koran and of the works of

Mohammedan writers, we meet with distorted views, and even where prejudices did not blind writers, their judgment was warped by being obliged to view facts and conditions through the eyes of others, instead of by the exercise of their own powers of vision. But when, with the rise of the historical spirit, scholars gathered their inspiration directly, prejudices disappeared, and fair sympathetic estimates began to take the place of the former caricatures which were taken for descriptions of Islam.

Similarly, through the impulse given to Sanskrit studies at the close of the last century, totally changed views arose with regard to Buddhism, and it is a direct result of the zeal with which Sanskrit texts were studied that Hindu thought was once more brought into touch with the Western world. Indeed, if for no other purpose than as an effective means of clearing men's minds of prejudices, the study of religious literatures in their original form should be strongly advocated; and it may not be inappropriate here to urge upon teachers of religion not to form judgments regarding other religions without such study. The position of the religious guide gives him exceptional opportunities for either encouraging his followers in their prejudices, or for aiding them to get rid of them.

A public utterance is a most serious matter, and it is therefore incumbent upon the Christian divine, for example, not to content himself with repeating parrot-like views regarding the Jews, which have reached him through the medium of tradition, but since they affect the relationship of men towards their fellows, to investigate these views for himself. This example is chosen because of the frequency with which totally erroneous and absurd judgments regarding the spirit of the Old Testament are still heard from Christian pulpits; and when such is the case it will be found that the preacher in question has never attempted to make a study, in its original form, of the production which he is discussing. It may safely be asserted that it is impossible to understand the remarkable evolution of which the Old Testament furnishes the trace, except by study of the books in the Hebrew tongue.

Despite the close bonds uniting Christianity to post-exilic Judaism, the student of Christianity cannot understand the spirit of the religion out of which Christianity arose without a prolonged study of the sources of that religion as embodied in the Old Testament, and in part in Rabbinical literature. What applies to the Old Testament is applicable of course also to the New Testament as one of the sources of the study of Christianity proper. Jewish divines, in protesting against erroneous views spread about the Jews, would make their protest more effective if they gave evidence of not committing the same fundamental error in forming a judgment about Christianity and other religions without a direct study of sources. Public opinion ought to severely condemn all utterances embodying judgments regarding religions made by those whose position lends to them a measure of authority, unless their judgments are based upon independent researches pursued by the application of scientific methods.

Until the public mind is educated up to this point, we cannot look forward to an amelioration of the present conditions in the religious world, which must be depressing to the earnest student, who sees what a strong hold prejudices and long-exploded erroneous judgments still retain upon even intelligent minds. It is not, of course, possible for every one to enter upon such a study of religion, but, on the other hand, it is not necessary for every one to have an opinion about any religion, except, of course, his own. The suppression of an opinion through a becoming recognition of one's inability to form one is indicative of a state of mind which it should be the aim of all to reach. The excuse of ignorance cannot, however, be urged in palliation of the religious teacher. It is an important part of his business to study religions, and one may therefore expect of him that he should study them properly and thoroughly.

V.

The point may, however, be urged—and with force—that it lies beyond the limit of human efforts to study more than a limited number of religions direct from their sources. The conclusion to be drawn from this perfectly correct proposition, is that a single individual cannot be regarded as an authority for a larger number of religions than he studies directly. To the scholar it is no hardship to realise that there are limitations to his powers, and so far as the public is concerned, it is essential that it should learn to distrust any one who poses as an authority in more than a very limited number of domains. For most of us it is a sufficient task to become a master within a single well-defined field, and those are fortunate indeed who possess the ability, and can secure the advantages needed, to make themselves authorities over a larger territory.

In discussing the sources for the study of religions without fixed literatures, it has been pointed out that the direct observation of a people living in a state of primitive culture needs to be supplemented by wide reading, so as to secure the necessary perspective in which to view the facts observed. Similarly, the study of any particular religion from its literary sources is of little avail, unless we also bring a certain amount of comparative material to bear upon our special knowledge. It has been well said that he who knows only one language knows none. With equal truth it may be asserted that, in order to understand one religion, we must be acquainted with more than one. Religions with literatures differ far more from one another than those which possess none. Hence it is not sufficient to study merely one religion direct from the sources. Studying two in this way may be set down as a minimum for acquiring that firmness of method and keenness of judgment needed for the chief problem of religious research — the interpretation of facts. This does not imply that the two are to be cultivated with equal intensity, or that the entire field of both must be covered, but only that in addition to the one religion which forms one's special object of research, one should be able to acquire a sufficient knowledge of a second religion, direct from its sources, as to be able to penetrate into the spirit of that religion. It will be observed that the special study of one religion on the part of the student is taken for granted. Such a course is indeed essential, not that every student of religion need necessarily develop into a specialist, qualified to speak with authority on some particular religion, but as a means of acquiring a thorough grasp of the historical method; the beginning must be made by picking out some religion, and then investigating it *ab ovo*—by a direct study of its sources.

For obvious reasons, a religion with a literature should be chosen in preference to a phase of primitive religion, and even if the opportunity is afforded of direct contact with tribes living in a state of primitive culture, the mental training acquired in the study of a new language, and with the help of that language in laying bare, as it were, the machinery of the religious instinct, is indispensable to fruitful and accurate observation. How far the special study of one religion from its sources should be carried, is a matter that will depend upon the immediate objects that the student has in view. If his chief interest lies in the study of primitive beliefs, only so much is required as to enable him to adopt a proper method ; if, on the contrary, the higher manifestations of the religious life are to form his chief object of study—the more intricate problems of religious history—it is indispensable that he should first acquire a detailed knowledge of one of the higher historical religions before branching out into a wider survey.

Let us assume that the study of Christianity is the ultimate goal of a student. The best, and also the most natural preparation for this task, would be the study of Hebrew, so as to fit himself for investigating direct from the sources the problems of Old Testament history, as the precursor of Christianity. The student will utterly fail to appreciate the condition which led to the rise of Christianity—nay, he cannot understand the character of Jesus himself—unless he can trace the course of religious development among the Hebrews, and is able to discern the special traits manifested by the religious instinct or the religious function among the Hebrews. Naturally, he cannot carry these studies to the extent of making himself a specialist in this branch, but the deeper he lays this foundation for his subsequent studies the better. Advancing to his specially chosen field, his next step will naturally be the thorough and critical study of the New Testament in the original tongue. In the course of this study he will soon be led to define more sharply the special purpose of his researches. The study of Christianity as a whole will loom up before him as a task too stupendous for a single individual, and he will select some particular period or some special phase. It will depend upon this choice just how far his New Testament studies will be carried, but in any case they must cover a thorough knowledge of the chief problems engaging the attention of specialists, and he must place himself in a position to follow modern investigation independently, by a direct appeal to the sources upon which the work of all specialists is based. In thus studying the Old and the New Testaments, he will have acquired that knowledge of two religions which we have set down as the minimum equipment for a thorough training in the methods of historical research.

It would for obvious reasons be preferable, perhaps, in case Christianity be chosen as one's special field, to select as the second religion one more removed

than Biblical Judaism—let us say Islam, or one of
the more ancient religions, the Egyptian or Babylonian, or even the Greek or Roman; but offsetting
the close connection between Judaism and Christianity
is the circumstance that the Old Testament contains
the record of the Hebrew religion in its various phases,
from a period when it is hardly to be distinguished
from the general religious practices of the Semites, to
the time when it presents an entirely unique appearance. Besides the fact, therefore, that in the earlier
phases the resemblance of the Hebrew religion to
Christianity is remote, the value of studying so complete a religious development as is furnished by the
Old Testament can hardly be over-estimated. In
this respect Old Testament study stands almost alone,
and only in the case of the material for the religions
of India, have we an approach to so complete a cycle
of religious development.

But even if the special object of one's research
should happen to be some of the comparative aspects
of religion,—say the development of the general belief
in life after death,—the mental training to be secured
by the study of one or two religions from their sources
would still be imperative as a preliminary to larger
researches. For comparative studies, a sound method
and a strict adherence to such a method is even more
important than for other branches of the study of
religion. The comparative history of religion offers
a fertile field for generalisation, and is therefore
always particularly attractive to dilettanti. It is
only the most thoroughly equipped and completely
trained scholar who can hope to make contributions
of permanent value in this difficult field, and in no
other way can this equipment and training be secured

than by a study of a number of particular religions from their sources.

The chief reason, therefore, for thus advocating the study of the sources as a *conditio sine qua non* for all researches in the history of religions are, in the main, two: to acquire a sound critical method, and to obtain a direct knowledge of the workings of the religious instinct in its manifold manifestations. The method having been once acquired, it will be possible to compare the researches of others in fields which we are unable to cultivate for ourselves, and to avail ourselves of these researches. With a thorough knowledge of one historical religion, and a fair knowledge of a second, we are in a position to extend the scope of our studies without danger of becoming superficial or of being led astray by the unsound investigations of others. Indeed, our judgment can be sharpened only by enlarging the circle of our knowledge as much as possible, when once we have become certain of our ground. This enlargement is fully as essential in the case of the study of religions with literatures as we have seen it to be the case in the study of primitive forms of religion.

In order to interpret facts correctly a proper perspective is required, and this element of our training demands as broad a horizon as it is possible to attain by extensive reading in religious literatures, and by the study of scholarly researches based upon these literatures. Such supplementary reading is equally essential whether we choose a particular religion as our special field, or prefer to branch out into the comparative aspects of religious beliefs or practices, or to make primitive manifestations of the religious instinct our particular province. The true specialist is not the person who confines his interest to a single point. He gathers material far and wide, he constantly aims to enlarge his mental horizon, and the greater his general knowledge the better is he equipped for penetrating into the remotest corners of the restricted field in which alone he can become an authority

CHAPTER XIV.

THE STUDY OF RELIGION IN COLLEGES, UNIVERSITIES, AND SEMINARIES.

I.

THE impetus to both the historical and psychological study of religion must come from our colleges and universities. The recognition of the subject in higher institutions of learning ensures the normal growth of the science, and by maintaining a high standard of equipment as a preliminary to conducting researches in this field, it will effectively discourage dilettanti who, by virtue of the peculiar attraction that the study of religion affords, have done so much to bring the study into disrepute among sober-minded scholars, and have promoted the prejudice which still exists against it.

Considering for a moment educational conditions as they exist in the United States, it is clear that the study cannot occupy the same position in the college curriculum as in the university course. The distinction between college and university being fairly well recognised, the study of religion enters into the college course only in so far as it forms part of the general equipment of culture which, viewed as the training school for professional studies or for a business career, it is the primary function of the college to supply. It will hardly be questioned that some

knowledge of religious history is part of the requirements of a liberal education.   The young man or
woman who enters upon the duties of life without
some knowledge of the actual part played in the
history of the race by so important a factor as
religion, has certainly missed something which may
properly be regarded as essential, and yet there is
scarcely a single American college in which the study
has been accorded a place—even of the most modest
proportions.   That this defect has not hitherto been
more seriously felt is due to the fact that it has been
partially remedied by the religious training accorded
in the home and in the church.   Such training is
invariably associated with instruction in the history
of religion, and not only in the history of the religion
in whose tenets the child is reared, but of other
religions as well.   While it is true that such instruction, besides being imparted generally in an indirect
manner, is necessarily imperfect, and in many instances also one-sided, it nevertheless serves an
important function, and until the college takes up
this work it is well that the church should continue
it.   Clearly, however, it belongs more properly to
the college.   At the college alone can instructors be
secured who have fitted themselves to teach this
subject thoroughly and adequately.   Moreover, the
mixed character of the students at a college forces
the instructor into an attitude of fairness and impartiality for which there is, in the nature of things, not
the same guarantee in the case of religious history
imparted from a particular point of view, and with
the definite purpose to make such instruction merely
an accessory in training the individual in practical
religious duties.

Another advantage of transferring the teaching of religious history to the college is, that it can be imparted at a more suitable age.   When the young man or young woman enters college, his or her religious training is practically finished.   The church has had them in hand for a considerable number of years, but this period, so important for laying the foundation of character, is not the one in which the full meaning of religion, and the part it has played in the history of the world, can be grasped.   Instruction in the subject at this period of life cannot therefore be effective, or in any sense of the word adequate.   The years spent at college, however, are the ones in which mental development makes great strides.   The horizon is for the first time enlarged to the extent of recognising the factors that have combined to produce modern civilisation.   This therefore is the appropriate time for giving the student at least some general knowledge of the various kinds of religions that the world has seen, what the past religions have stood for, and what the present ones represent.

Doubts may, however, arise in the minds of many, whether such instruction can be imparted in such a manner in a college as not to wound or shock the sensibilities of some sections of the religious community, or of religious people in general; and secondly, whether the effect of such instruction will not prove disastrous to students in confusing their thoughts, rather than beneficial in enlarging their sympathies.

II.

It may at once be admitted that such instruction as is here contemplated is difficult, and requires delicate handling, but so do many other subjects—

notably Philosophy and Political Economy—which nevertheless are included in the college curriculum. In the hands of a poor teacher, one lacking in that sympathy for religions which is an essential pre-requisite in the interpretation of religious facts, or of one too much concerned with impressing his own particular views upon his surroundings, instruction in the history of religion could indeed prove a deadly undertaking, but surely such fears are to a large extent purely hypothetical, if not imaginary; and secondly, it is the business and within the power of an institution to guard itself against securing the wrong kind of a teaching force, no matter what the subject may be. There is no reason why it should be more difficult to obtain the right kind of an instructor for dealing with the history of religion in an impartial and purely scientific, albeit sym-pathetic spirit, than to secure an instructor who will be able to teach a class of young men or women the philosophical systems of Spinoza, Kant, Hegel, or Herbert Spencer. Still, it is idle to disguise the fact that the fear of the consequences of imparting in-struction in religious history has hitherto restrained the officers of American colleges from giving the subject a place in the curriculum. Some decades, and possibly generations, must elapse before this prejudice against the subject will disappear. Meanwhile, it will devolve upon investigators within the field to aid in removing this prejudice by the character of the work they produce; and if, in addition to this, some leading institutions will once set the example, others will soon follow.

It may perhaps not be inappropriate to point out the manner in which the subject could and should

be taught in the college without realising any of
the contingencies feared. Naturally, the method of
the specialist cannot be introduced. The general
purpose of the college course, and the necessary
plan upon which it is laid out, forbid the expendi-
ture of the time required to study the sources of
any particular religion. In this case, it will be perfectly appropriate to begin with the general aspects
of religion as revealed in the history of mankind.
The purpose of including the subject in the college
curriculum being to illustrate its place in human
culture, a general introduction to the subject, followed by outlines of the history of the more important religions in ancient times and in the present,
will form the natural programme. Surely, a course
which will illustrate the manner in which religion
manifests itself among savages, and among people
in a state of primitive culture, can be given without
wounding any religious sensibilities. The subjects
included in such a course are touched upon in connection with instruction in psychology and anthropology, and the history of early civilisations, and
there is therefore no reason why they should not be
supplemented by a course in which certain aspects
can be treated more fully.

Coming to the religions of the past, no conflict
with current religious sentiments is conceivable in
presenting outlines of such religions as those of the
Egyptians, Babylonians, Phœnicians, Greeks, Romans,
and Teutons; and it will be admitted that it is
essential for an understanding of ancient history
that the religious ideas and ideals prevalent in
antiquity should be set clearly before students. So
far as the Greeks and Romans are concerned, this

subject is already represented in many colleges, but inasmuch as the classical nations were indebted for much in their religion and mythology to the influence of Oriental culture, a consideration of the religions of the ancient Orient forms a natural corollary to the study of Greek and Roman mythology, and of the cults of these two nations. The situation is somewhat different when on the one side, religions of China, Japan, and India are broached, and on the other, the religion of the ancient Hebrews, later Judaism, Islam, and Christianity. Here one must be on one's guard against the predominance of the personal factor, which could easily lead an instructor to impart prejudicial views or to come into more or less violent conflict with the religious sentiments held by a large section of the community; but the danger can be averted by a strict insistence upon a purely historical treatment of religions which belong to the present, or which have helped to shape the religions of our days. This simple condition once fulfilled, all further fears are idle. Naturally, if the results of historical investigation in regard to certain religions run counter to views traditionally held, the instructor must set these results before his students. If they are of such a character as to have been generally accepted, no further discussion of them is required; if, however, they are uncertain, the more important of the conflicting opinions should be explained as clearly and as impartially as possible.

It will, upon practical experience, be found that the disposition to impose personal views is not very common among instructors, particularly in a college course. The college professor feels too keenly the responsibility of the situation to think himself justified in instilling into youths at an impressionable age his own opinions on themes in regard to which uncertainty prevails. Were the student able to judge for himself, dogmatic assertions on the part of the instructor would be in place, but where this is not the case, the conscientious instructor will probably err on the other side, and become too impartial for fear of misusing the influence that he could exert upon his pupils in favour of his own attitude on controverted questions.

So far as the treatment of the history of religions, directly or indirectly connected with the present, is concerned, the situation is not different from that of the treatment of philosophical and economic problems. The same possible dangers and the same difficulties confront us in the case of these disciplines, and the escape from these dangers and difficulties is also the same. No one would think of excluding philosophy or political economy from a college curriculum because, forsooth, the instructor might misuse his position to promulgate Pantheism, or Atheism, or Materialism, or for fear that a professor would use his chair as a means of launching socialistic or communistic schemes. Besides, even in the divisions of the subject under consideration, the difficulties are not as formidable as on the surface they appear to be. In the case of the religions of India, China, Japan, and Islam, a fair and sympathetic exposition is all that is demanded, and if, as a result, the college instruction leads to the weakening of the prejudices entertained against these religions, there is surely cause for rejoicing, and not for condemnation. In helping to spread a spirit of appreciative consideration of these great religions, the college would fall in line with the commendable disposition at present manifested in many church organisations to do justice to religions that were formerly swept to one side as merely temptations put into the world by an evil spirit.

There remain the religion of the ancient Hebrews, post-Biblical and modern Judaism, and Christianity, which, it must be admitted, require particularly delicate and careful handling. Should they be excluded from the course on the ground that the churches ought to be permitted to teach the history of these religions in their own way? The course would be lamentably imperfect if such a policy were adopted, and, moreover, it is a question whether more injury to the cause of practical religion would not be done by an omission which would naturally raise suspicion in the minds of the students. On the other hand, it is but a proper concession due to the direct interest that Christians of all denominations, and Jews, whether orthodox or advanced, have in the presentation of their religious history that the greatest possible care be exercised to secure for the subject an impartial, strictly historical, and at the same time sympathetic treatment. In setting forth the doctrines and rites of Judaism and Christianity, there is no need of any discussion of their value, but merely of their historical aspects. Indeed such discussion should be rigidly excluded, and similarly, in unfolding the development of the religion of the ancient Hebrews, all doctrinal questions should be left to one side. A conscientious instructor will not only find no difficulty in adopting this policy, but he will be anxious to do so in the interest of the subject which he is treating.

Let it be emphasised once more, that after all only an outline of the history of religions is to be included in the college curriculum, and since naturally the disputed territory lies for the most part quite beyond the limits of such an outline, the task is still further lightened. On the whole then, while tact, judgment, and, above all, a sympathetic attitude in the treatment of the general subject are indispensable, with the help of these three factors, the difficulties involved in introducing the history of religions into the college curriculum can be overcome.

Before leaving the subject, it may be well to set down the programme suggested for a college course.[1] The subject could be covered in one year, and the last year of the college course is the one naturally adapted for this purpose. The instruction itself would be imparted chiefly by means of lectures, with supplementary reading on the part of the students. Before the history proper is taken up, an introduction to the subject should be given, furnishing a survey of the field covered by the subject itself, with some account of the history of the science, and such preliminary themes discussed as the position of religion in human history, the methods of classifying religions, the definitions that have been proposed for religions, and the various views that have been brought forward to account for the origin of religion. No exhaustive treatment of these themes is required, but the mind of the student should be prepared for understanding views and discussions that he is sure sooner or later to come

---

[1] See also the outlines for an elementary and an advanced course in Maurice Vernes, *L'Histoire des Religions* (Paris, 1887), pp. 231-256.

across, either through reading or through intercourse
with his fellow-men.

The introduction should be followed by the
outlines of the history proper.   Sub-divisions will
naturally suggest themselves.   The religions of
primitive peoples should be treated in a group, their
general traits defined, and some account given of
primitive rites and ceremonies.   In the case of the
more advanced religions likewise, certain groups
should be distinguished.   The religions of the ancient
Orient, of Egypt, Babylonia, Phœnicia, Palestine, and
Arabia, will form one group; India, China, and
Japan another; the Greeks and Romans a third;
while Teutonic and Celtic heathenism may be taken
up as a fourth.   The great religions occupying the
first rank, Buddhism with its ramifications, Zoroastrianism, Judaism, Christianity, and Islamism, should
naturally receive special treatment, their chief doctrines and rites should be set forth, and the important
periods in their history indicated and briefly discussed.
In the supplementary reading suggested, care should
be exercised not to recommend too much, for fear of
confusing the mind of the student.   A good comprehensive manual[1] might be chosen as a guide for
the course, and then out of the abundance of literature on the subject, a careful selection should be
made, the preference being given to works which
are suggestive, arousing the interest of the student,
rather than such as belabour him with abundance
of facts.

By means of a course of this kind, the student

---

[1] Such as Menzies, *History of Religion;* or Chantepie de la Saussaye,
Lehrbuch der Religionsgeschichte (2nd ed.), by far the best of its kind,
but of which, unfortunately, an English edition does not exist.

will come to realise the vast scope of the subject, and receive a general view of the direction taken by the religious development of man. The part taken by religion in the history of civilisation will become clear to him. He will see for himself the points at which religion and history intersect each other. His own mental horizon will be enlarged, his sympathies with mankind in general quickened, and he will also be in a better position to appreciate and take his part (whatever that may be) in the religious movements of his day and with which he will necessarily come into contact. In a word, a general knowledge of the history of religion acquired in this way may properly be regarded as part of the mental equipment which we have a right to expect the man or woman, laying claim to liberal culture, to possess.

III.

The educational conditions in England and on the continent of Europe being so totally different from what they are in the United States, the place to be accorded to the study of religion is naturally also different. In the United States, the question whether the history of religion should be introduced as a course of study into the public schools, hardly merits serious discussion. Belonging as it does to the group of culture-studies, there is no occasion for taking it up before the college is reached.

Indeed one cannot see what purpose would be served by introducing students at an immature age to a consideration of facts which would only result in confusing their minds in a most thorough fashion.

The nearest approach to the American college is represented in England by such institutions as Rugby and Eton, which serve as preparatory schools for Oxford and Cambridge, and on the Continent by the French Lycées or the German and Dutch Gymnasiums, which lead directly to the university. The age at which students leave the English and Continental institutions is about the same as the average age at which in the United States students enter college, so that the objection which applies to including the subject in a public school curriculum might seem to cover our higher schools as well. This is correct in so far as the higher schools in England are concerned; they are in the nature of private institutions, but on the Continent, where the government takes upon itself to provide for religious instruction in the public schools, the question of introducing the history of religion as a fit study for the Lycées and Gymnasiums takes on a different aspect. The religious instruction is introduced for purely practical purposes, namely, to educate the children in attendance in the tenets of the religious faith professed by their parents, and hence the instruction is imparted by religious guides.[1] Still, since the course covers the history of the religions whose doctrines and rites are thus taught, it is natural that the proposition should have been made to actually introduce the general history of religions into these schools.

In a measure this has been done in France,[2]

---

[1] In Germany, Holland, Austria, and France, special provision is made, *e.g.*, for the religious instruction of Jewish children, by teachers of their own faith.

[2] See Vernes, as above, pp. 130-137.

where the religions antecedent to Christianity are treated in outline, while in Germany, Holland, and Belgium, at all events, the mythology of the Greeks and Romans is included, and incidental references made to the religions of other ancient nations. The total disregard, however, of any attempt at furnishing a systematic course, and the omission of all references to Judaism and Christianity, is not satisfactory to such representatives of the historical study of religions as Vernes, Van Hamel, Goblet d'Alviella, and others, who strongly advocate extending the historical phases of religious instruction, so as to make it practically an outline course in the general history of religions. The wisdom of the procedure, even with due consideration to the educational condition prevailing in Europe, might be called into question, for the simple reason already suggested, that those in attendance at Lycées and Gymnasiums are too young to profit by such instruction ; and naturally this objection would apply with even greater force in the lower public schools, into which some zealous advocates also are disposed to introduce the subject.

Still, with the alternative of confining the subject entirely to university instruction, there is much to be said in favour of giving the subject *some* place in the curriculum of the higher schools. It is surely a serious defect for the student to come to the university or to enter into active life without any knowledge at all of a subject which affects his own position in the world. It is admitted that there is as much necessity for the study of Greek and Latin mythology in the higher schools as for Greek and Roman history, so long as an important place is accorded to the Greek and

Latin languages in the curriculum. With this as a starting-point, a brief course could be arranged for the last year of the course in the Lycée or Gymnasium, which could take up the more important religions of the past and present; but while the instruction could only be of an elementary character, and not as complete as the course adapted for the curriculum in American colleges, enough could be given in this way to make a lasting impression on young minds, and enough stimulus imparted to prompt them towards a maintenance of their interest upon reaching more mature years, in following the fascinating narrative of the religious development of mankind.

The main purposes, then, for which the study of religions should be introduced into the curriculum of American colleges, and of the higher schools on the Continent leading to the university proper, are two —as part of the equipment of a liberal education, and as a necessary adjunct for appreciating and understanding the religious movements and the religious needs of the present time. History, no matter of what period or of what country, is unintelligible without a knowledge of the part played by religion, and an intelligible grasp of one's own religious position is materially aided by such knowledge.

IV.

The position of the subject among university studies is quite different, and here no account need be taken of the traits peculiar to the universities of the various civilised countries. At all of them the main reason why the historical study of religions should be accorded a prominent place in the university curriculum is its importance as a branch of research; and the chief aim to be held in view is to provide, by means of a thorough training, a body of scholars in each generation, equipped for contributing to the further progress of the science.

While in the college and in the higher schools a single individual can cover the subject so far as it needs to be introduced into institutions of this order, it is manifest that for the training of specialists a different system is required. No single individual can possibly cover the entire field in such a way as to serve as a guide for a student desirous of cultivating some special corner, and hence sub-divisions are necessary. The study of the sources being the first requisite for thorough training, the services of specialists are required, and indeed in such numbers that a faculty for the study of religion is the natural outcome.

The recognition of this need led to the establishment in 1885 of the section for the study [1] of Religions at the École des Hautes Études—which is itself a section of the Paris University. No less than twenty members make up the faculty, among whom the work is divided. Each year courses are offered in the study of the sources of the religions of the past and present, extending from the religions of Egypt and Babylonia, through those of Greece, Rome, Judæa, Persia, and India, down to Christianity and Islam, besides general courses covering the history of those religions; and recently there has been added to the programme the study of primitive

---

[1] Section des Sciences Religieuses. See, for an account of this work and organisation, an article by Jean Réville, " The Rôle of the History of Religions in Modern Religious Education " (*The New World*, i., pp. 503-519).

religions, customs, and folk-lore. The comparative aspects, too, come in for their share, and the work on this branch is further supplemented by the chair for the general History of Religions, established at the Collège de France in 1880. The courses are assigned in every case to specialists in the respective languages and literatures, so that a strict philological training is assured with the introduction into the historical method. Paris is particularly fortunate in having in its midst at all times a sufficient body of scholars occupying some post, who can give the additional time needed for work in this special section, but it may well be questioned whether the example is one that can be generally followed. It is indeed not essential that every university in the United States, in England, or in Germany should make such ample provision as is made in Paris, though not a few of them are in a position to do so. It will be sufficient if, in addition to the general and comparative aspects, needed as a supplement to the special studies, a certain number of the religions of the past or present are represented by complete courses. In this way one institution may content itself with providing for the special study of the religion of the Greeks and Romans, another for the religions of the ancient Orient, and still another for the investigation of primitive religions.

As the opportunity presents itself, or the growing interest calls for it, the courses could be gradually extended. At all the leading universities of America and Europe, the Latin and Greek departments are sufficiently large to permit one member in each to direct his particular attention to the reli-

gious texts and the other sources for the study of
the religion of the one or the other of these two nations.
The study of Sanscrit and of the Semitic languages is
closely bound up with the religious literature produced in India and among the Semites, so that many
of the courses now offered on these subjects are practically a part of the programme for the study of religions.
By a readjustment, involving no profound modifications, provision could thus be made at many institutions for a considerable portion of the entire field.
Naturally, the chair for the general and comparative
aspects should not be wanting, but even without such
a chair a beginning could be made, by encouraging
students to take up some special language and its
literature, and to direct their energies into the channel
of the religious thought of the people as expressed
in its literature. It seems indeed timely that some
active steps should be taken by the leading universities of America and Europe to recognise the study
of religions as part of the legitimate university
curriculum. Outside of Paris, Holland is the only
continental country where the subject is placed on
a par with others, and a student who is a candidate for the Doctor's degree can choose the
history of religions as a major or minor. The
reorganisation of the Dutch Theological Seminaries
in 1876 led to this happy issue by providing at each
of the four universities a special chair for the history
of religions, and in making other provisions for the
subject, even if not on so large a scale as in Paris.
Neither in Germany, Austria, nor England has the
subject received formal recognition by university
authorities, while in the United States, only two or
three institutions have bestowed it. It is precisely this

formal recognition of the history of religions as a subject admissible for a major or a minor on the part of a student, who is a candidate for the Doctor's degree, which is needed before any further steps can be taken for its adequate or partial representation in the curriculum.

V.

The objections which might be urged against introducing the subject into the college curriculum, or into that of the higher schools, have even less force, if indeed any at all, in the case of the university curriculum. All fears of undue influence that might be exerted upon students are groundless in the case of persons who are sufficiently matured to be regarded as capable of making a choice of subjects to which they desire specially to devote their attention. The studies themselves being based to so large an extent upon the philological study of texts, which have almost exclusively a theoretical interest, there is scarcely any opportunity to touch upon the larger questions of religious belief which occur to the layman and dilettante the moment that the phrase " history of religions " is uttered. It may again be urged that it is in the interest of practical religion, as much as for the progress of the science itself, that the universities should become centres for research in the history of religions. In no other way can the dilettante be driven from the field, and until the universities do occupy it, he will be under the strong temptation to usurp it as his own. The university will naturally make its requirements before the degree can be granted so high as to place the prize beyond the reach of any but the thoroughly trained student.

Taken as a major subject, a study of at least two religions direct from the sources will be demanded, besides a general knowledge of the religious history of mankind. The thesis for the degree, chosen from the field which the student desires to make particularly his own, will afford him an opportunity for applying a strict historical method to some particular point, while in the preparation for the final examination he will be further led to make his equipment as thorough as possible. As a minor, the requirements will be less in quantity, but the method to be pursued will be the same, and a partial knowledge of two religions studied from the sources should still be held up as the minimum needed to enable a student to control the researches of others, and to continue the study of the subject for himself.

VI.

Besides the College and the University, there is another institution in which the study of religion should decidedly find a place—the Theological Seminary. If we have a right to expect from the liberally educated layman some knowledge of so important a subject as the religious history of the race, this is all the more necessary in the case of religious guides and teachers of mankind. It is indeed a matter of surprise to note the shameful manner in which the study of religions was until recently entirely neglected in institutions established for the training of ministers. Even for the purely practical purpose of the profession, a good knowledge of religious history, of the doctrines and tenets of other religions than their own, seems an essential

24

requirement. Mission work among foreign nations becomes a hopeless muddle, if entrusted to those who know little or nothing of the religious habits and the religious disposition of those among whom they expect to labour. The modern pastor is almost inevitably apt to be placed in a community made up of organisations representing various beliefs. How can he expect to act as a guide unless he knows what these beliefs are, how they arose, and why they are entertained? Religious thought constantly presents new aspects; and he is left hopelessly behind, who does not fit himself to follow these changing conditions. The theoretical value of a knowledge of religious history is even more to a religious teacher. Nothing, it may be safely asserted, is so well qualified to lend a forcible character to the system of religious philosophy (or theology) for which he stands, as the ability to compare it with others, and to note the points of agreement and difference. Sympathy with the religious struggles of mankind is properly demanded of the religious guide, and in no better way can this sympathy be acquired than by an extension of one's knowledge of what religion has actually accomplished, and what it has stood for in the past. In whatever direction the religious teacher turns he must experience the need of a knowledge of religious history.

As yet the institutions are few in which adequate provision for the subject has been made. In the United States more has been done than elsewhere,[1] but at Oxford, Manchester College alone includes the subject in its curriculum, while in Germany

---

[1] Andover Theological Seminary and the Theological Department of the University of Chicago call for special mention.

only a few of the theological departments connected with the universities offer some courses of a very general character. In Holland alone, the theological seminaries maintained in collaboration with the universities demand a knowledge of the general history of religions as part requirement of the candidate for ordination.

Something more, however, than a general knowledge is required in the seminary curriculum. A part of the time spent by the student in training for a clerical career should be utilised in making himself more particularly familiar with some branch of so large a subject. Not that he should go through the training required to make him a specialist, but it seems essential that he should be introduced by direct contact with strict historical methods into religious researches. And this can only be accomplished if he is taught to go directly to the sources for at least *one* of the great religions. It is quite possible, and indeed probable, that practical duties, when once he has entered upon his active career, will prevent him from continuing his studies in the history of religions, but the impression made upon him by contact with the sources of some great religion will be lasting, and will become a part of his mental store. In consequence of such contact he will come to recognise aspects of religion totally unknown to him before. In the case of the theological seminary or theological department of a college or university, therefore, the general course, which should form part of the college curriculum, needs to be supplemented by opportunities to study more specially the sources of the history of some religion. It matters little which one is chosen, and the choice will often depend upon peculiar circumstances. In seminaries for training Christian divines, the study of Judaism or of Islam or of Buddhism suggests itself, and of these the preference might be given to the former, in view of the strange misconceptions regarding it which are common among the Christian clergy. In those seminaries established for equipping guides in the Jewish church, it will be well to urge the importance of a study of the New Testament as an essential towards understanding Christianity, in which respect Jewish Rabbis are sadly and inexcusably deficient.[1]

VII.

Apart from the value to themselves, which an adequate knowledge of the subject would have for the members of the clerical profession, there is another and even more urgent reason why the study of religions should be encouraged and promoted in every possible way among this class. There is no body of men who exert such an influence upon public opinion as do the occupants of pulpits. Despite the oft heralded decline of practical religion, fully nine-tenths of the members of a community come, either at an early age or later, under some species of religious influence. The Church still has the opportunity of moulding, to a large extent, the religious spirit of mankind. It receives the young under its guidance at the most impressionable age, and for the great masses the instruction received through the religious school is a permanent acquirement, the truth of which is never questioned in later life. In view of this, the

---

[1] See an article by Claude G. Montefiore in the *Jewish Quarterly Review*, vol. viii., pp. 193-216.

responsibility resting upon religious guides should weigh heavily upon them. It is their province to promote the healthy growth of religious thought, and they also have it in their power to check that growth by instilling the poison of intolerance, illiberality, and fanaticism into innocent minds, or into minds incapable of judging things for themselves. How large a share of the misunderstandings, bickerings, hatred, and cruel deeds with which the pages of religious history are soiled is due to the pernicious influences spread through religious guides it is hard to say, but it is easier to under-estimate than over-estimate this share.

Such a state of affairs should not blind us to the other side of the picture, in which we behold the Church, through the influence of its representations, leading men to deeds of valour and promoting the welfare of human society, but it should prompt us to consider the power for good or evil which has thus been placed in the hands of religious teachers. It is of supreme importance, therefore, in the interests of the highest ends after which humanity strives, that its guides should be equipped with an adequate knowledge of the religious history of the race. It is part of their work, with the aid of earnest study of one or the other of the great religions of the past or present, to recognise the function of the religious spirit, its scope and significance, and to become filled with a spirit of intense sympathy for the manifestations of religions everywhere, recognising in these manifestations the struggles and throes of the human soul in its longing for truth and in its desire to attain to a perception of the Infinite. To impart this spirit of sympathy to their followers is one of the functions of religious guides.   Happy those who succeed in doing so.   To have implanted in the heart of an individual the sentiment of human love and general sympathy, is to have equipped him with three-fourths of the true religious spirit.

To sum up.   (1.) In the American college the historical study of religions should form part of the curriculum during the last year of the course as an essential feature of a liberal education.   By means of lectures, supplemented by required reading, the general phases of the subject should be imparted to the student, together with an outline of the development of religious thought among mankind, and an account of the important religions of the past and present.

(2.) In the higher schools of England and the Continent—the preparatory colleges, the Lycées, and Gymnasiums—owing to the somewhat lower age at which the students finish their course, only the general outlines of the subject should be presented during the last year of the course, but enough to give the student, before entering upon professional studies or on a business career, some grasp of the part played by religion in history, and of the scope of its functions.   The instruction should take the form of lectures, general phases—such as the classification of religions, the origin of religion, and the like— being omitted.   The character of the existing literature, suited only for more mature minds, makes it undesirable to supplement so elementary a course by any required reading.

(3.) In the university curriculum the attempt should be made to cover the entire field, or as large a part of the field as possible.   A chair should be found at every leading university for the general history of religion, and the comparative aspects of the subject, to be supplemented by courses in the sources and history of special religions, to be in charge of members of the faculty who are specialists in the language in which the sources for the study of the religion in question are found. The ultimate goal of such a programme is the formation of a special section within the general department of philosophy (or whatever its name may be), though, even without such a section, provision can be made for recognising the historical study of religions as a subject admissible as a major or minor for the doctor's degree.

(4.) In the curriculum of the theological seminary or theological department of a university, provision should be made (*a*) for the general aspects and outlines of the history of religions by means of lectures with supplementary reading, corresponding to the course proposed for American colleges, but in addition to this, (*b*) the history of one religion outside the one for whose service the student is being trained, should be studied up to a certain point of proficiency directly from the sources, as a means of familiarising the student with the method of historical research. Opportunities should also be provided for such students as show a special bent, to carry their studies in the history of religions into special directions, either through co-operation with a university or by the introduction of supplementary courses. Two years of the curriculum should be covered by the course required for all students, the first to be directed to general aspects and outlines, the second to the initiation into methods of research by a study of the sources of one or other of the great religions.

In this outline for the study of religions, we have hitherto considered only the historical aspects. There are, however, other points of view from which religion and religions are to be regarded, notably, the philosophical and the psychological. It cannot be emphasised too strongly that the basis for both of these points of view must be the actual course taken by religion.[1] Mere speculation as to the meaning of certain currents in religious thought, or as to the character of certain emotions and experiences commonly regarded as religious, is futile unless built upon a structure of solid fact—and the facts in religion can be obtained only by the application of the historical method and by the study of religious phenomena. The obvious conclusion from this position is, that the philosophy and the psychology of religion are phases of the study which come after the training in the historical method has been secured, and also after a student has, by actual contact with the sources, made himself thoroughly at home in the history of at least one religion. Religious statistics, however carefully gathered, do not suffice as a starting-point for the psychological study of religious phenomena. The religion itself, or the religions furnishing the statistics, must be studied as they have actually manifested themselves in history, before we can advance to the investigation of the psychological substratum of the facts; and similarly, to trace the course of certain philosophical principles in the domain of religion can lead to results of an enduring character only if the history of the religions has been thoroughly grasped.

From what has been said in this chapter, it will

[1] See pp. 276-279.

have become clear that the main function of the college, seminary, and university is to supply—each in its way—training in the historical method. In addition to this, the seminary and the university can point the way, by some general courses, to the study of the philosophical and psychological aspects of religious phenomena. These courses should run parallel with the special work in the historical study, but it hardly seems advisable, even in the case of the university curriculum, and much less therefore in the seminary work, to go beyond the general course, introduced more as a means of stimulating the mind of the student and of directing his attention to the philosophical and psychological problems involved, than as definite attempts at the solution of these problems. The course in the philosophy of religion would naturally fall within the province of the scholar occupying the chair for the general history of religions, while the psychology of religion should be entrusted, for the time being at least, to the specialist in psychology, whose interest should be broad enough to include religious phenomena within his horizon. As yet but few of the psychologists of the new school have seriously entered upon this field, but in time no doubt the number will increase; and it cannot be long before those interested in this branch of psychological study will recognise the necessity more fully than at present, of combining historical studies with purely psychological observations.

Desirable as the inclusion of general courses on the philosophy and psychology of religion in the seminary and university curriculum is, the loss is not a serious one if provisions of an adequate

character cannot be made. For some time to
come, historical investigations, particularly in the
domain of ancient religions, will have to absorb
the attention of students. It is in this field that
workers are needed, and the higher institutions of
learning can perform no better service than to train
and encourage young men for this task. In the
career of the individual, the active study of the
philosophy or of the psychology of religion will
lose nothing by being postponed to a mature age,
after the mind has been thoroughly disciplined, a large
fund of experience as well as of knowledge has been
acquired, and one's spurs have been won by attempts
less ambitious than the solution of the vexed problems
in the domain of philosophy or psychology, on which
so many careers have been shipwrecked in the past.
Let it be emphasised once more, that solid work
in the philosophy and psychology of religion can
be done only after the university or seminary stage
of one's career is past. While, so far as the historical
study of religions is concerned, the university and
seminary can actually take a student some way
along the road leading to permanent results, for
the philosophical and psychological aspects, they
can only point the way leading to the road itself.

Confining ourselves, then, so far as the seminary
and university are concerned, to the general course,
such a one would embrace, in the field of philosophy,
an exposition of the leading ideas in the religions
of the world, a classification of these ideas, and a
summary account of their development; in the
field of religious psychology, the course would
cover an investigation of the conditions under
which the religious emotions are aroused, the

various kinds of such emotions, studies of mental phenomena at important physical crises in the life of the individual, with special attention to abnormal phenomena in the domain of religious history, both of entire peoples and of individuals, religious hallucinations, periods of unusual religious excitation, religious revivals, and the like. It need perhaps hardly be pointed out that the philosophy of religion here contemplated differs in essential particulars from courses parading under this name at universities and seminaries a few generations ago, and still given at some places. As for the psychology of religion, I know of no institution where such courses, with utilisation of modern researches in physiological psychology, are given. What we have had hitherto has been a treatment of the psychology of religion from the point of view of the philosopher, but this is something totally different from a treatment of the subject from the standpoint of the trained psychologist.

CHAPTER XV.

MUSEUMS AS AN AID TO THE STUDY OF RELIGION.

I.

THE museum as a factor in popular education, and as an aid in the training of special students, has come to stay; and this is due to the modification that the museum idea itself has undergone. Instead of being a general gathering place for curios, the modern museum is characterised as much by what it excludes, as by what it contains. Special museums for special subjects are the order of the day, and even where the attempt is made to make the museum representative of all phases of history and culture, and of all the sciences, the field is divided into groups, and we have practically an aggregate of individual museums. Systematic arrangement, according to carefully conceived plans, counts for more than one-half of the value of any collection; and in view of this, it is not the number of objects that is important, but their quality and character. The value of an object is proportionate to the amount and kind of illustration that it furnishes. Next to arrangement comes labelling as an important means of making a collection accessible and useful; and here we cannot quote too often the remark of the late G. Brown Goode, when he

characterised the ideal museum as "a good collection
of labels with objects attached as illustrations."

II.

These preliminary remarks will prepare us for
estimating the place to be accorded to the museum of
religious history as an adjunct to the study.   There
are naturally some subjects of investigation for which
the museum is of more importance than for others.
Zoology, anatomy, anthropology, can hardly be
carried on without a museum, which is as important
to these subjects as the laboratory is for chemistry,
physics, biology, and psychology; but there is scarcely
any subject which cannot be all the better taught
by the aid of an illustrative and properly arranged
museum.

It is the merit of Émile Guimet to have demonstrated the value of a museum of religious history for
the study of the subject.   Guimet is a man whose
entire life has been devoted to a single purpose—the
furtherance of research in the field of religious history.
His own special interest in the religions of China and
Japan and India led him to direct most of his energies
towards collecting objects illustrative of the doctrines
and rites of the religions prevailing in these countries,
but he also included others in his scope.   In 1888 he
brought his collection to Paris and formally presented
it to the city.   A handsome building was erected for
housing the treasures.   An extensive library was
added as part of the equipment, and facilities for
research afforded to students, so that the Musée
Guimet, as it is officially styled, forms a most valuable adjunct to the *Section des Sciences Religieuses*

at the Paris University. On a much smaller scale the Smithsonian Institution organised, a number of years ago, a section for objects illustrative of religious worship;[1] while at the British Museum three rooms have been devoted to religion.

III.

Extensive as the Musée Guimet is, it is far from covering the whole range of the study.[2] It may be argued that a completely equipped museum is impossible, and in a certain sense this is correct, but it is quite within the range of feasibility to organise a collection which will illustrate the entire history of religion from the earliest period to which it can be traced back, down to the present time. In order to do this, however, the term museum must be extended so as to include maps, books, photographs, models, diagrams, and descriptive drawings.

A three-fold division suggests itself — general, special, and comparative. Assuming a special building erected to house the museum, a large hall should form, as it were, the introduction to the museum proper. By a series of diagrams the divisions of the history of religions should first be indicated, a list given of the most important classifications of religions that have been suggested, and of the most

[1] For an account, see the reports of the Curator, Dr. Cyrus Adler, in the *Annual Smithsonian Reports.* Special exhibitions of a temporary character have been held in various places. See Adler's article, "Museum Collections to Illustrate Religious History and Ceremonials," in *Memoirs of the International Congress of Anthropology,* pp. 324-328.

[2] See Appendix II., in which an outline of the arrangement of the Musée Guimet is given.

significant definitions that have been proposed by the most eminent thinkers. These diagrams need to be supplemented by a series of maps illustrating for the various periods the distribution of the special religions. In all six maps would be required, (1) illustrating the distribution of religions prior to the days of Alexander the Great, (2) Religion at the time of the birth of Jesus, (3) The period just before the rise of Mohammedanism, (4) Mohammedanism in its prime, (5) Religion after the Reformation, (6) Religion at the present time. Naturally, opinions might vary as to the divisions to be proposed, but this is of comparatively little moment as long as periods are chosen in which significant changes in the distribution of religions took place. Statistical tables should form an important adjunct to the maps, indicating in detail, as far as possible, the number of adherents of the various religions and sects in each of the countries represented.

For the second grand division of the museum, a proper classification is the first requisite. In the Musée Guimet the classification is geographical, but clearly the more scientific plan would be to place religions in groups, according to a scheme of classification which should indicate the position they occupy in the development of religious thought. Adopting, by way of illustration, the division proposed in this work, there would be four distinct sections—

The Religions of Savages.

The Religions of Primitive Culture.

The Religions of Advanced Culture.

The Religions emphasising the co-extensiveness of religion with life.

In the construction of a building for a religious

museum there would be no difficulty in so arranging
the sections as to form a continuous series, which would
enable the visitor to follow with ease the principle of
religious development underlying the arrangement.
A prominent feature in each section would be a
large map, or series of maps, illustrating the distribution of the religions belonging to the group.
In the case of the first two sections, no further geographical sub-divisions would be called for, since the
religion of savages and those of people living in a
state of primitive culture, are marked by certain
common traits, rather than by an individual character, distinguishing a certain group of savages or of
people of primitive culture. By means of charts the
general traits of savage beliefs should be pointed out, as
also the chief features of primitive religions. The objects collected will serve as illustrations of these traits
and features, consisting as they would of talismans,
objects used in the cults, models of primitive altars and
temples, images of the gods and spirits worshipped,
and either models or photographs illustrative of
religious worship, of religious dances and processions,
of incantations and magic ceremonies, as well as of
marriage and burial customs. Particular stress should
be laid upon the latter, as furnishing in most instances
a key to the most significant of a people's religious
beliefs.

In connection with objects, models, and photographs, belonging more particularly to the religious
life, some attempt should also be made to illustrate the
general state of culture reached, by an exhibition of
the arts and manufactures, so far as found, among the
various people in question—their style of dress, of
their dwellings, their food, and their games.

In the third and fourth sections, each religion should, in a sense, form a unit, but a number should again be united into a group. Charts should illustrate the religions included in each section, and the further sub-divisions proposed. In the third section we should thus have a group, (1) Religions of the ancient Orient, embracing (*a*) Egypt, (*b*) Babylonia and Assyria, (*c*) Phœnicia, (*d*) Arabia and Palestine; (2) another group would be formed by the religions of Greece and Rome, and a third (3) by the religions of the distant East antecedent to the rise of Buddhism. Objects illustrative of the cult would naturally be much more abundant in this section than in the preceding two. Each religion being treated separately, the endeavour would naturally be made to exhibit as far as possible the traits of each. The objects themselves would need to be supplemented by models and charts. So in the case of Egypt and Babylonia, the religious architecture, so important as an expression of religious ideals, could only be made clear by models, based, of course, upon careful studies; and it might be appropriate to emphasise here, that for the purpose of a religious museum, casts, whether of statues, columns, monuments, inscriptions, or tablets, are quite as useful as originals.

In the case of religions belonging to the third and fourth sections, a prominent place should be accorded to the illustration of religious literature. In addition to charts furnishing a survey of the literature in each instance, there should be specimens either in the shape of original inscriptions, tablets, manuscripts, as the case may be, or of casts, facsimiles, and printed books. Full explanations, with translations of characteristic passages, should make clear the nature of

25

the literature, and its importance as a means for understanding the religion of which it is the expression. The natural interest attaching to the religions of the present will lead to giving a much larger space to these than to those which belong to the past. The hopelessness of a complete exhibit suggests in this instance selection rather than collection as the best policy.

Two groups suggest themselves for the religions of the present: (1) Christianity, Judaism, and Islam on the one side ; (2) the religion of India, China, and Japan on the other, with Zoroastrianism as a kind of link between the two, though more closely allied to those in the first group. Each religion, however, should be illustrated independently, and in the selection of objects, casts, photographs, and models forming the exhibit, the point to be kept in mind must be the bringing out of the salient traits only. More than this would lead to confusion by the very multiplicity of the exhibit itself. By means of models or photographs the chief types of religious architecture and of art-temples, altars, sculptures, and paintings characteristic of each of the religions of the present could be brought out. In the case of models, casts, or photographs of images of the gods, a complete series might be aimed at, and lies within the range of possibility, but so far as the objects used in religious worship are concerned, little would be gained by trying to embrace everything, for instance, that is used in connection with the rites of all of the numerous sects into which Christianity is divided. So far, *e.g.*, as the dress of the priests and clergy represent peculiar traits, it should be exhibited, but manifestly there are many features in this dress without special significance. Again, in illustration of the ritual, characteristic features should be chosen with an intentional neglect of unimportant details. By a careful execution of this policy, a collection could be formed covering the fourth section, which would answer all purposes.

IV.

There is, however, another aspect of the religious museum which needs to be included in this survey of its scope. The large entrance hall of the ideal building should be taken up with maps, diagrams, and statistical tables illustrating the general aspects of religions—classification, definitions, distribution, and the like. There would follow the series of rooms devoted to the illustration of the four sections into which we have divided the religions of the world; but in order to obtain a bird's-eye view, as it were, of the course taken by religion, and above all, to trace its general features, there should be included in the museum, provision for illustrating the comparative aspects. The proper place for this third division is after the special religions have been disposed of, corresponding to the place assigned to the comparative study of religions.[1]

In this comparative section the beginning should again be made with maps showing the historical relationship of the various religions to one another. Statistical tables should furnish facts regarding their relative scope and distribution, while by means of diagrams, the range covered by certain leading doctrines — such as monotheism, immortality of the soul, incarnation, and the like—could

[1] See p. 348.

be traced. No less interesting would be a series of diagrams illustrating the comparative study of leading myths and folk-tales; and lastly, the religious customs, their distribution, the points of agreement and points of divergence among different peoples should be presented in an elaborate series of tables, for which Herbert Spencer's *Descriptive Sociology* furnishes an appropriate model. The objects themselves—originals or casts—together with the models and photographs in the section, would largely illustrate the maps and diagrams. They would naturally be duplicates of what has already been included in the second division of the museum devoted to the illustration of the various religions, but the arrangement of them would be made from the comparative point of view. A series of models or photographs would enable us to make a comparative study of religious architecture. An important subdivision would be a selected series of objects used in the various cults, which should illustrate points of agreement and the salient features of each of the cults. Religious customs—as, for example, birth, marriage, and burial rites—should similarly be presented from the comparative point of view; and lastly, the comparative study of the traits of the vast number of gods in the various religions should be facilitated by a collection of images chosen from all sides and from all periods in the history of religious development.

V.

Having thus set forth the general plan for a religious museum on a comprehensive scale, it will be in order to consider exactly what purpose will be served by it.

Religion being, by virtue of its practical relationship to life, a subject of interest to all classes of the community, it is manifestly of direct importance to spread a knowledge of its history as widely as possible. As long as religion remains a factor in public and private life—and one cannot conceive of a time when this will not be the case—every community has a natural concern in the direction of the exercise of the religious function into proper channels. If it is possible, therefore, to supplement the work of the churches without interfering with the liberties or encroaching upon the domain of the church organisation, the opportunity should be embraced, and should be welcomed by those who have the religious training of the members of the community particularly at heart. The museum of religious history, properly conceived, is well fitted to act as such an educational supplement. The plan of such a museum should be so conceived as to have in mind, in the first instance, the needs of the general public. The arrangement of the rooms, the display of the objects, the labelling, and the explanatory guide-book, should all be prepared with a view of arousing and chaining the interest of those who have neither the opportunity nor the inclination to make a special study of religions. The impression will be all the more profound because of this lack of preparation ; and in order that this impression may not have its outcome in a mental confusion, the arrangement should follow, so far as possible, the natural and logical order in which the various sub-divisions of the study of religions would be taken up.

To the objection that is sometimes urged against

educational projects, that the public is not prepared
for them, it may be pointed out in reply that we are
apt to under-estimate the intellectual calibre of what
is called the masses. Time and again it has been
demonstrated that the masses possess more discrimination than they are usually given credit for,
that good music, good art, and substantial lectures
appeal to them, and that it is not difficult to arouse
their interest in subjects frequently supposed to be
beyond their reach. Public museums of all kinds,
if opened at a time when the working classes can
attend, soon become popular, and the educational
advantages of collections illustrating man's achievements and his history can hardly be over-estimated.

VI.

There is another aspect from which museums of
religious history should be regarded. The two
extremes are apt to be found in large numbers in
every community—those who in revolt from ecclesiastical authority, or for other reasons, have assumed a
hostile attitude towards religion, and deceive themselves by the repetition of superficial arguments into
the belief that they have demolished the foundations
of faith, and those who become so centred in their
own religious views as to lose all sympathy with
other forms of belief. The cultivation of the sympathetic attitude, which we have seen [1] constitutes the
very corner-stone of all fruitful investigation of
religious phenomena, is as important for the masses
—if not more so—as for the student. In no more
effective way can this broad spirit be infused into

[1] Chap. xii.

people than by showing them the numerous aspects assumed by religious belief, the various roads that have been taken in the hope of reaching the goal of existence, and the general path followed by the religious unfolding of mankind. Nay, the mere suggestion once borne in upon them, that there is such a thing as religious development, is sufficient to impart a new conception of the function and scope of religions.

The further progress of religious thought being dependent not merely upon the labours of thinkers, but upon raising the general intellectual level, any step in that direction should be heartily welcomed. The establishment of popular religious museums in our large cities is such a step, and, fortunately, the possibility of organising at least a section for religious history in connection with the public institutions already existing in both the larger and smaller intellectual centres of the civilised world removes the suggestion from the province of Utopian schemes. The beginning may be made in a modest way, but there is no reason why, in many cities that might be mentioned, this beginning should not be made on a large scale.

It is hardly necessary to dwell upon the various ways in which such a museum would be of direct service to the student—whether in the college, in the higher schools, in the university, or in the seminary. The opportunities of extensive travel are given to but few. Illustrations of objects used in cults are scattered through many volumes, and do not afford that clear view which the object itself, or the cast, can give. Moreover, the possibility, while studying any particular religion, of obtaining, in a convenient manner, a general view of the field covered is an advantage that represents a saving of months of patient labour. To this must be added the mental stimulus acquired by direct contact, as it were, with the subject which is engrossing one's attention. All this is too obvious to require any further comment ; but a word might, in conclusion, be said regarding the general effect that religious museums would have in arousing interest in the study, and in promoting further investigation of the many unsolved problems in the field of religious history.

The study of religion, the method for which it has been the chief aim of this book to illustrate, is still in that stage which requires what may properly be called propagandism. There is no reason for shrinking from this oft misunderstood term. Despite the popular adage to the contrary, the worthiest cause needs advocates ; and when that cause is one which is apt to encounter popular prejudices, it is all the more important that those who feel convinced of its worthiness and significance, who are earnestly devoting themselves towards furthering its objects, should, even at the risk of temporarily deserting their books, step into the arena of public debate and plead its cause. Whatever may be done to call attention to the practical and theoretical value of the historical study of religions will also help to remove prejudices and misunderstandings as to the scope and purpose of the study itself.

But more effective than pleadings by word of mouth, or through the pen, is the object-lesson furnished by an illustration of religious history, such as is possible in a museum alone. The immediate result of the establishment of such a museum would be the quickening of the general interest in the subject, thus presenting itself in a new light to many, while its presence in the midst of a community would be a permanent aid and incentive to those more particularly interested in the subject. The greater the general interest in a subject, the greater the intensity with which students will apply themselves to the work in hand. The museum of religious history would form a bond between the public and the investigators. It would be the means of rendering generally accessible the results of research ; and, in return, the consciousness of thus directly contributing towards the education and liberalising of the masses will give the scholar that courage and cheer which constitutes the chief reward of his labours.

The historical study of religions is pre-eminently a subject that should be pursued with the ultimate purpose of reacting on the intellectual life of the general public. Many of the problems involved, though of a purely historical character, have a more or less direct bearing upon those which confront us to-day. It is therefore a healthy and encouraging symptom to find a more general interest spreading in the study; and it is not only proper for scholars to aid and promote this interest, but it is their duty to do so. It is only through the reaction of the work of thinkers and investigators upon the general mind that intellectual progress is brought about. This applies particularly to the further progress of religious development, which is dependent upon the establishment and maintenance of harmonious relations between the leaders in thought and their followers, between the zealous teachers and those who stand in the no less honourable rank of willing pupils, between the scholar whose happy lot it is to be engaged in an intellectual pursuit which makes him useful and the world at large which reaps the benefits of the scholar's labours. Leaders and followers alike are concerned in promoting the two main objects of the study of religions, namely, the determination of the nature, scope, and achievements of the religious spirit in all its various manifestations, from the earliest times to the present, and the cultivation of that spirit of intense sympathy with one another, which is the basis of mutual esteem, and constitutes an important factor in establishing peace and good-will among individuals and among nations.

APPENDIX I.

Courses given during the Second Semester, 1899-1900, in the Section for the Science of Religion of the École des Hautes Études, Paris.

Religions of Non-civilised Peoples.

L. Marillier.—1. The worship of the dead, and the condition of souls after death. 2. Human sacrifices and cannibalistic rites.

Religions of the extreme Orient and of the American Indians.

Leon de Rosny.—1 Tao and the idea of God in ancient China. 2. The Trinity-idea in primitive Shintoism. 3. The Buddhistic doctrine of the Re-incarnation and of the Extinction of Personality. 4. Interpretation of sacred writings of the extreme Orient and of ancient Armenia.

Religions of India.

A. Foucher.—1. Buddhistic Archæology and Iconography. 2. Interpretation of the Laws of Manu.

Religions of Egypt.

E. Amelineau.—1. The recent excavations of Abydos (second year). 2. The life of St. Macarius Ægyptius (Coptic).

Religions of Israel and of the Western Semites.

Maurice Vernes.—1. The traits of the ancient religion of Israel: sanctuaries, festivals, public and private worship. 2. Interpretation of the second part of Isaiah.

Talmudic and Rabbinical Judaism.

Israel Levi.—1. Critical study of the Midrash Bereshit Rabba. 2. Interpretation of the recently discovered Hebrew fragments of Ecclesiasticus.

Islam and the Religions of Arabia.

Hartwig Derenbourg.—1. Chronological study of the Koran. 2. Interpretation of Sabæan and Himyaritic inscriptions.

Religions of Greece and Rome.

J. TOUTAIN.—The Gallic-Roman Religion.

Christian Literature.

A. SABATIER.—1. The composition of the Gospels. 2. Interpretation of certain texts embodied in the Gospels and in the Epistles of St. John.

History of Dogmas.

ALBERT RÉVILLE.—Evolution of ecclesiastical doctrines in Rome as evidenced by the work known under the name of "Philosophoumena" (end of second and beginning of third century).

F. PICAVET.—1. Aristotle's *About the Soul* (third book) in comparison with the Greek, Arabic, and Christian commentaries, and with Cicero's *De Fato.* 2. Bibliography of Scholasticism—Thomas Aquinas and Neo-Thomism.

History of the Christian Church.

JEAN RÉVILLE.—1. History of the Christian Church from the end of the reign of Marcus Aurelius till the advent of Constantine. 2. The various types of the Reformation in the sixteenth century.

Byzantine Christianity.

G. MILLET.—1. Ecclesiastical ownership. 2. The decoration of churches, and symbolical doctrines.

History of Canon Law.

ESMEIN.—1. Testaments in canon law. 2. Interpretation of texts regarding the electoral system of the church.

History of the Ancient Churches of the East.

J. DERAMEY.—History of the church of Jerusalem from the commencement of the fourth century to the Arabic conquest.

Assyro-Babylonian Religion.

C. FOSSEY.—1. The Babylonian traditions regarding Creation and the Deluge. 2. The religious invocations in the royal inscriptions of Assyria.

APPENDIX II.

THE MUSÉE GUIMET AT PARIS.[1]

Established in Lyons in 1879 by M. Émile Guimet, and
transferred to Paris in 1888.

The following religions are represented at present in the
Museum :—

1. Religions of India.
2.   „   Thibet.
3.   „   China.
4.   „   Indo-China.
5.   „   Japan.
6.   „   Ancient Egypt.
7.   „   Greece and Rome.

The disposition of the objects displayed is as follows :—

Ground Floor.

1. Exhibition of Chinese and Japanese Ceramics.
2. Monuments from Siam and Cambodia.

First Floor.

1. Library of 24,000 volumes, with reading-room for students.
2. The Religion of the Parsees (one room).
3. Religions of Thibet and China (five rooms).
4. Religions of Indo-China, Cambodia, Burma, Siam, Anam,
   Tonkin, Siberia, and the popular religion of the southern
   Chinese province (five rooms).
5. Religions of Japan (six rooms, with two additional apart-
   ments devoted to Japanese art).

Second Floor.

1. Miscellaneous collection of paintings illustrative of religious
   cults.
2. Religions of Greece, Italy, and Gaul.
3. Cappadocian Monuments.
4. Mohammedan Art of Central Asia.
5. Ethnography and Religion of Crete.
6. Religion of Ancient Egypt.

[1] *Petit guide illustré au Musée Guimet, par L. Milloüe, conservateur*
(Paris, 4th ed., Leroux, 1900).

BIBLIOGRAPHY.

NOTE.

FOR greater convenience, the Bibliography has been divided into thirteen sections, as follows :—

The first two sections lie somewhat beyond the scope of this volume, which is concerned chiefly with the method, and only incidentally with the actual history of religions, but it was thought to be useful to indicate, as aids to the student, some of the general works on the history proper. In the case of the histories of religions, the more notable of the older and now antiquated works have been included, because of their historical interest and value in following the history of the study of religion.

In order, however, that the student may not go amiss, those histories which can be recommended as reliable guides have been marked with an asterisk. A selection of the numerous works and articles on the Philosophy of Religion has been given in the second section as a kind of supplement to the general works on the History. The selection has been made as inclusive as possible, so as to represent the various points of view from which the philosophy of religion has been approached. This section must be distinguished from the tenth section, which is devoted to monographs dealing with the *relationship* of religion to philosophy. In the third section, the manuals specially recommended have been marked with an asterisk. Be it understood that in the first and third sections *only* has this procedure, to mark with asterisk works particularly singled out for the needs of students, been followed. In the case of the sixth, seventh, and eighth sections it was difficult to avoid overlapping, and yet it seemed preferable to divide the general works on religion from such as deal with the nature and origin of religion, and the latter again from monographs on the religious sentiment and on the nature and analysis of belief. The selection in the case of these sections was also entailed with considerable difficulties, but the writer hopes that he has achieved his chief aim, which was to represent again the various points of view from which the problems involved may be considered. In the eleventh section, some works dealing with the methodology in the study of mythology have been included because of their bearing on the relationship of religion to mythology. In the last section monographs discussing the *practical* aspects of the relationship between religious belief and scientific investigations have been excluded as lying beyond the scope of this work. For the history of this relationship, the works of Draper and White (included in this section) suffice, though, naturally, others might have been added.

Be it emphasised once more that, for the reason set forth in the Preface (p. x.), the Bibliography as a whole, and in its sections, represents merely a *selection*, and in this selection the author has been guided by what might best serve the needs of students and readers for whom this book is intended, and who, with the indications given, will have no difficulty in completing any section of the Bibliography.

ABBREVIATIONS.

A.J.T.—American Journal of Theology.
A.R.—Archiv für Religionswissenschaft.
B.W.—Biblical World.
I.J.E.—International Journal of Ethics.
I.M.—International Monthly.
J.A.O.S.—Journal of the American Oriental Society.
J.P.T.—Jahrbücher für Protestantische Theologie.

N.W.—New World.
R.C.—Revue Chretienne.
R.Cr.—Revue Critique.
R.H.R.—Revue de l'Histoire des Religions.
T.S.K. — Theologische Studien und Kritiken.
T.T.—Theologisch Tijdschrift.
Z.W.T.—Zeitschrift für Wissenschaftliche Theologie.

I.

Dictionaries, Encyclopædias, and General Histories.

Those recommended are marked with an asterisk.

Benham, William.—The Dictionary of Religion. London, 1887.
*Crozer, John Beattie.—History of Intellectual Development. 2 vols. London, 1897-1901.
*Deussen, Paul. — Allgemeine Geschichte der Philosophie mit besonderer Berücksichtigung der Religionen. Leipzig, 1894.
Dupuis, Charles. — Origine de tous les Cultes ou Religion Universelle. Paris, 1795; new ed., Paris, 1870.
Geden, Alfred.—Studies in Comparative Religion. London, 1898.
Gould, F. J.—A Concise History of all Religions. 3 vols. London, 1893-98.
*Herzog, Plitt, and Hauck.—Real-Encyklopäedie für Protestantische Theologie und Kirche. 3rd ed. (in course of publication), Leipzig, 1896-
    Very wide in its scope, and includes general history of religions.
Ingram, John K.—Outlines of the History of Religion. London, 1900.
    One-sided from Positivist's point of view.

*Jastrow, Morris, Jun.— Editor of Handbooks on the History of Religions. Ginn & Co., Boston.
    I. The Religions of India. By E. W. Hopkins. 1895.
    II. The Religion of Babylonia and Assyria. By Morris Jastrow, Jun. 1898.
    III. The Religion of the Ancient Teutons. By P. D. Chantepie de la Saussaye. 1901.
    In Preparation.
    IV. The Religion of Persia. By A. V. Williams Jackson.
    V. Introduction to the History of Religions. By C. H. Toy.
    VI. The Religion of Israel. By Rev. John P. Peters.
    VII. The Religion of Islam. By Morris Jastrow, Jun.
Kellogg, S. H.—A Handbook of Comparative Religion. Phil., 1899.
    Narrow in scope and view.
*Lichtenberger, F. — Encyclopédie des Sciences Religieuses. 12 vols. Paris, 1877-83.
Meiners, Christoph.—Allgemeine kritische Geschichte der Religion. 2 vols. Hanover, 1806-7.
Meiners, Christoph. —Grundriss aller Religionen. Lemgo, 1785; 2nd ed., 1816.
*Menzies, Allen. — History of Religion. London and New York, 1895.
Moffatt, James C.—Comparative History of Religions. New York, 1873.

26

*Orelli, Conrad von.—Allgemeine Religionsgeschichte. Freiburg, 1899.

*Picart, B. [and Bernard, J. F.].—The Ceremonies and Religious Customs of the various Nations of the known World. 6 vols. London, 1733.

*Preiss, Hermann. — Religionsgeschichte — Geschichte der Entwickelung des religiösen Bewusstseins in seinen einzelnen Erscheinungsformen — eine Geschichte des Menschengeistes. Leipzig, 1888.

Price, E. D. — The Story of Religions. London and New York, 1898.
Unsatisfactory and defective.

Reichenbach, A.—Die Religion der Völker nach den besten Forschungsergebnissein bearbeitet. 2 vols. München, 1885.

Ross, Alexander. — Pansebeia, or a View of all Religions in the World. London, 1653.

*Saussaye, P. D. Chantepie de la.—Lehrbuch der Religionsgeschichte. Freiburg, 1887-88; 2nd ed. 1897, entirely modified.
English translation of the 1st vol. (Phenomenology of Religion) of the 1st ed., by Beatrice S. Colyer-Fergusson. London, 1892.

Scholten, J. H.—Geschiedenis der Godsdienst en Wijsbegeerte. Leiden, 1863.
French translation by Albert Réville (Paris, 1861), under the title "Manuel de l'Histoire comparée de la Philosophie et de la Religion."

*Tiele, C. P.—Geschiedenis van den Godsdienst in de oudheid tot op Alexander den Groote. Vols. i., ii. Amsterdam, 1891-97.
(In course of publication.) German translation by G. Gehrich, "Geschichte der Religion im Alterthum bis auf Alexander den grossen." Gotha, 1895.

*Tiele, C. P.—Outlines of the History of Religions. London, 1877.
Translation from the Dutch, by

J. E. Carpenter. French translation appeared in 1886 (2nd ed.), under the title "Manuel de l'Histoire des Religions," translated by Maurice Vernes, and revised by the author; German translation by F. W. T. Weber, "Compendium de Religionsgeschichte." Berlin, 1880; 2nd ed., 1887; new revised German edition by Nathan Soederblom, in co-operation with the author, in preparation.

II.

Philosophy of Religion.

Apelt, C. Fr.—Religionsphilosophie. Leipzig, 1860.

Bascom, John.—A Philosophy of Religion on the rational Grounds of Religious Belief. New York, 1876.

Berger, J. G.—Ideen zur Philosophie der Religionsgeschichte (C. F. Ständlin Beiträge, etc., 1797).

Beneke, Friedrich Ed.—System der Metaphysik und Religionsphilosophie. Berlin, 1840.

Biedermann, G.—Moral, Rechts und Religionsphilosophie. Prag, 1891.

Biedermann, G.—Religionsphilosophie. Leipzig, 1887.

Billroth, Joh. Gustav Friedr.—Vorlesungen über Religionsphilosophie. Herausgegeben von Johann Eduard Erdmann. Leipzig, 1877.

Caird, John.—An Introduction to the Philosophy of Religion. Glasgow, 1880; 2nd ed., London, 1889.

Caird, John.—Lectures on the Philosophy of Religion. London, 1876.

Caldecott, Alfred.—The Philosophy of Religion in England and America. London, 1901.

Carrau, L.—La Philosophie religieuse en Angleterre depuis Locke jusqu'à nos jours. Paris, 1881.

Carus, F. A. — Moralphilosophie und Religionsphilosophie,

"Nachgelassene Werke," vol. vii. Leipzig, 1810.

Drobish, Moritz Wilhelm. — Grundlehren der Religionsphilosophie. Leipzig, 1840.

Druskowitz, H.—Religionsphilosophie auf modern wissenschaftlicher Grundlage. Leipzig, 1886.

Eschenmayer, C. A.—Religionsphilosophie. 2 vols. Tübingen, 1818.

Fairbairn, A. M.—Studies in the Philosophy of Religion and History. London, 1876.

Fraser, A. C.—Philosophy of Theism, "Gifford Lectures." Edinburgh, 1900.

Fries, G. F.—Handbuch der Religionsphilosophie. Heidelberg, 1832.

Glogau, G.—Vorlesung über Religionsphilosophie. ·Kiel, 1898.

Groenewegen, H. Y.—De Nieuwere wijsbegeerte van den godsdienst. T.T., xxx. 117-155, and xxxii. 283-301.

Hartmann, Eduard v.—Religionsphilosophie. Erster-historisch kritischer Theil: Das Religiöse Bewusstsein der Menschheit - Zweiter - systematischen Theil—Die Religion des Geistes. Leipzig, 1888.
Hartmann's comprehensive work embraces Prolegomena, the history of religions in outline, the Psychology and Metaphysics of Religion, and also Ethics.

Hegel, C. F. W.—Vorlesungen über die Philosophie der Religion, "Sammtliche Werke." Vols. xi. and xii. Berlin, 1832.
See the new edition with commentary by G. J. P. J. Bolland. Leiden, 1890; English translation by E. H. Speirs and J. B. Sanderson. 3 vols. London, 1895.

Kant, Immanuel. — Vorlesungen über die Religionslehre. Ed. L. Politz. 2nd ed., Leipzig, 1830.
See Timothy Colany, "Exposè Critique de la Philosophie de Religion

de Kant," Strassburg, 1854; and H. Holtzmann, "Kant's Religionsphilosophie mit Bezug auf neuere Darstellungen." Z.W.T., xviii. 161-190.

Krause, Karl Christian Friedrich. —Die Absolute Religionsphilosophie. 2 vols. Dresden, 1834-43.

Krause, Karl Christian Friedrich. —Zur Religionsphilosophie und speculative Theologie. Leipzig, 1893.

Lasson, A.—Ueber Gegenstand und Behandlungsart der Religionsphilosophie. Leipzig, 1879.

Lindsay, James.—Recent Advances in Theistic Philosophy of Religion. Edinburgh, 1827.

Lotze, Hermann. — Grundzüge der Religionsphilosophie. Leipzig, 1882.
English translation by G. T. Ladd. Boston, 1885.

Morell, J. D.—The Philosophy of Religion. London, 1849.

Pfleiderer, Otto.—Religionsphilosophie auf geschichtlicher Grundlage. 3rd ed., Berlin, 1896.
English translation, "The Philosophy of Religion on the Basis of its History." 2 vols. London, 1886. See article by A. Bruining, "Wijsbegeerte van den godsdienst," T.T., xv. 365-428.

Pfleiderer, Otto.—Philosophy and Development of Religion, "Gifford Lectures." 2 vols. Edinburgh, 1899.

Pfleiderer, Otto. — Genetisch-spekulative Religionsphilosophie. Berlin, 1889.

Pünjer, G. Ch. B.—Geschichte der Christlichen Religionsphilosophie seit der Reformation. 2 vols. Leipzig, 1881-83.
English translation by W. Hastie. Edinburgh, 1887.

Pünjer, G. Ch. B.—Grundriss der Religionsphilosophie. Braunschweig, 1886.

Rauwenhoff, L. W. E.—Wijsbe-
geerte van den godsdienst. 2
vols. Leiden, 1887.
German transl. by J. R. Hanne,
"Religionsphilosophie." Braunschweig, 1889.
Rettberg, F. M.—Religionsphilosophie. Marburg, 1850.
Rhétoré, F.—Philosophie de la
Religion. Paris, 1896.
Richard, Jean.—Essai de Philosophie Religieuse. Heidelberg,
1872.
Sabatier, Auguste. — Esquisse
d'une Philosophie de la Religion d'après la Psychologie et
l'Histoire. 4th ed., Paris, 1897.
English translation, London, 1897;
German translation, Freiburg, 1898.
Sabatier, Auguste.—Quelques Re-
flexions sur la Philosophie de
la Religion. R.C., 1897, pp.
330-341.
Saisset, Emile Edmond.—Essais
sur la Philosophie et la Religion du XIXme siècle. Paris,
1845.
Schmidt, Ulrich Rudolf.—Zur Religionsphilosophie. Jena, 1888.
Schultze, H. — Religionsphilosophie auf modern wissenschaftlicher grundlage. Herausgegeben von Baumann. Leipzig,
1886.
Seydel, Rudolf.—Religionsphilosophie im Umriss, mit historisch-
kritischer Einleitung über die
Religionsphilosophie seit Kant.
Freiburg, 1893.
Siebeck, H.—Lehrbuch der Religionsphilosophie. Freiburg,
1893.
Taute, G. F.—Religionsphilosophie vom standpunkt der Philosophie Herbart's. 2 vols. 2nd
ed., Leipzig, 1852.
Teichmüller, G.—Religionsphilosophie. Breslau, 1886.
Vatke, Wilhelm.—Religionsphilosophie oder allgemeine philosophische Theologie. Heraus-

gegeben von Hermann G. S.
Preiss. Bonn, 1888.
Wernicke, Alex.—Zur Religions-
philosophie. J.P.T., viii. 193-
227.
Methodology.

III.

*Manuals for the Science and
History of Religion.*
Those specially recommended are
marked with an asterisk.
Bettany, G.—Primitive Religion:
Being an Introduction to the
Study of Religion. London,
1892.
*Burnouf, Eugene.—La Science
des Religions. 3rd ed., Paris,
1876.
English translation, "The Science
of Religions," by Julie Liebe. Lon-
don, 1888.
Cave, Alfred.—An Introduction
to Theológy. Edinburgh, 1886.
Includes general history of Re-
ligions.
Chabin, P.—La Science de la
Religion. Paris, 1898.
*D'Alviella, Goblet. — Introduc-
tion à l'Histoire Generale des
Religions. Bruxelles, 1886.
*Jevons, Frank Byron.—An In-
troduction to the History of
Religion. London, 1896.
Lamers, G. H.—De Wetenschap
van den godsdienst. Leiddraad
ten gebruike bij het hooger
onderwijs. Utrecht, 1891.
Introduction.
*Max-Müller, Friedrich.—Intro-
duction to the Science of Re-
ligion. London, 1873; 2nd ed.,
1880.
*Réville, Albert.—Prolégomènes
de l'Histoire des Religions.
Paris, 1881.
English translation by A. S. Squire.
London, 1884.
Rhétoré, F.—Science des Re-
ligions. Paris, 1894.
*Tiele, C. P.—Hoofdtrekken der
Godsdienstwetenschap. Am-
sterdam, 1901.
Compendium.

*Tiele, C. P.—Elements of the Science of Religion. Part I., Morphological; Part II., Ontological, "Gifford Lectures." 2 vols. Edinburgh, 1897-99.
Also in Dutch and German. See A. Réville, "Un Essai de Philosophie de l'Histoire religieuse." R.H.R., xxxvi. 370-398; xl. 374-413; and xli. 201-219, 359-389.

Tischhauser, C.—Grundzüge der Religionswissenschaft zur Einleitung in die Religionsgeschichte. Basel, 1891.

Van den Gheyn, J.—La Science des Religions: Essai historique et critique.
La Controverse et Le Contemporain, 1886.

IV.

The Study of Religion—General Aspects, History, and Present Status.

Briggs, Charles A.—The Scope of Theology and its Place in the University. A.J.T., i. 38-70.
Includes scope of "Study of Religions."

Carpenter, J. Estlin.—A Century of Comparative Religion, 1800-1900.
Reprinted from "The Inquirer," London.

Carpenter, J. Estlin.—The Place of the History of Religion in Theological Study. London, 1891.

D'Alviella, Goblet — Des préjugés qui s'opposent à l'étude scientifique des Religions, "Revue de Belgique." Bruxelles, 1885.
See Vernes, Maurice, R.Cr., Sept. 28, 1885.

D'Alviella, Goblet.—De la necessité d'introduire l'histoire des religions dans notre enseignement public, "Revue de Belgique." Bruxelles, 1882.

Gubernatis, A. de. — L'Avenir de l'Histoire des Religions. R.H.R., xlii. 198 219.

Hardy, E.—Die Allgemeine Vergleichende Religionswissenschaft im Akademischen Studium unsere Zeit. Freiburg, 1887.

Hardy, E.—Zur Geschichte der vergleichenden Religionsforschung. A.R., vol. iv., 45-66, 97-135, and 193-229.

Jastrow, Morris, Jun.—The Historical Study of Religions in Colleges and Universities. J.A.O.S., xx. 317-325.

Jastrow, Morris, Jun.—Recent Movements in the Historical Study of Religions in America. B.W., i. 24-32.

Meyer, Friedrich.—Die Religion und die Religionswissenschaft. Z.W.T., x. 121-131.

Réville, Albert. — L'Enseignement des Sciences Religieuses à l'École des Hautes Études.
In "Sciences Religieuses," i. pp. i.-xxx., published as vol. i. of the "Bibliothèque de l'École des Hautes Études." Paris, 1889.

Réville, Jean.—The Rôle of the History of Religions in Modern Religious Education. N.W., i. 503-519.

Réville, Jean.—L'Enseignement de l'histoire des Religions aux Etats Unis et en Europe. R.H.R., xx. 209-216.

Saussaye, P. D. Chantepie de la. —Die Vergleichende Religionsforschung u. der Religiöse Glaube. Freiburg, 1898.

Snell, M. M.—The Speculative Value of Comparative Religion. B.W., 1898, 342-345.

Snell, M. M. — The Practical Value of Comparative Religion. B.W., 1899, 88-93.

Tyler, Charles Mellen.—Study of the History and Philosophy of Religion. Ithaca, N.Y., 1891.

Van Hamel, G.—Aperçu general des principaux Phénomènes Religieux. R.H.R., ii. 377-386.

Van Hamel, G.—L'Enseignement

406 BIBLIOGRAPHY.

de l'Histoire des Religions en
Hollande. R.H.R., i. 379-385.
Vernes, Maurice.—De la Théo-
logie considerée comme science
positive et de sa place dans
l'enseignement laïque.
With Review by E. Littre, in
Vernes' "Mélanges de Critique Religieuse." Paris, 1880, pp. 301-313,
and 329-345.

V.

The Study of Religion—Method and Scope.

Appeldoorn, J. G.—Het Object
der Religie. T.T., xxxv. 240-
252.
Discussion of method.
De Broglie, l'Abbè.—Problèmes et
Conclusions de l'Histoire des
Religions. Paris, 1885.
From the standpoint of Catholic
theology.
Cara, P. Cesare A. de.—Esame
critico del sistema filologico e
linguistico applicato alla mito-
logia et alla scienza delle Reli-
gioni. Rome, 1884.
Collins, J.—La Question de l'Instruction Religieuse historique
dans l'enseignement secondaire
en Hollande. See R.H.R., iv.
243-247.
D'Alviella, Goblet. — Maurice
Vernes et la Methode comparative dans l'histoire des Religions. R.H.R., xii. 170-178.
Hardy, E. — Was ist Religionswissenschaft? A.R., i. 9-42.
Harnack, Adolf. — Die Aufgabe
der theologischen Facultaten
und die allgemeine Religionsgeschichte. Giessen, 1901.
Hökstra, S. — Gedachten over
wesen en de methode van de
godsdienstleer. T.T., vi. 1-44.
Hookyas, I.—Étude générale des
differentes Religion. R.H.R.,
ii. 386-389.
Outline of course.
Hugenholtz, Ph. R.—Over de
methode der wijsgeerige Gods-

dienstwetenschap. T.T., xv.
1-32.
See reply by A. Bruining, ib.,
200-246.
Hugenholtz, P. R.—Godsdienst en
Godsdienstwetenschap. T.T.,
xvii. 358-376.
Jastrow, Morris, Jun.—The His-
torical Study of Religions : Its
Scope and Method, "Memoirs
of the International Congress of
Anthropology." Chicago, 1894,
pp. 287-297.
Jevons, F. B.—The Science of
Religion : Its History and
Method. I. M., 1901, 464-
494, 550-569.
Knappert, L. — De Beteekenis
van de Wetenschap van het
Folklore voor de Godsdienst-
geschiedenis. Amsterdam, 1887.
Labanca, Baldassare. — La reli-
gione per le università è un
problema non un assioma.
Turin, 1886.
Place of subject in Universities.
Lamers, G. H.—De Wetenschap
van den godsdienst. 2 parts.
Utrecht, 1896-97.
Max-Müller, Friedrich. — The
Principles of the Science of
Religion or Comparative Theo-
logy, "Progress," vol. iii., pp.
17-30. Chicago, 1898.
Pfleiderer, O.—Das Recht der
Entwickelungstheorie in der
Religionswissenschaft, "Zeits.
f. Missionskunde und Religions-
wissenschaft," 1889, 4-11.
Rauwenhoff, L. W. E.—Wereld-
godsdiensten. T.T., xix. 1-33.
Discussion of term "Universal
Religions."
Réville, Jean. — L'Histoire des
Religions sa méthode et son
rôle d'après les travaux recents
de MM. Maurice Vernes, Goblet
d'Alviella, et du P. van den
Gheyn. R.H.R., xiv. 346-
363.
Tannenberg, H. — Religionsge-
schichtliche Bibliothek, I.

"Die Religionsforschung und das historische Princip." Berlin, 1898.

Tiele, C. P.—De Plaats van de Godsdiensten der Natuurvolken in de Godsdienstgeschiedenis. Amsterdam, 1873.
Reply J. I. Doedes, "De toepassung van de Ontwikkelingstheorie niet aantebevelen voor de Geschiedenis der Godsdiensten," Utrecht, 1874; see also Pfleiderer in J.P.T., i. 65-116; and Tiele, T.T., ix. 170-192.

Tiele, C. P.—De Ontwikkelingsgeschiedenis van den Godsdienst en de Hypotheze waarvan zij uitgaat, "De Gids," 1874, No. 6.

Tiele, C. P. — Eenige Woorden ter inleiding van den nieuwen cursus over de Wijsbegeerte van den Godsdienst. T.T., 1892.

Tiele, C. P.—Godsdienstwetenschap en Theologie. T.T., i. 38-52.

Tiele, C. P.—Godsdienstwetenschap en Wijsbegeerte in het jongste Ontwerp van Wet op het hooger Onderwijs, "De Gids," 1869, No. 7.

Tiele, C. P.—Over de Geschiedenis der oude Godsdiensten haar Methode, Geest en Belang. T.T., vii. 573-589.

Tiele, C. P.—Over de Wetten der Ontwikkeling van den Godsdienst. T.T., viii. 225-262.

Tiele, C. P.—Theologie en Godsdienstwetenschap, "De Gids," 1866, No. 5.

Tiele, C. P.—Tweërlei godsdienstgeschiedenis. T.T., xxi. 253-271.

Usener, H.—Götternamen. Bonn, 1896.

Vernes, Maurice.—L'Histoire des Religions, son Esprit, sa Méthode et ses Divisions, son enseignement en France et a l'Étranger. Paris, 1887.
See Th. Reinach, R.Cr., April 4, 1887.

Vernes, Maurice.—Les abus de la méthode comparative dans l'histoire des religions en general et particulièrement dans l'étude des religions semitiques, "Revue Internationale de l'Enseignment," Paris, 1886; also in Vernes' "L'Histoire des Religions," pp. 67-118.
See criticism in "Museon," 1887, 56-65.

Woods, Jas. Houghton. — The Value of Religious Facts : A Study of some Aspects of the Science of Religion. New York, 1889.

VI.

Religion—General Discussion and Aspects.

D'Alviella, Goblet.—La Loi du progrès dans les Religions, "Revue de Belgique." Bruxelles, 1894.

Darmesteter, James.—The Future of Religion, in "Selected Essays," translated by Helen B. Jastrow. Boston, 1895.

De Wette, M. L.—Vorlesungen über die Religion. Berlin, 1827.

Frazer, J. G.—Magic and Religion in "The Golden Bough," vol. i., pp. 7-128. 2nd ed., London, 1900.

Hume, David. — The Natural History of Religion. Vol. II. of Green and Grose's edition of "Hume's Essays." London, 1882.

Hume, David.—Dialogues concerning Natural Religion, ib.

Kant, Immanuel.— Religion innerhalb der Grenzen der blossen Vernunft. Königsberg, 1793.
See Wilhelm Mengel, Kant's "Begründung der Religion." Leipzig, 1900.

Köstlin, Julius.—Article "Religion" in "Real-Encyklopædie für Protestantische Theologie und Kirche." 2nd ed.

Lang, Andrew.—Magic and Religion. London, 1901.

Lang, Andrew.—Myth, Ritual, and Religion. 2nd ed., London, 1899.

See Victor Henry, R.Cr., Feb. 17, 1896; French translation, with Introduction by L. Marillier, Paris, 1895.

Lefevre, A.—La Religion. Paris, 1892.

Bibliothèque des Sciences Contemporaines.

Letourneau, Ch. — L'Évolution Religieuse dans les divers races humaines. Paris, 1892.

Marillier, L.—Article "Religion" in the "Grande Encyclopédie."

Max-Müller, Friedrich.— Gifford Lectures. 1. Natural Religion, 1889; 2nd ed., 1892; 2. Physical Religion, 1890; 3. Anthropological Religion, 1891; 4. Theosophy or Psychological Religion, 1892; 2nd ed., 1899.

Mill, John Stuart.—Three Essays on Religion. 1. Nature; 2. Utility of Religion; 3. Theism. London, 1874.

See John Morley, "Critical Miscellanies," 2nd series, London, 1877.
See Henri Gast, "La Religion dans Stuart Mill." Montauban, 1882.

Molinari, G.—La Religion. Paris, 1892.

Naquet, Alfred J.—Religion, Propriété, Famille. Paris, 1869.

Newbolt, W. C. E.—Religion. London, 1899.

Christian theology.

Nitzsch, Immanuel.—Ueber den Religionsbegriff der Alten. T.S.K., 1828, 527-545, and 725-754.

Olshausen, H.—Ueber den Begriff der Religion. T.S.K., 1830, 632-650 (criticism of Schleiermacher and Twesten).

Opzoomer, C. W. — De Godsdienst. Amsterdam, 1864.

German translation by Friedrich Mook, "Die Religion." Elberfeld, 1868.

Schleiermacher, Friedrich. — Ueber die Religion—Reden an

die Gebildeten unter ihren Verächtern. 1799.

English translation by John Oman. London, 1893.

Seydel, Rudolf. — Die Religion und Religionen. Leipzig, 1872.

Stokes, George Gabriel.—Natural Theology, "Gifford Lectures." London, 1891.

Taylor, Henry Osborn.—Ancient Ideals : A study of intellectual and spiritual growth from early times to the establishment of Christianity. 2 vols. New York, 1896.

Tiele, C. P.—Article "Religion" in "Encyclopædia Britannica," 9th edition.

Tiele, C. P.—Article "Comparative Religion" in "Johnson's Universal Encyclopædia."

Van Ende, M.—Histoire Naturelle de le Croyance. Paris, 1887.

VII.

Religion—Nature and Origin.

Bacon, T. S.—The Beginnings of Religion: An Essay. London, 1887.

Baissac, Jules.—Les Origines de la Religion. Paris, 1877.

Nouvelle ed., 2 vols., 1899.

Baring-Gould, S. — Origin and Development of Religious Belief. London, 1882.

Bassermann, H.—Was ist Religion ? "Deutsche Revue," 1900, 201-208.

Bell, F. W. B.—Het wesen der godsdienst. T.T., iii. 410-430.

Bender, Wilhelm.—Das Wesen der Religion und die Grundgesetze der Kirchenbildung. 4th ed., 1888.

Berlin, I.—Neue Gedanken über die Entstehung der Familie und der Religion. Bern, 1898.

Biedermann, A. E.—Eine Bilanz ueber die rationellan grundbegriffe der Religion. Z.W.T., xiv. 1-30.

Borchert, Aloys. —Der Animismus oder Ursprung und Entwickelung der Religion aus dem Seelen-Ahnen- und Geisterkult. Freiburg, 1900.

Bosanquet, Bernard. —Evolution of Religion. I.J.E., v. 432-443.

Carnere, Moritz. —Die Religion in ihrem Begriff, ihrer weltgeschichtlichen Entwicklung und Vollendung. Weilburg, 1841.

Clemen, Carl. —Der Begriff Religion und seine verschiedene Auffassungen. In T.S.K., 1896, 472-505.

Constant de Rebecque, Henri Benjamin. — De la Religion considerée dans sa source, ses formes et ses developpements. 6 vols. Paris, 1824-31.

Cook, F. C. —The Origins of Religion and Language considered in five essays. London, 1884.

Dorner, August. —Einige Bemerkungen zu neueren Ansichten über das Wesen der Religion. Z.W.T., xliv. 497-531.

Dorner, August. — Ueber das Wesen der Religion. T.S.K., 1883, 217-277.

Duhm, Bernhard. —Das Geheimniss in der Religion. Freiburg, 1896.

Ehni, I. —Ursprung u. Entwickelung der Religion. T.S.K., 1898, 581-648.

Elwert. —Ueber das Wesen der Religion, "Tübinger Zeitschrift f. Theologie," 1835, Heft iii., 1-116.
With reference to Schleiermacher's theory.

Feuerbach, Ludwig. —Vorlesungen über das Wesen der Religion. Stuttgart, 1846.
English translation by A. Loos, "Essence of Religion." New York, 1873.

Hagenmacher, Otto. —Zur Frage nach dem Ursprung der Religion und nach der ältesten

Religionsformen : eine Studie. Leipzig, 1883.

Harrison, Frederic, and Spencer, Herbert. — The Nature and Reality of Religion : A Controversy. New York, 1885.

Hartmann, Ed. v. —Die Anfänge der Religion, "Westermann's Illustrierte Deutsche Monatshafte," 1897, 325-341.

Helmersen, A. von. —Die Religionen : ihr wesen, ihr entstehen und ihr vergehen. Graz, 1875.

Heman, C. F. —Der Ursprung der Religion. Basel, 1868.

Hillen. — Die religiösen Vorstellungen im Anfänge der Geschichte der Menschheit. Coesfeld, 1880.

Holsten. C. — Ursprung und Wesen der Religion. Berlin, 1886.

Holtzmann, H. —Der Religionsbegriff der Schule Herbart's. Z.W.T., xxv. 66-92.

Hugenholtz, Ph. R. —Het Wezen en het Recht van den godsdienst. T.T., viii. 410-425, ix. 207-225 and 511-527.

Kaftan, Julius. —Das Wesen der Religion. 1881.

Kellogg, S. H. — Genesis and Growth of Religion. New York, 1892.

Köstlin, Julius. —Ursprung der Religion. T.S.K., 1890, 213-294.

Martineau, James —A Study of Religion : Its Source and Contents. 2 vols. London, 1888.
Analysis by Richard A. Armstrong in Series "Small Books on Great Subjects." London, 1900.

Müller, Johannes G. —Bildung u. Gebrauch des Wortes, "Religio." T.S.K., 1835, 121-148.
See also T.S.K., 1835, Heft i.

Paret, H. —Ueber die Eintheilung der Religionen. T.S.K., 1855, 261-296.

Peyton, W. W.—Anthropology
and the Evolution of Religion,
"Contemporary Review," 1901,
213-230 and 435-446.

Pfleiderer, Otto.—Zur Frage nach
Anfang und Entwickelung der
Religion. J.P.T., i. 65-116.
See Section V., sub. Tiele.

Pfleiderer, Otto.—Die Religion,
ihr Wesen und ihre geschichte
auf Grund des gegenwärtigen
Standes der Philosophie u. des
historischen Wissen. Leipzig,
1869.

Powell, J. W.—The Evolution
of Religion, "Monist," 1898,
183-204.

Pressensé, E. de.—L'origine de
la Religion. R.C., January
1881.

Rauwenhoff, L. W. E. — Het
onstaan van den godsdienst.
T.T., xix. 257-320.
Cf. W. Scheffer.—"Ein drietal
vragen aan. Professor Rauwenhoff
bettreffende het ontsaan van den
godsdienst." T.T., xx. 137-148.

Reischle, Max.—Die Frage nach
dem Wesen der Religion.
Grundlegung zu einer method-
ologie der Religionsphilosophie.
Freiburg, 1889.

Ruge, A.—Reden über die Religion, ihr Entstehen und Vergehen. 2nd ed., Berlin, 1869.

Saussaye, P. D. Chantepie de la.
— Methodologische bijdrage
tot het onderzoek naar den
oorsprong van den godsdienst.
Utrecht, 1871.

Schwarz, K. H. W.—Das Wesen
der Religion. 2 vols. Braunschweig, 1847.

Staes-Brame.—De l'Évolution de
l'Idee Religieuse. Lille, 1898.

Stein, Ludwig. — Origine psy
chique et caractère sociologique
de la religion, "Revue Internationale de Sociologie," 1897,
40-67.
See Th. Achelis, A.R., i. 188-190.

Tannenberg, H. — Religionsge-
schichtliche Bibliothek. II.

Was ist Religion? Berlin,
1898.

Tiele, C. P.—Het Wezen en de
Oorsprong van den Godsdienst.
T.T., v. 373-406.

Tiele, C. P.—Max Müller und
Fritz Schultze über ein Prob-
lem der Religionswissenschaft.
Leipzig, 1871.
Discussion of origin of religion.

Tiele, C. P.—Over den Aanfang
en de Ontwikkeling van den
Godsdienst. T.T., ix. 170-192.
Critique of Pfleiderer's article
(above).

Vernes, Maurice.—Article, "Religions, classement et filiation
des," in Lichtenberger's "Encyclopédie des Sciences Religieuses," vol. xi.

Ward, Jas. Henders Durer.—
How Religion arises: a psychological study. Boston, 1888.

Wette, W. M. L. de.—Vorlesungen ueber die Religion—ihr
Wesen, ihre Erscheinungsformen und ihren Einfluss auf's
Leben. Berlin, 1827.

Wyttenbach, Joh. Hugo. — Der
Geist der Religion. Frankfort,
1886.

Zeller, E.—Ursprung u. Wesen
der Religion (Vorträge u.
Abhandlungen II.), 2te Samm-
lung. Leipzig, 1877.
Originally published in "Theologische Jahrbücher," 1845, 26-75 and
393-430.

VIII.

*Religion—Belief and the
Religious Sentiment.*

Balfour, Arthur James. — The
Foundations of Belief; being
Notes Introductory to the Study
of Theology. London, 1895.

Brinton, D. G.—The Religious
Sentiment. New York, 1876.

Byles, John Barnard. — Foundations of Religion in the Mind
and Heart of Man. London,
1875.

Caird, Edward.—The Evolution of Religion, "Gifford Lectures." 2 vols. Edinburgh, 1893.
See L. Marillier, R.H.R., xxx. 243-318; and xxxiii. 177-208.

Coe, George A.—The Spiritual Life: Studies in the Science of Religion. New York, 1900.

Eucken, Rudolf.—Der Wahrheits gehalt der Religion. Leipzig, 1901.

Fechner, Gustav Theodor.—Die drei Motive und Gründe des Glaubens. Leipzig, 1863.

Fiske, John. — Through Nature to God. Boston, 1899.

Fox, William Johnson.—On the Religious Ideas. London, 1849.

Frickhöffer, H. — Die Grund-frage der Religion. Hamburg, 1887.

Gehring, Albert.—The Genesis of Faith. N.W., viii., 460-470.

Happel, Julius.—Die Anlage des Menschen zur Religion. Haarlem, 1877.

Holtzmann, H.—Die Entwickelung des aesthetischen Religions-begriffes. Z.W.T., xix. 1-30.

Lang, Andrew.—The Making of Religion. London, 1898.

Liddon, H. P.—Some Elements of Religion. London, 1872.

Long, George.—An Inquiry concerning Religion. London, 1855.

Martineau, James.—The Seat of Authority in Religion. London, 1891.

Momerie, Alfred Williams. — The Basis of Religion. 2nd ed., Edinburgh, 1886.

Murphy, Joseph John. — The Scientific Bases of Faith. London, 1873.

Reich, E.—Die Entwickelung der Religiosität und das Werk der Religion. Zürich, 1898.

Richard, Jean.—Le Sentiment Religieus fondement de la Meta-physique. Lausanne, 1893.

Russell, John, Viscount Amberley. —An Analysis of Religious Belief. 2 vols. London, 1876; 2nd ed., 1897.
See C. P. Tiele, "Eine ontleding van het godsdienstig geloof." T.T., x. 583-604.

Steinmann, Th.—Der Primat der Religion im menschlichen Geistesleben. Leipzig, 1899.

Thompson, Daniel Greenleaf.— The Religious Sentiments of the Human Mind. London, 1888.

Tyler, Charles Mellen.—Bases of Religious Belief, Historic and Ideal. New York, 1897.

Upton, Chas. B.—Lectures on the Bases of Religious Belief, "Hibbert Lectures." London, 1894; 2nd ed., 1897.

Wilson, W. D.—The Foundation of Religious Belief. New York, 1883.

Wiseman, M. W.—The Dynamics of Religion. London, 1898.

Ziegler, Theodor.—Religion und Religionen. Stuttgart, 1893.

IX.

Religion and Ethics.

Adler, Felix.—Creed and Deed. New York, 1877.

Adler, Helene. — Religion und Moral. Frankfort, 1882.
From a pedagogical point of view.

Bender, Wilhelm.—The Relations of Religion and Morality. N.W., ii. 453-478.

Buckley, Edmund.—Relation between Early Religion and Morality. I.M., 1900, 577-617.

D'Alviella, Goblet.— Des Rapports historiques entre la Religion et la Morale. R.H.R., xliii. 30-46.

Everett, Walter Goodnow.—The Relation of Ethics to Religion. I.J.E., x. 493-502.

Fox, James J. — Religion and Morality: their natural and

412   BIBLIOGRAPHY.

mutual relation, historically
and doctrinally considered
(from a Catholic standpoint).
New York, 1899.
Göransson, Nils Johann.—Utkast
till en Undersökung af Religionen med till Moralen. Up-
sala, 1899
Grave, .—Die Seelbstständliche
Stellung der Sittlichkeit zur
Religion. J.P.T., xviii. 341-
404, 493-574, and 643-716.
Gropelli, Emilio Serra.—Teorica
delle Religione considerate nel
rapporto etico. Rome, 1886.
Guyau, J. M.—Esquisse d'une
Morale sans obligation ni sanc-
tion. Paris, 1885.
Heidel, W. A. — Metaphysics,
Ethics, and Religion, "Philo-
sophical Review," 1900, 30-
41.
Hering, H.—Sittlichkeit und Re-
ligion, "Deutsch Evangel.
Blätter," 1898, 643-660.
Herrmann, Wilhelm.—Die Reli-
gion im Verhältniss zum Wel-
terkennen und zur Sittlichkeit.
Halle, 1879.
Hoekstra, S. — Godsdienst en
Zedelijkheid, ii. 117-155.
Hugenholtz, Ph. R.—Theologie
en Ethiek. T.T., xv. 501-
522.
Kidd, James.—Morality and Re-
ligion. Edinburgh, 1895.
Köstlin, Julius. — Religion und
Sittlichkeit. T.S.K., 1870, 50-
122.
Lamers, G. H. — Godsdienst en
Zedelijkheid beschouwd in
onderling verband. Utrecht,
1883.
Lühr, Karl.—Ist eine Religions-
lose Moral möglich. Berlin,
1899.
Mackenzie, J. S.—Source of Moral
Obligation. I.J.E., 1900, x.
464-478.
Marcus, E.—Die exacte Aufdeck-
ung des Fundamentes der

Sittlichkeit und die Konstruk-
tion der Welt aus den Elementen
des Kant. Leipzig, 1899.
Martineau, James. — The Re-
lations between Ethics and
Religion. London, 1881.
Momerie, Alfred.—The Ethics of
Creeds. N.W., ii. 676-687.
Pfleiderer, Otto. — Moral und
Religion nach ihrem gegen-
seitigen Verhältniss. Haarlem,
1871 [and Leipzig, 1872].
Potter, Robert.—The Relation of
Ethics to Religion: An Intro-
duction to the Critical Study
of Religion. London, 1888.
Rade, M.—Religion und Moral.
Giessen, 1898.
Rupp, W.—Ethical Postulates in
Theology. A.J.T., iii. 654-
678.
Schultz, Hermann.—Religion und
Sittlichkeit in ihrem Verhält-
niss zu einander. T.S.K.,
1883, 60-130.
Seeley, J. R.—"Ethics and Reli-
gion," in volume of Essays by
various writers, under title of
"Ethics and Religion," pp.
1-28. London, 1900.
Spir, African M.—Moralität und
Religion. Leipzig, 1874. I.,
3rd ed. in "Gesammte Schrift-
en," 1884, vol. iii., pp. 1-192.
Sullivan, W. R. Washington.—
Morality as a Religion. Lon-
don, 1898.
Thieme, Karl. — Die Sittliche
Triebkraft des Glaubens. Leip-
zig, 1895.
Wallace, William.—Lectures and
Essays on Natural Théology
and Ethics. Edited by Edward
Caird. Oxford, 1899.
Watson, J.—Art, Morality, and
Religion, "Queen's Quarterly,"
v. 287-296.
Weygoldt, G. P.—Darwinismus
Religion und Sittlichkeit. Lei-
den, 1878.

X.

Religion and Philosophy.

Allier, R.—Religion, Theologie, und Philosophie. R.C., Feb. 1889.

Bascom, John.—Science, Philosophy, and Religion, "Lowell Lectures." New York, 1871.

Blanc, J.—De la Philosophie et de ses rapports avec la theologie, "L'Université Catholique," 1898, 161-182.

Delff, Heinrich Karl Hugo.—Die Hauptprobleme der Philosophie und Religion. Leipzig, 1886.

Fichte, J. H.—Spekulation und Theologie. Heidelberg, 1846.

Fichte, J. H.—Religion u. Philosophie in ihrem gegenwärtigen Verhältnisse. Heidelberg, 1834.

Franck, Adolphe. — Philosophie et Religion. 2nd ed., Paris, 1869.

Gillet, L.—Religion, Philosophie et Litterature. Paris, 1898.

Gloatz, Paul.—Spekulative Theologie in Verbindung mit der Religionsgeschichte. Gotha, 1884.

Hughes, Henry.—Religious Faith: An Essay on the Philosophy of Religion. London, 1896.

Lamers, G. H.—De Wijsbegeerte van den godsdienst. Amsterdam, 1881.

Lipsius, R. A.—Philosophie und Religion. Leipzig, 1885.

Matter, Jacques.—Histoire de la philosophie dans ses rapports avec la religion depuis l'ére chrétienne. 2 vols. Paris, 1854.

Mehmal, C.—Ueber des Verhaltniss der Philosophie zur Religion. Erlangen, 1805.

Royce, J. R.—The Religious Aspect of Philosophy. Boston, 1886.

Saint-Hilaire, J. Barthelemy.—La Philosophie dans ses rapports avec les Sciences et la Religion. Paris, 1889.

Schelling, F. W. — Philosophie und Religion, "Sämmtliche Werke," Abth. i., vol. 6, pp. 11-70. Stuttgart, 1858.

Solms, Fürst Ludwig. — Zehn Gesprache über Philosophie und Religion.

Stirling, Jas. Hutchinson.— Philosophy and Theology. Edinburgh, 1890.

Strong, Augustus Hopkins.— Philosophy and Religion. New York, 1888.

Thikötter, J.— Das Verhältniss von Religion und Philosophie, historisch und kritisch belenchtet. Bremen, 1888.

Tulloch, John.—Modern Theories in Philosophy and Religion. London, 1884.

Wilken, L.—Kritische Darstellung des Verhältnisses in dem nach Kant Philosophie und Theologie zu einander stehen. Z.W.T., xxi. 1-13.

XI.

Religion and Mythology.

Bender, Wilhelm.—Mythologie und Metaphysik. Stuttgart, 1899.

Cox, G. W.—An Introduction to the Science of Comparative Mythology and Folk-lore. London, 1881.

Lang, A. — Custom and Myth. London, 1885.

    C. P. Tiele.—"Le Mythe de Kronos a propos d'une nouvelle methode en Mythologie comparée." R.H.R., xii. 246-277.

    Ch. Ploix.—"Mythologie et Folklorisme." R.H.R., xiii. 1-46, and reply of A. Lang, *ib.* 197-205.

Lang, Andrew. — Art. "Mythology" in "Encyclopædia Britannica," 9th edition.

Lang, Andrew.—Modern Mythology. London, 1897.
Exposition and illustration of anthropological method.

Lang, Andrew.—Myth, Ritual, and Religion. 2nd ed., London, 1899.

Lefevre, A.—Religions et Mythologies comparées. 2nd ed., Paris, 1879.

Max-Müller, Friedrich.—Comparative Mythology. 1858.

Max - Müller, Friedrich. — The Philosophy of Mythology, "Contemporary Review," Dec. 1871.

Müller, K. O.—Prolegomena zu einer wissenschaftlichen Mythologie. Göttingen, 1825.
English translation, "Introduction to a Scientific System of Mythology," by John Leitch. London, 1844.
See A. Réville, "Étude sur la Mythologie grecque d'après Otfried Müller." R.H.R., ix. 133-166 and 273-306.

Noack, Ludwig.—Mythologie u. Offenbarung. Die Religion in ihrem Wesen, ihrer Geschichtlichen Entwickelung und ihrer absoluten Vollendung. 2 vols. Darmstadt, 1845.

Regnaud, P.—Quelques Observations sur le Méthode en Mythologie comparée. R. H. R., xi. 286-297.

Réville, Jean.—De la Complexité des Mythes et des Legendes a propos des recentes controversies sur la méthode en mythologie comparée. R.H R., xiii. 169-191.

Saussaye, P. D. Chantepie de la.—Mythologie en Folk-Lore, "De Gids," August, 1885.

Schelling, F. W. — Philosophie der Mythologie, " Sämmtliche Werke," Abth. ii., vols. 1-2. Stuttgart, 1856.
"Philosophie der Offenbarung," Abth. ii., vols. 3-4.

Schjott, P. O.—Questions scientifiques modernes. I. Religion

et Mythologie. Copenhagen, 1898.
"Videnskabselsk Skrifter." II. Hist. filos Klasse, No. 3.

Schwarz, W.—Der Ursprung der Mythologie. Berlin, 1860.

Tiele, C. P.—De oorsprong van Mythologie en godsdienst naar Anleidung der Theorien van de Quatrefages en Brinton. T.T., iv. 1-27.

Vignoli, Tito.—Myth and Science. New York, 1882.

Vodskov, H. S.—Sjaeledyrkelse og Naturdyrkelse, Bidrag tel bestemmelsen af den mytologiske metode. Copenhagen, 1897.

XII.

Religion and Psychology.

Braasch, Ernst. — Das Psychologische Wesen der Religion. Z.W.T., xxxvii. 161-175.

Grasserie, Raoul de la.—De la Psychologie des Religions. Paris, 1899.

Kierkegaard, S.—Zur Psychologie der Sünde, der Bekehrung und des Glaubens. Leipzig, 1890.
German translation by Schrempf.

Kinast.—Beiträge zur Religions-Psychologie. Erlangen, 1900.

Koch, Emil. — Die Psychologie in der Religionswissenschaft. Freiburg, 1896.

Lechler, Karl. — Bemerkungen zum Begriffe der Religion mit besonderer Rücksicht auf die psychologischen Fragen. T.S.K., 1851, 755-825.

Leuba, James H.—Introduction to a Psychological Study of Religion, "Open Court," 1901, pp. 195-225.

Leuba, James H.—Religion : its Impulses and its Ends. Bibliotheca Sacra, 1901, 751-773.

Marillier, L.—De la Rôle de Psychologie dans les Études de

Mythologie comparée. R.H.R., xxxii. 116-141.
Introduction to French translation of Lang's "Myth, Ritual, and Religion."

Schultze, Fr. — Psychologie der Naturvölker. Leipzig, 1900.
Book III. treats of Religion of Primitive Man, psychologically considered.

Starbuck, Edwin D.—The Psychology of Religion: an empirical study of the growth of Religious Consciousness, "Contemporary Science Series." London, 1899.

Taute, G. F.—De psychologico religionis fundamento. Munich, 1825.

Vierkandt, A.—Zur Psychologie des Aberglaubens. A.R., ii. 237-257.

Vorbrodt, Gustav.— Psychologie des Glaubens. Göttingen, 1895.

Weir, James.—Psychical Correlation of Religious Emotion and Sexual Desire.

Ziemssen, O.—Die Religion im Lichte der Psychologie. Gotha, 1880.

XIII.
Religion in relation to Science, History, and Culture.

Delff, Heinrich Karl Hugo.—Kultur und Religion. Gotha, 1875.

Draper, W. F.—History of the Conflict between Religion and Science. New York, 1875.

Ely, Richard T. — Religion as a Social Force, "Christian Quarterly," 1897, 321-328.

Fairbairn, A. M. — Religion in History and in Modern Life. London, 1895.

Franke, J. H.—Ueber den Kulturwerth der Religion vom Standpunkte der Kunst. Zürich, 1896.

Grasserie, Raoul de la. — Des religions comparées au point de vue sociologique. Paris, 1899.

Hase, J. C A.—Die Bedeutung des Geschichtlichen in der Religion. Leipzig, 1874.

Herder, Joh. Gottfried v.—Ideen zur Philosophie der Geschichte der Menschheit. Vols. 13 and 14 of Suphan's edition. Berlin, 1889.

Hinrichs, Hermann Fr. W.— Die Religion im innerem Verhältniss zur Wissenschaft. Heidelberg, 1822-28.

Hunt, W. Holman. — Religion and Art, "Contemporary Review," 1897, pp. 41-52.

Lefevre, A.—La Science des Religions dans ses rapports avec l'ethnographie. Paris, 1892.

Mellone, S. H.—Present Aspects of the Relation between Science and Religion. N.W., v. 506-526.

Partridge, W. O.—The Relation of Art to Religion, "Arena," Dec. 1897.

Rade, Martin.—Die Religion im modernen Geistesleben. Freiburg, 1898.

Riehm, Ed.—Religion und Wissenschaft. T.S.K., 1881, 104-130.

Romanes, G. J. — Thoughts on Religion. 3rd ed., edited by Charles Gore. London, 1895.
Contains Influence of Science on Religion.

Sabatier, Auguste.—La Religion et la Culture moderne. Paris, 1898.
German translation, Freiburg, 1898. English translation, "Religion and Modern Culture," in the "New World," viii. 91-110.

Soederblom, Nathan.— Die Religion und die Soziale Entwicklung. Freiburg, 1898.

Temple, F.—Relations between Religion and Science. London, 1884.

Thode, Henry.—Kunst, Religion und Kultur. Heidelberg, 1901.

Wasson, D. A.—Religion and Social Science. Boston, 1869.

White, A. D.—A History of the Warfare of Science with Theology in Christendom. 2 vols. New York, 1897.

INDEX.

—•●•—

27

28*

THE END.

PRINTED BY WALTER SCOTT, NEWCASTLE-ON-TYNE.